Vocabulary *in use* Intermediate

Second Edition

100 units of vocabulary practice in North American English

with answers

Stuart Redman

with Lawrence J. Zwier

CAMBRIDGE
UNIVERSITY PRESS

CAMBRIDGE
UNIVERSITY PRESS

79 Anson Road, #06-04/06, Singapore 079906

Cambridge University Press is part of the University of Cambridge.

It furthers the University's mission by disseminating knowledge in the pursuit of education, learning and research at the highest international levels of excellence.

www.cambridge.org
Information on this title :www.cambridge.org/9780521123754

© Cambridge University Press 1999, 2010

First published 1999
Second edition 2010
7th printing 2015

Printed in China by Golden Cup Printing Co. Ltd

ISBN 978-0-521-12375-4 paperback Intermediate Student's Book with answers
ISBN 978-0-521-12367-9 paperback Basic Student's Book with answers
ISBN 978-0-521-12386-0 paperback High Intermediate Student's Book with answers

Contents

v

Acknowledgments

I wish to thank the following reviewers, whose comments were so helpful in improving this book: Julien Park, English Language Academy, South Korea; Nick Taggert, Instructor, Interactive College of Technology, Chamblee, Georgia; and Nina Ito, Academic Coordinator, American Language Institute, California State University, U.S.A.

I also wish to acknowledge the insightful suggestions provided by reviewers at Cambridge University Press: Emeric Lau, Singapore; Jinhee Park, South Korea; Satoko Shimoyama, Japan; and Alex Martinez, Mexico.

Many thanks are due to the *Corpus* consultant Randi Reppen, who made sure the text was faithful to contemporary American usage. But above all, I am indebted to my American adapter Lawrence J. Zwier. Without Lawrence's collaboration, this second edition would not be published.

I would also like to express my appreciation to the following editorial staff at Cambridge University Press: Caitlin Mara, Katherine Wong, Kathleen O'Reilly, Keiko Sugiyama, Maya Lazarus, and Richard Walker. My special thanks go to Bernard Seal, who guided this book through the editorial process with his usual calm and professionalism.

Finally, I would like to thank all those who helped in the making of the first edition of *Vocabulary in Use Intermediate*, especially Ellen Shaw, my original American adapter.

Stuart Redman
December 2009

Layout and design: Transnet Pte Ltd
                     based on a design by Tanky Media
Cover design: Studioleng

Illustrations by Jonathan C. Shih, LiDan Illustration & Design Studio, Richard Peter David, and Tanky Media.

The author and publishers would like to thank Guy de Villiers and Stephen Forster, and would also like to thank the following for permission to reproduce copyright material and photographs:

p.6, definition of "seat": adapted and reprinted with permission from *Cambridge Advanced Learner's Dictionary* Third Edition © Cambridge University Press, 2008; p.20, *(clockwise from top left)* ©iStockphoto. com/DamianPalus, ©iStockphoto.com/OneO2, ©iStockphoto.com/Garry518, ©iStockphoto.com/seraficus, ©iStockphoto.com/bluestocking, ©iStockphoto.com/Floortje; ©iStockphoto.com/yzak, ©iStockphoto.com/ skodonnell, ©iStockphoto.com/AndrewJohnson; p.48, ©iStockphoto.com/mbbirdy; p.62, *(bottom left to right)* ©iStockphoto.com/robas, ©iStockphoto.com/Yuri_Arcurs, ©iStockphoto.com/jerryhat, ©iStockphoto. com/wiktorbubniak, ©iStockphoto.com/gollykim; p.114, *(left)* ©iStockphoto.com/Lighthousebay, *(right)* ©iStockphoto.com/jrsower; p.128, ©iStockphoto.com/oksanaphoto; p.134, 135 *(clockwise from top)* ©iStockphoto.com/fotoVoyager, ©iStockphoto.com/RedBarnStudio, ©iStockphoto.com/jallfree, ©iStockphoto. com/mladn61, ©iStockphoto.com/fjdelvalle; p.154, *(left to right)* ©iStockphoto.com/RapidEye, ©iStockphoto. com/DNY59, ©iStockphoto.com/jgroup, ©iStockphoto.com/RapidEye; p.168, *(top)* ©iStockphoto.com/ bibikoff, *(bottom)* ©iStockphoto.com/shapecharge; p.180, *(top)* image by Corbis; p.182, *(clockwise from top left)* ©iStockphoto.com/rest, ©iStockphoto.com/lopurice, ©iStockphoto.com/MattGrant, ©iStockphoto.com/ joecicak, ©iStockphoto.com/saints4757, ©iStockphoto.com/YinYang, *(bottom)* Image Source/Getty Images; p.184, *(top left)* ©iStockphoto.com/tilo, *(top right)* ©iStockphoto.com/The-Tor

Introduction

This new edition of *Vocabulary in Use Intermediate* still retains the features that made the first edition so popular:

- The format of presentation on the left-hand page and practice on the right-hand page.

- Approaching vocabulary in a variety of ways: topics (e.g., Food), word formation (e.g., Prefixes), words and grammar (e.g., Uncountable and plural nouns), collocation and phrases (e.g., *Make, do,* and *take*), functions (e.g., Request, invitations, and suggestions), concepts (e.g., Time), varieties of English (e.g., Formal and informal English), etc.

- A student-friendly Answer key, including not only correct answers to right/wrong exercises, but also possible answers for more open-ended exercises.

- Usage notes that are ideal for self-study learners.

- A complete Index, which lists all the target words and phrases.

What is different about the new edition?

Color

The first thing you will notice is that the new edition is in color. This makes the text and the artwork more attractive, and it also makes the book easier for you to use: the different headings and sections are now clearer, and the usage notes are shown against their own color background, so you can find them and read them more easily.

Updated content

The content has been updated in several ways:

- All the artwork is new: the full-color illustrations are clearer and more attractive, and they reflect recent changes in technology.

- Collocation and phrases: the new edition focuses even more on showing words in common collocations and phrases. For example, when you study different meanings of *see* (Unit 26), you will learn that it often appears in these phrases: *I see, I see what you mean, I don't see the point,* etc. In a unit on physical appearance (Unit 47), you will meet these common collocations: *blond hair, medium height, broad shoulders,* etc.

- New units: in response to suggestions from teachers and students, there are now four completely new units in the book:

  Likes, preferences, and interests (Unit 19)
  Common responses (Unit 21)
  Have and *have got* (Unit 24)
  Leave, catch, and *let* (Unit 27)

- Many other units have been significantly revised: for example, City life (Unit 64), Country life (Unit 65), The office (Unit 71), On the phone (Unit 79), and Computers and the Internet (Unit 80).

- The Index is now organized unit by unit, allowing learners to see at a glance the key words and phrases of any unit.

Use of the *Cambridge English Corpus*

This new edition has made use of the *Cambridge English Corpus* of written and spoken English. This is important in several ways:

- The *Corpus* has been used to check that all language and content is contemporary, natural, and accurate.

- The frequency information in the *Corpus* has helped guide the selection of words and phrases in the book and ensure that the vocabulary will be suitable for learners of English at an intermediate level.

- Example sentences are the same or similar to those in the *Corpus*. In other words, the examples show you words and phrases being used in their most typical contexts.

Using this book

Who is this book for?

Vocabulary in Use Intermediate has been written to help learners at this level to improve their English. The material corresponds approximately to level B1 of the Council of Europe's CEFR (Common European Framework of Reference for Languages). It has been designed for students who are studying on their own, but it can also be used by a teacher in the classroom with a group of students.

How is the book organized?

The book has 100 two-page units. The left-hand page explains the new words and phrases chosen for that unit. Most units contain approximately 25 new words or phrases and they are all highlighted in **bold**. The right-hand page gives you a chance to check your understanding through a series of exercises which practice the new vocabulary.

There is an Answer key at the back of the book. This gives *correct* answers to exercises with "right" or "wrong" solutions, and also possible answers for exercises which do not have "right" or "wrong" solutions.

There is also an Index at the back of the book. This lists all the words and phrases introduced in the book. It is organized unit by unit.

The left-hand page

The left-hand page introduces the new vocabulary for each topic or area of language. The vocabulary is divided into a number of sections (A, B, C, etc.) with simple, clear titles. New words and phrases are explained in a number of different ways:

1. A short definition
   e.g., **unemployed** [without a job]; **give** me **a hand** [help me]; **honest** [tells the truth]

2. A short explanation
   e.g., He **admitted** stealing her money, but **denied** taking the camera. [He said "yes" he took her money, but "no" he didn't take the camera .]

3. A synonym or opposite
   e.g, **select** [choose]; **weak** [not strong]

4. Sentence examples. For many of the new words/phrases there are also sentence examples which show the words in context in order to illustrate their meaning and any special grammatical features. For example:

   My girlfriend gets **jealous** when I talk to other girls.

We saw the plane in the sky, but then it **disappeared** behind a cloud.

He can't **get along with** his parents. [have a good relationship with] (verb + adverb + preposition)

5. A situation. With some words and phrases it is easier to see their meaning when they are in context. The following is from a text about a car accident:
"Both drivers were **badly injured**, and both cars were very **badly damaged**."

6. A picture or diagram. This is the clearest way to illustrate a large number of concrete nouns and verbs.

e.g.,

saxophone

You have to **press** that button to start the machine

Finally, a big effort has been made to introduce new words alongside other words that often appear with them (this is called "collocation"):

commit a crime; fasten your seat belt; miss the bus; tell the truth; terribly sorry; tight schedule; etc.

The right-hand page

The right-hand page contains the exercises to practice the new vocabulary presented on the left-hand page. In general, the first exercise practices the form of some of the new words, and then additional exercises focus on the meaning. In most units there is at least one exercise which gives learners a chance to think about and practice new vocabulary in relation to their own lives, and/or a task which invites learners to do something with the vocabulary outside of the book. In every unit, there is a range of exercise types to help maintain your interest.

How should I use the book?

The first four units teach you some important words and phrases; they also give you information about vocabulary, plus ideas and techniques to help you learn vocabulary. Do these units first, then work through the book studying the units that interests you.

If you go to English classes, it is a good idea to study Unit 5. This introduces vocabulary that is often used by teachers or needed by students in the classroom, e.g., **notebook;** look up a word; **What does** *highlight* **mean? How do you pronounce** it?

Everything you need is in the book. The new vocabulary is explained on the left-hand page, and the exercises have an Answer key at the back of the book. But if you need a dictionary to help you with any of the words or exercises, you can go to http://dictionary.cambridge.org/, where you can look up words you are not sure of and learn more about words you already know.

Companion Web site: www.cambridge.org/vinu

On the *Vocabulary in Use* Companion Web site, you will find a range of free additional activities for vocabulary and listening practice.

We hope you like this book. When you have finished it, you can go to the highest level in the series, *Vocabulary in Use High Intermediate*.

Good luck!

Learning and reviewing with this book

Look at Exercise 1.1 on the next page before you read this page.

A Establish a routine

September						
Mon	Tue	Wed	Thu	Fri	Sat	Sun
		1	2 study	3	4	5 study
6	7 study	8	9 study	10	11	12 study
13	14 study	15	16 study	17	18	19 study
20	21 study	22	23 study	24	25	26 study
27	28 study	29	30 study			

In a **routine**, you do certain things **regularly** [often] in the same way. It's a good idea to have a routine, especially if you are using this book for self-study [studying alone]. **Schedule** [plan] enough time each day or each week to learn and review the vocabulary. Some suggestions:

- Take **at least** [a minimum of] 30 or 45 minutes to study a unit for the first time.
- Take 5 or 10 minutes to review a unit for the second or third time.

B Be an active learner

As you use the book, do different things to **maintain your interest** [keep your interest high]. Be <u>active</u> when you are learning. For example:

- Use a highlighter pen to mark new or interesting vocabulary on the left-hand page.
- Pronounce the words **silently** [without noise or speaking] in your head, and also **out loud** [with noise or speaking].
- Use some of the ideas from Unit 2 to add words **effectively** to your own notebook. [If something is **effective**, it works well and produces good results.]
- Try different combinations to study the material on the left- and right-hand pages:
  a) Read all of the left-hand page, then do the exercises.
  b) Read part of the left-hand page. Then do one or two exercises.
  c) Try the exercises first. Then use the left-hand page when you have a problem.
- Don't study the units in the same order as the book. Choose units that interest you.

C Review

Review regularly, even for short periods. This will help you remember words and make them part of your "active" vocabulary. Here are some ideas to help you review:

- If you write in your book, use a pencil. Check the answers and then **erase** them [remove them using an eraser]. Later, come back and do the exercises again.
- Review each word in **bold** [darker type] on the left-hand page. Study each definition/ explanation in **brackets** [ ] or **parentheses** ( ). Test yourself afterwards.
- Keep lists of new words and definitions in a notebook, on your laptop computer, or in an electronic organizer.
- Create vocabulary games for yourself; **set goals/targets** [decide on what you want to be able to do by a particular time].

Exercises

1.1   **Answer these questions for yourself.**

1. Is it better to establish a regular study schedule or to study whenever you have some free time?
2. Is it a good idea to write down new words in a notebook while you study a unit?
3. When you learn a new word, do you practice saying it silently, out loud, or both?
4. What are some ideas for reviewing vocabulary?
5. Is it better to review vocabulary occasionally for long periods of time or to review frequently for short periods of time?

1.2   **Find your way around the book.**

1. Find the Contents in the front of this book. Turn to the Topic units (Units 42–92) on pages 84–185. Cover the examples on the right.
2. For each unit topic, write down your own examples – one or two for each topic.
3. Are there any unit titles you don't understand? Are there any units where you can't think of examples? If so, turn to that unit and find out what it is about.

1.3   *True* or *false?* **If the sentence is false, correct it. Write your answers in pencil. Don't look at page 2.**

1. In this book, new words are often shown in **bold** print.
2. Definitions/explanations of new words are often in **parentheses** after the word.
3. A **routine** means doing certain things in **a different** way **each** time.
4. If you **maintain** something, it means you keep it at the same level.
5. If something is **effective**, it doesn't work very well.
6. "**At least** 50 people" means "a maximum of 50 people."
7. If you write something, then **erase** it, you remove it from the page.
8. If you do something **silently**, you do it without making noise.
9. **Reviewing** means studying something for the first time.
10. If you have a **goal** or **target**, you have something you want to be able to do or achieve by a particular point in the future.

Now check your answers (see page 2) and look carefully at any incorrect ones. Then erase your answers and come back to this exercise again tomorrow. Find out how much you can remember.

1.4   **Plan your study.**

Now set your own goals and make a schedule for learning vocabulary with this book. Decide how much time you can spend each week, including some short periods for review. Also, decide how many units you want to finish each week.

Keeping a vocabulary notebook

A **Organize your notebook**

Give a title to each page or section (e.g., Sports, Education, Phrasal verbs). **Record** [write] each new word or phrase on an appropriate page. You could put a general index in the back of your notebook. As you learn new words, you can enter them alphabetically in the index.

B **What do I need to record?**

Here is a listing of the kind of information you will record in your vocabulary notebook.

What?	How?	Example
Meaning	a. definition/explanation	A **pond** is an area of water smaller than a lake.
	b. translation	to **remember** = *lembrar* (Portuguese)
	c. synonym or opposite	**awful** (= terrible); **tight** (= not loose)
	d. picture	**cell phone** 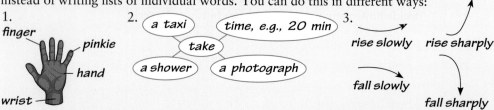
	e. example sentence	My hands were cold, so I **put on** my **gloves**.
Pronunciation	phonetic symbols *or* your own system	**ache** /eɪk/ **ache** (like "make")
Part of speech	(n.), (v.), (adj.), etc.	**gloves** (n.), **careful** (adj.), **ache** (n., v.)
Grammar	make a note + example sentence	**enjoy** + *-ing* form: I enjoy going to parties. **weather** (uncountable): We had beautiful **weather** in Rio.
Common word partners	phrase or sentence	make a **mistake**; make a **decision**; do my **job**; I'm on a **tight schedule**.
Special style	make a note	**purchase** (= buy; *formal*); **kids** (= children; *informal*)

> **note** You will not record everything about a word or phrase the first time you add it to your notebook. Leave space on the page so you can come back and add more information later.

C **Organize words on the page**

Certain words often appear together (common word partners). Record them together, instead of writing lists of individual words. You can do this in different ways:

1.
finger
pinkie
hand
wrist

Don't pronounce the "w" in "wrist" or the "b" in "thumb."

2.
a taxi
time, e.g., 20 min
take
a shower
a photograph

3.
rise slowly   rise sharply

fall slowly

fall sharply

Note both verbs are irregular: rise/rose/risen; fall/fell/fallen.

Exercises

2.1 Arrange these words into three groups and give each group a title for the topic.

glove	homeless	painful	plane	put on
shirt	ticket	trip	airport	careful
careless	get on	helpful	jacket	jeans

2.2 Circle the correct answer.

1. I really enjoy:
   a) play tennis   b) to play tennis   c) playing tennis
2. When we were on vacation, we had:
   a) beautiful weathers   b) beautiful weather   c) a beautiful weather
3. The underlined letters in **a<u>ch</u>e** are pronounced the same as in:
   a) ma<u>ch</u>ine   b) cat<u>ch</u>   c) <u>sch</u>edule
4. When we were in Seoul, we .... lots of pictures.
   a) did   b) took   c) made
5. The .... is also called the little finger.
   a) thumb   b) wrist   c) pinkie
6. The past tense of **fall** is:
   a) fell   b) felt   c) falled
7. You can **put on:**
   a) a cell phone   b) a decision   c) shoes
8. **Rise sharply** means:

a) 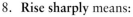   b)   c)

2.3 What is the best way to record the meaning of each word below? What other information should you record with it (e.g., pronunciation, part of speech)? Use a dictionary to help you.

awful	hand	purchase	kids
pond	tight	remember	cell phone

2.4 Write at least two more common word partners for each verb.

1. take *a picture* ....   2. make *a mistake* ....   3. do *my job* ....
....
....
....

Using a dictionary

A What dictionaries do I need?

If possible, have two dictionaries: a good **bilingual** dictionary and an **English-English** learner's dictionary. The bilingual dictionary is quicker and easier for you to understand, but the English learner's dictionary may give you more information about a word or phrase.

B What information does a dictionary give me?

Notice the parts of a dictionary **entry:**

pronunciation   part of speech

grammatical feature
(see page 64)

definition

examples

seat FURNITURE /siːt/ *n* [C] an item of furniture that has been designed for someone to sit on • *Chairs, stools, sofas and benches are types of seat.* • *The chairs are taken, so you'll have to use this table as a seat.* • *A car usually has a* **driver's** *seat, a* **front/passenger** *seat and* **back/rear** *seats.* • *Why don't you sit down* **on** *that seat over there while we're waiting?* • If you tell someone to **have/take a seat** you are asking them politely to sit down: *Have a seat, Mr. Jones, and tell me what I can do for you.* *(formal) Please* **keep** *your seats* (= stay sitting down) *until asked to leave.* • *adj* **seat of the pants** *(informal)* made up without much planning • *Josh made a seat-of-the-pants decision to take a left turn.*

collocations

idioms

usage labels

C Finding the best meaning

Many words in English have **multiple** meanings, and some words can be more than one part of speech (or word class). For example, the word **treat** can be a noun or a verb, each with several different meanings:

- Verb meanings include "behave toward someone in a certain way" (often used with *like*), and "give (someone) medical attention" (often used with *for*).
  I'm 21, but my mother still **treats** me like a child.
  The hospital **treats** hundreds of patients every day.
- Noun meanings include "a special, nice thing you do for someone," and "nice surprise."
  We're going out for dinner – it's my birthday treat.

When you meet a new word, look at the **context** it is in (the words and sentences around it). Which part of speech **fits** the **grammar** of the context? Which definition fits the meaning of the context?

D Finding phrases in a dictionary

Dictionaries explain the meanings of single words, compound words, and phrases. Phrases often contain one **key word,** an important word in the phrase. Try to identify the key word. For example, you may find these phrases by looking up the key word *time:* **take your time, for the time being, (give someone) the time of day.**

Exercises

3.1 Use a dictionary to find/check the answers to these questions.

1. What is the definition of **dreadful**? *very bad, terrible*
2. How do you pronounce **lose**? (Is it like *choose* or *chose*?)
3. Grammar: What part of speech is **choose**?
4. What part of speech is **homesick**?
5. **Homework** and **chaos** are both nouns, but what type of noun are they?
6. Write two adjectives that are often used before **chaos**.
7. How many syllables does **chaos** have?
8. Pronunciation: Is the *ch* in **chaos** like the *ch* in *character* or in *change*?
9. Collocations: What two prepositions are often used after **choose**?
10. Example: Write a sentence using **choose** with a preposition.

3.2 Use your dictionary to help you answer these questions.

1. **Choose** is a verb. What is the noun with the same meaning? *choice*
2. **Advice** is a noun. What is the verb with the same meaning?
3. **Advice** is uncountable. You can make it countable using another word. Complete this sentence: "He gave me a very useful .... of advice."
4. What adjective is formed from **chaos**?
5. What is the opposite of **dirty**?
6. What is the difference between **homework** and **housework**?
7. What is the opposite of **lose a game**?
8. What is the opposite of **lose weight**?
9. **Law** often appears in the phrase **law and** ....
10. If you want to invite someone to sit down in an empty **seat**, what can you say?

3.3 Look at your dictionary's entries for these words/phrases. Write any usage labels you find.

1. grungy ..*informal*..........................   4. thereby ....
2. bye-bye ....   5. incision ....
3. childish ....   6. put someone down ....

3.4 Use your English-English dictionary to find these idioms and expressions. Underline the key word(s) you found them with.

1. the <u>tip</u> of my <u>tongue</u>
2. in other words
3. better late than never
4. on second thought
5. break a promise
6. no hard feelings
7. the sooner the better
8. a matter of opinion
9. every now and then
10. beside the point

Words for talking about English

A **Parts of speech**

noun	e.g., chair, information, happiness
verb	e.g., choose, tell, complain
adjective	e.g., happy, tall, dangerous
adverb	e.g., slowly, carefully, fast, often
preposition	e.g., in, at, on
pronoun	e.g., me, you, him, we, it, she
article	e.g., the (definite article); a/an (indefinite article)

B **Special terms**

uncountable noun: a noun that has no plural form and cannot be used with the indefinite article, e.g., *information*.

plural noun: a noun that has a plural form but no singular form and cannot be used with the indefinite article, e.g., *scissors*.

infinitive: the base form of a verb used with *to*, e.g., *to work, to stop, to be*.

phrasal verb: a verb + adverb and/or preposition, e.g., *turn on, look over, give up, put up with*.

idiom: a group of words with an overall meaning different from the combined meanings of its individual parts, e.g., *have second thoughts, have something in mind, keep an eye on something*.

transitive verb: a verb that needs a **direct object**, e.g., "Police caught the thief" (*the thief* is the direct object of the verb *caught*).

intransitive verb: a verb that does not need a direct object, e.g., "The books arrived on time" (there is no direct object after *arrived*).

synonyms: words with the same meaning. For example, *big* is a synonym of *large*. The **opposite** of *large* is *small*.

C **Word building**

The word *uncomfortable* contains a **prefix** (*un-*), a **root** (*comfort*), and a **suffix** (*-able*). Other common prefixes include: *re-, in-,* and *dis-*. Suffixes include: *-ity, -ment,* and *-ive*.

D **Pronunciation**

Dictionaries show pronunciation with **phonetic symbols**, e.g., book /bʊk/, before /bɪˈfɔːr/, Internet /ˈɪnt·ər,net/.

Each word contains one or more **syllables**: *book* has one syllable, *before* has two, and *Internet* has three. To pronounce a word correctly, put the main **stress** on the proper syllable.

Note: Your dictionary may mark stress with bold type (re·**turn**), capital letters (re-TURN), or with a ' before the stressed syllable (re'turn).

E **Punctuation**

period	.	comma	,	parentheses	( )	brackets	[ ]
hyphen	-	question mark	?	semicolon	;	colon	:

Exercises

4.1 One word is missing from each line of this text. Put a caret (∧) where the word should be. Then write the missing word in the blank. Indicate what part of speech the word is (noun, verb, etc.).

Last year I went to∧for my vacation. I spent the first week Seville staying with a couple of friends, and then I took a train to Barcelona, where spent another ten days. It is beautiful city, and I had a marvelous time. I stayed in a very hotel right in the center of town, but I didn't mind spending a lot money because it has a relaxed, and is also very convenient. My brother recommended it; he goes Spain a lot and he stays anywhere else.

1. ...*Spain (noun)*...........................
2. ....
3. ....
4. ....
5. ....
6. ....
7. ....
8. ....
9. ....

4.2 In the conversation below, underline at least one example of an idiom, an infinitive, a phrasal verb, a plural noun, and an uncountable noun. Label your choices.

A: What <u>time</u> is it? ...*uncountable noun*.........
B: It's 8:00. We'd better hurry up to make the 8:30 show. ....
A: OK, just let me go change into some jeans real quick. ....
B: No. We don't have time. I don't want to be late. ....
A: Take it easy about the time. We'll be all right. ....

4.3 Label the underlined verbs as transitive (T) or intransitive (I).

1. She <u>broke</u> her leg. ...*T*.......
2. Question marks <u>show</u> uncertainty. ....
3. We <u>arrived</u> late. ....

4. <u>Take off</u> your jacket. ....
5. I <u>got up</u> at 7:30. ....
6. In phonetic symbols, bag <u>is</u> /bæg/. ....

4.4 Write the number of syllables in each word. Underline the main stress in each word.

<u>brac</u>kets ..*2*.......   root ....   hyphen ....   parentheses ....
understand ....   period ....   comma ....   pronunciation ....
before ....   opposite ....   preposition ....   semicolon ....

4.5 Complete the chart.

Word	Part of speech	Adverb with "-ly" suffix	Prefix for "opposite"	Synonym
happy	adjective			
correct		correctly		
lucky			un- (unlucky)	
sure				
probable				likely

A Equipment

These are some things you may use in your classroom or school.

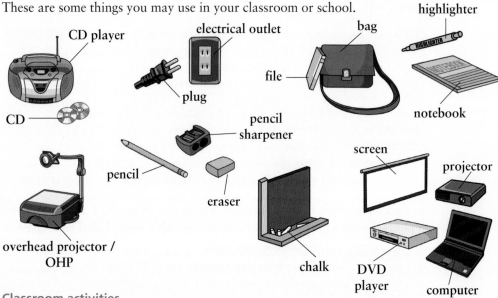

CD player · electrical outlet · bag · highlighter · CD · plug · file · notebook · pencil sharpener · pencil · eraser · screen · projector · overhead projector / OHP · chalk · DVD player · computer

B Classroom activities

Things students or teachers do in the classroom:

Look up a word if you don't understand it. [find its meaning in a dictionary]
Borrow someone's dictionary or eraser. [use it and then return it]
Plug in the CD player. [put its plug into an outlet]
Erase things in a notebook / from the board. [remove writing from a notebook / the board]
Correct students' English. [tell them which words to use if they **make mistakes**]
Highlight vocabulary words. [mark them with a bright-colored pen]
Sharpen a pencil. [give it a point]

Things a teacher may ask students to do in the classroom:

Write down these words. [write these words on a piece of paper / in a notebook]
Kim, could you **share** your book **with** Lorena? [use it together and at the same time]
Repeat this sentence after me. [say it again]
If you have a question, **raise your hand**. [hold up your arm]
Open your books and **do exercise** 3. [complete the activity]
Turn in / hand in your **homework**. [give it to your teacher]

C Questions about vocabulary

What does *highlight* mean? (*not* What means *highlight*?)
How do you pronounce it?
How do you spell *bicycle*?
How do you use *anyway* in a sentence?
What's the difference between *do* and *make*?

Exercises

5.1   Look around your classroom and write down six things that you see that are also pictured on page 10.

1. ....   3. ....   5. ....

2. ....   4. ....   6. ....

5.2   Use the words in the box below to complete the sentences.

erase	plug in	pencil	notebook
repeat	highlight	LCD projector	borrow

1. I didn't bring my book. Can I .... yours?
2. Remember to use a .... to write your answers in this book.
3. I like to .... vocabulary after my teacher pronounces it.
4. We need to .... the OHP before we can use it.
5. I like to .... words in my vocabulary ....
6. Hiro likes to help the teacher .... the board.
7. The teacher couldn't get the .... to work.

5.3   Match the verbs on the left with the nouns on the right.

1. look up   a classmate
2. sharpen   a word
3. turn in   mistakes
4. share with   an exercise
5. erase   homework
6. do   a pencil
7. make   the board

5.4   Think about your last class. Put a check next to any of the things you did. Compare your answers with a classmate if possible.

☐ use an eraser   ☐ look up a word   ☐ hand in your homework
☐ borrow something   ☐ make or correct a mistake ☐ highlight a vocabulary word
☐ raise your hand   ☐ write a word down   ☐ use a computer

5.5   Here are some answers. What are the possible questions?

A: .... ?
B: It means to use something that belongs to someone else and then return it.
A: .... ?
B: /ˈbɑr·oʊ/ Like *tomorrow*.
A: .... ?
B: B-O-R-R-O-W.
A: .... ?
B: If you borrow something, you take it. If you lend something, you give it.

A Adjective prefixes with the meaning "not"

Some prefixes give adjectives a negative meaning.

happy	**un**happy	like	**un**like
possible	**im**possible	legal	**il**legal [against the law]
correct	**in**correct	regular	**ir**regular, e.g., irregular verbs

un- is the most common, e.g., **unfriendly, unable, unemployed**. [without a job]

in- / im- / ir- / il- are all different spellings of the same negative prefix for adjectives that come from Latin roots:
- *il-* before adjectives starting with "l" (**illegal, illogical**)
- *im-* before "m" or "p" (**impatient, impolite**)
- *ir-* before "r" (**irrelevant, irresponsible**)
- *in-* before other letters (**invisible, informal**)

dis- is used before some adjectives, e.g., **dishonest**, and a few verbs, e.g., **dislike, disagree**.

> **note** A prefix does not normally change word stress, e.g., h<u>a</u>ppy/unh<u>a</u>ppy; p<u>o</u>ssible/imp<u>o</u>ssible.

B Verb prefixes: *un-* and *dis-*

With some verbs, these prefixes can mean "to do the opposite of an action" or "to reverse an action."

I lost the key so I couldn't **unlock** the door.
After I **unpacked** [took everything out of] my suitcase, I put my clothes in the closet.
I got **undressed** [took off my clothes] and went to bed.
We saw the plane in the sky, but then it **disappeared** behind a cloud.
I really **dislike** waiting in long lines.
Briana **disagreed** with the group's decision.

C Other verb prefixes

re- [again]	My homework was all wrong, so I had to **redo** it.
	The store closed down, but it will **reopen** next month.

over- [too much or too long]	I went to bed late and **overslept** [slept too long] this morning.
	The cashier **overcharged** me. [charged too much money]
mis- [badly or incorrectly]	Speak clearly so people don't **misunderstand** what you say.
	A lot of people **misspell** the word *misspell*.

Exercises

6.1 Write a prefix to form the opposite of each word. The first three columns contain adjectives; the last column contains verbs.

1. _un_.... happy	5. .... correct	9. .... logical	13. .... appear
2. .... patient	6. .... regular	10. .... friendly	14. .... pack
3. .... polite	7. .... visible	11. .... employed	15. .... lock
4. .... legal	8. .... possible	12. .... honest	16. .... like

6.2 Complete each conversation by agreeing. Use a synonym for each underlined word or phrase. Choose words from page 12.

1. A: He, <u>doesn't have a job</u>, does he?
   B: No, ..._he's unemployed._.... .

2. A: <u>It's against the law</u>, isn't it?
   B: Oh, yes. It's ....

3. A: This bill can't be right. They've <u>charged me way too much</u>.
   B: You're right. They've .... you.

4. A: Bacteria <u>can't be seen</u> without a microscope.
   B: That's right. They're practically ....

5. A: His argument <u>doesn't make any sense</u>.
   B: Yes, I know. It's ....

6. A: She <u>can never wait for five minutes</u>, can she?
   No. She's very ....

7. A: I thought it was <u>rude</u>, didn't you?
   B: Yes, it was very ....

6.3 Complete the verbs.

1. If you mis ...._understand_................ the directions, you will go to the wrong place.
2. We un .... our bags as soon as we got to the hotel.
3. She was here a minute ago, but then she dis ....
4. I totally dis .... with his opinion on this subject.
5. The teacher said I have to re .... my homework.
6. Her alarm clock didn't work, so she over ....
7. There's no need to dress up for the party. It will be very in ....
8. My computer's spell-checker corrects any word I mis ....

6.4 Complete the chart. Use a dictionary to help you find new words.

re-	un-	in-	im-	ir-
reopen	undressed	incorrect	impossible	irrelevant

Noun suffixes

A Verb + suffix

These common suffixes can change verbs to nouns.

Verb	Suffix	Noun
improve [get better]	-ment	improvement
manage [direct or control a business]		management
select [choose]	-ion	selection
discuss [talk about something seriously]		discussion
inform [give (someone) facts]	-ation	information
administer [manage an organization]		administration
spell [say each letter of a word]	-ing	spelling
post [put (a message) where many can see it]		posting

B Adjective + suffix

The suffixes -ness and -ity make nouns meaning "the quality of being the adjective."

Adjective	Suffix	Noun
weak [not strong]	-ness	weakness [being weak]
dark [without much light]		darkness
happy		happiness
stupid [not intelligent]	-ity	stupidity
punctual [arriving on time]		punctuality
similar [almost the same]		similarity

C Stressed syllables

Adding a suffix may move the main stress to a different syllable. Stressed syllables are underlined in these tables.

Verb	Noun
educate	education
inform	information
explain	explanation

Adjective	Noun
similar	similarity
stupid	stupidity
punctual	punctuality

D -er, -or, and -ist

These suffixes can be added to nouns or verbs. They often describe people and their jobs.

-er	-or	-ist
driver	actor	artist
manager	director	economist
writer	translator	journalist
programmer	educator	guitarist

Exercises

7.1 Underline the syllable with the main stress in each verb or adjective. Then complete the table with the noun forms. Underline the stressed syllable in each noun.

Verb	Noun	Adjective	Noun
1. educate	....	8. stupid	....
2. improve	....	9. dark	....
3. discuss	....	10. weak	....
4. inform	....	11. similar	....
5. spell	....	12. punctual	....
6. hesitate	....	13. happy	....
7. arrange	....	14. popular	....

7.2 Combine the words on the left with the suffixes on the right. Then complete the text. Change some words to plurals. Make small spelling changes as necessary.

improve	post	select
educate	weak	manage
administer	active	

-ment	-ion
-ation	-ness
-ity	-ing

According to a (1) ..*posting*............... this morning on President Garvin's Web site, the university has completed its (2) .... of a company to operate a new campus e-mail system. ClariNet Services, Inc., has been chosen to take over the (3) .... of all electronic communication systems on campus as of July 1. Because of (4) .... in the present system, faculty and students sometimes lose access to their accounts. High levels of (5) .... often cause the system to shut down entirely. The Garvin (6) .... has long promised to make (7) .... to the campus network. ClariNet is the nation's largest provider of network services to business and (8) ....

7.3 Complete the definitions.

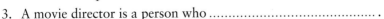

1. An economist is a person who ..*studies economics.*.........................
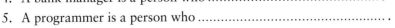
2. An actor is a person who ....

3. A movie director is a person who ....
4. A bank manager is a person who ....
5. A programmer is a person who ....
6. A songwriter is a person who ....
7. A translator is a person who ....
8. A guitarist is a person who ....
9. A driver is a person who ....
10. An artist is a person who ....
11. A journalist is a person who ....

Adjective suffixes

A Noun or verb + suffix

These suffixes can change a noun or verb to an adjective.

Noun or verb	Suffix	Adjectives
danger, fame	-ous	**dangerous, famous** [well known] e.g., "San Francisco is **famous** for its hilly streets."
music, politics, industry	-al	**musical, political, industrial, practical** [sensible; can be realistically done] e.g., "Texting is a **practical** way to send short messages."
cloud, fog, sun, dirt	-y	**cloudy, foggy, sunny, dirty** [opposite: clean] e.g., "Please put your **dirty** dishes into the sink."
attract, create	-ive	**attractive** [pretty, nice to look at]; **creative** [able to produce new ideas; with imagination] e.g., "This poet uses familiar words in **creative** new ways."

B -able (-ible)

This suffix creates adjectives from nouns or verbs: **enjoyable, comfortable, knowledgeable.** [knowing a lot]

Sometimes *-able* means *can be done*. For example, something that is **washable** can be washed. Other examples: **drinkable, reliable.** [can be relied on or trusted]

Sometimes the suffix is spelled *-ible*, e.g., **flexible** [easy to bend], **comprehensible** [can be comprehended or understood].

flexible

Many words with *-able* can add the prefix *un-* to mean "not": **undrinkable, unreliable, unbreakable** [cannot be broken], **uncomfortable.** Words ending with *-ible* usually add the prefix *in-* instead: **incomprehensible, inflexible, inedible** [cannot be eaten].

C -ful and -less

The suffix *-ful* means "full of" or "showing the characteristic of":

If you are **careful,** you show care [caution] in what you do. Someone who is **helpful** is willing to help. **Helpful** advice contains information that can help. Other examples: **painful** [hurting a lot]; **useful** [able to be used]; and **thoughtful** [thinking about how others may feel].

The suffix *-less* means "without":

If you are **careless,** you do something "without care," and you usually make mistakes because you are not careful. Other examples: **painless, useless, thoughtless, homeless** [having nowhere to live].

painful

Exercises

8.1   Write an adjective (or adjectives) from these nouns or verbs.

1.	industry *industrial*	11.	pain
2.	attract	12.	knowledge
3.	create	13.	comprehend
4.	fog	14.	thought
5.	home	15.	music
6.	dirt	16.	comfort
7.	care	17.	fame
8.	danger	18.	rely
9.	politics	19.	wash
10.	enjoy	20.	break

8.2   Complete the sentences with adjectives from page 16.

1. You have to be very .... when you drive in wet weather.
2. Everyone in my country has heard of her; she's very ....
3. The tourist guides were very .... and answered all my questions.
4. This is a very .... road; there were three serious accidents on it last year.
5. It was extremely .... when I hit my leg against the corner of the table.
6. In five years we've had no trouble with our DVD player; it's been very ....
7. It is not .... for one person to call every club member. You need help.
8. I made some coffee, but it was horrible. In fact, my sister said it was ....
9. My working hours are very .... , from 9:00 to 5:00 every single day.
10. The floods destroyed the town and made hundreds of people ....

8.3   Which of these words can form opposites with the suffix *-less*? Circle them.

painful	wonderful	useful	hopeful
beautiful	careful	awful	thoughtful

8.4   Choose three adjectives from this unit to describe each of these people or things.
(You can use the same adjective more than once.)

1. the weather ..*cloudy, sunny, foggy*............................
2. a very bad driver ....
3. a soccer game ....
4. Albert Einstein ....
5. a new car ....
6. yourself ....
7. a speech ....
8. a large city ....

$E = mc^2$

A Similar or different meanings

A noun and verb with the same form may have the same (or very similar) meaning.

What's the **answer**? (n.)	Please **answer** the question. (v.)
Each **package** contains twelve pencils. (n.)	The company **packaged** twelve pencils together. (v.)
Ann put Jim's application into a **file**. (n.)	Ann **filed** Jim's application form. (v.)
I wrote a **reply** to the letter. (n.)	I didn't **reply** to the letter. (v.)

In other cases, the meaning is different.

Put your money in the **bank**. (n.) Don't **bank on** getting an A. (v.) [don't depend on it]	The pencil may **break** if I press hard. (v.) At work, I take a **break** every two hours. (n.)

You may know these words as one form (either a noun or a verb) but not the other. The definitions are for the verb.

 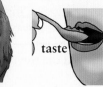 

smile

taste

smell

laugh

rain

dream

walk [travel by foot]

diet [eat less and lose weight]

guess [say or think something you're not sure of]

call [telephone]

push [opposite: **pull**]

tag [mark with a sign or label]

> *note*   Other words in this group include **drink**, **chat**, **rest**, **look**, **cost**, and **wait**.

B Which verb?

When each of these verbs is used as a noun, it may go with a certain new verb (*take*, *have*, *go*, etc.).

Verb	Noun
We **rested** for a while.	We **took/had** a short **rest**.
She **turned** quickly.	She **made** a quick **turn**.
He needs to **diet**.	He needs to **go on** a **diet**.
I'll **call** you next week.	I'll **give** you a **call** next week.
I **dreamed** about you last night.	I **had** a **dream** about you last night.
Runners **drink** water often.	Runners **take** frequent **drinks** of water.
The parents **smiled** at their son.	The parents **gave** their son a **smile**.
I **chatted** on the phone with a friend.	My friend and I **had** a **chat** on the phone.

Exercises

9.1 Rewrite each sentence. Change the underlined noun to a verb. The meaning should stay the same.

1. There was a lot of <u>rain</u> yesterday.
   It rained a lot yesterday.
2. We had a long <u>wait</u>.
   ....
3. Can you give me an <u>answer</u> to my question?
   ....
4. This orange has a strange <u>taste</u>.
   ....
5. I usually respond to jokes with a <u>laugh</u>, even if they are not funny.
   ....
6. I wrote a <u>reply</u> to his letter yesterday.
   ....
7. When the door gets stuck, you have to give it a <u>push</u>.
   ....

9.2 Rewrite each sentence. Change the underlined verb to a noun. The meaning should stay the same.

1. I'll <u>call</u> her tonight.
   I'll give her a call tonight.
2. The coach <u>smiled</u> at us after we scored our second goal.
   ....
3. We were very tired, so we <u>rested</u> after lunch.
   ....
4. I <u>turned</u> to the right and entered a large room.
   ....
5. I <u>dreamed</u> about our class last night.
   ....
6. My teacher <u>files</u> my homework in a folder with my name on it.
   ....
7. We <u>chatted</u> online for a while.
   ....

9.3 On a separate sheet of paper, write a one- or two-sentence answer to each question. Use any of the words from the list as a noun or a verb. Circle the items you use.

drink	package	tag	guess	pull
walk	cost	smell	look	diet

SHOPPING FOR GROCERIES [food you use in making meals]

1. How do you get to the store where you shop for groceries?
2. How can you tell whether the fruit or vegetables in the store are fresh?
3. How can you tell how much you have to pay for an item?

Compound nouns

A Formation

Most compound nouns are formed from two or more nouns that create a single new idea.

wedding rings

credit card

alarm clock

traffic light

DVD player

toothbrush

light bulb

cell phone

textbook

sunglasses

stop sign [a sign that tells drivers to stop]
dining room [a room used mostly for eating meals]
laptop [a small computer you can carry and use on your lap]
brother-in-law [your sister's husband; your spouse's brother]
income tax [the tax you pay on your income or salary]
haircut [the process or result of having someone cut your hair]
washing machine [a machine for washing clothes]
running shoes [shoes made for use in running for exercise]
babysitter [someone who watches children when the parents are out]
math teacher [someone who teaches mathematics]

B One word or two?

A compound noun may be written as one word (e.g., **bedroom** [a room where someone sleeps]), as separate words (e.g., **paper clip** [a bent piece of metal or plastic that holds papers together]), or as two or more words joined by a hyphen (e.g., **brother-in-law**). Use a dictionary to check how to spell a noun compound.

C Forming new compounds

One part of a compound may form the basis for many different compound nouns.

post **office**	brother-**in-law**	running **shoes**	**coffee** break
admissions **office**	father-**in-law**	dress **shoes**	**coffee** shop
front **office**	mother-**in-law**	tennis **shoes**	**coffee** cup

Exercises

10.1   Find compound nouns on page 20 connected with each of these topics.

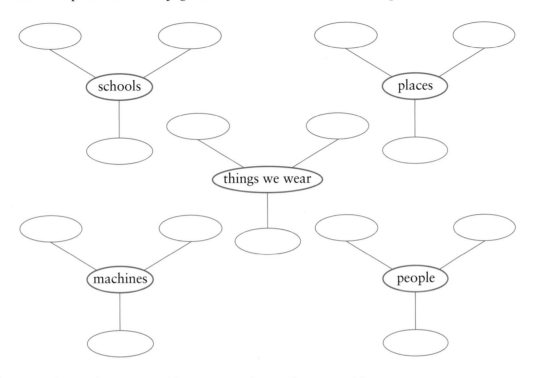

10.2   Complete each sentence with a compound noun from page 20.

1. The driver saw the .... at the corner but couldn't stop on the icy road.
2. You can't call me when I'm in the mountains. My .... doesn't work there.
3. My .... didn't go off this morning; I didn't wake up until noon!
4. For every four hours I work, I get a 15-minute ....
5. With no .... for their kids, the parents could not go out last night.
6. Long hair is uncomfortable in this hot weather. I need a ....
7. Each worker is supposed to pay .... on his or her earnings.
8. The papers are held together by a .... in the upper left corner.

10.3   Take one word (the first or second part) from each compound and create a new compound. Use a dictionary if necessary.

Examples   *brother-in-law*   *mother-in-law*
           dining room   *bathroom*

1. wedding ring ....
2. credit card ....
3. toothbrush ....
4. traffic light ....
5. sunglasses ....
6. front office ....

Compound adjectives

A Formation

A compound adjective is formed from two or more words. The second part is often a present participle (e.g., **good-*looking***) or a past participle (e.g., **well-*known***). Compounds with these participles are spelled with a hyphen before a noun (e.g., a **well-dressed** man, a **good-looking** actor).

Check a dictionary for help in hyphenating compound adjectives.

B Describing people

Many compound adjectives describe a person's appearance, character, and situation.

This is Bill. He isn't **well known** [famous], he isn't **well off** [rich], and nobody says he is **good-looking** [handsome/attractive]. But he's a nice man – kind, friendly, and **easygoing** [relaxed]. In this picture he's wearing a **short-sleeved** shirt and a **brand-new** hat [one he recently got]. Like most people he is **right-handed**.

> **note** **Short-sleeved** means having short sleeves. **Right-handed** means using mostly one's right hand. **Sleeved** and **handed** are not verb participles. They are adjectives made from nouns.

C With adverbs of quality (*well, nicely, badly, poorly*)

These combine with many past participles to form compound adjectives.

a **well-paid** job [one with a high salary]
a **well-educated** person [one who has learned a lot in school]
a **badly behaved** child [one who often does things he or she shouldn't do]
a **badly injured** person [one who has been seriously hurt]
a **nicely written** story [one that is told skillfully]
a **nicely done** project [one that has been done well]
a **poorly planned** project [one that has not been planned well in advance]
a **poorly understood** idea [one that few people understand correctly]

D With numbers and fractions

A compound with a number or fraction word plus a noun is spelled with a hyphen. The noun is always singular (e.g., a **five-minute** walk; *not* a five-minutes walk).

It's a **fifteen-minute** drive to the beach.
She has a **part-time** job.
He works in a **four-star** hotel.
I gave her a **five-dollar** bill.
The winner was a **ten-year-old** girl.
I found a **half-inch** nail in the flat tire.
I like to fly in the **first-class** section of a plane.
She wears **second-hand** clothes, but they look new.

Exercises

11.1 Combine words from the left box with words from the right to make ten compound adjectives.

good	well		done	known
easy	ten		written	dollar
short	badly		looking	sleeved
part	right		hand	handed
first	nicely		going	time

1. ..*good-looking*.......
2. ....
3. ....
4. ....
5. ....

6. ....
7. ....
8. ....
9. ....
10. ....

11.2 Make two compounds with each word.

1. poorly ..*planned*..........
   ....

3. badly ....
   ....

5. ....
   .... -handed

2. ....
   .... -time

4. twenty- ....
   ....

6. ....
   .... -inch

11.3 Complete the compound adjectives.

1. We stayed in a five- .... hotel.
2. Second- .... furniture costs a lot less than new furniture.
3. The .... -class cabins on a cruise ship are huge.
4. The TV has a .... -inch screen.
5. One little girl was very .... behaved during lunch.
6. He just got a .... -time job. He works twelve hours per week.
7. The painter Vincent van Gogh was not very .... known until after he died.
8. They're very well .... , so they can afford to go to expensive restaurants.
9. I can get home quickly. It's only a ten- .... walk to my house.
10. What would you do if you found a hundred- .... bill in the street?
11. She wore a .... -sleeved dress because it was very warm outside.
12. That sofa looks brand .... ! Did you just buy it?

11.4 Write about yourself, using ten different compound adjectives from page 22 or similar compounds. You can describe yourself, your personality, your family, your clothes, the place where you live, etc. Compare your answers with another student's if possible.

Collocations (common word partners)

A What is a collocation?

Certain words frequently go together. When this happens, we say the words **collocate**. The phrase that results is called a **collocation**.

I **missed the bus**. [I didn't **catch the bus**.] (*not* I "lost" the bus.)
He is a **heavy smoker**. [someone who smokes a lot] (*not* a "strong" smoker)
She **committed a crime**. (*not* She "made" a crime.)
The driver was **seriously injured** in the accident. [very badly hurt]

Good learner dictionaries list common collocations.

B Verb + noun

Some verbs form collocations with several nouns.

start	a car [turn on the engine] a family [have your first child] a fight	tell	a story the truth [opposite: tell a lie] a joke
run	a company [manage/control it] a race a (computer) program [use it]	miss	a chance a person [who is now gone] a target [opposite: hit the target]

C Adjective + noun

heavy	rain smoker accent	(a) hard	time [opposite: an easy time] work (*not* "a" hard work) look [a long, careful look]
deep	trouble breath sleep [opposite: a light sleep]	(a) straight	answer [is direct or honest] face [without a smile] A's [all top grades in school]

D Intensifier adverb + adjective

The adverbs in these collocations mean "very" or "to a great degree."

I was **terribly sorry** to hear about your accident.
It's **highly unlikely** he'll come now.
It is **virtually impossible** to see the ocean from here.
Sam gave his teacher an **utterly ridiculous** excuse for not doing his work.

Exercises

12.1 Complete the word webs. Use words from page 24.

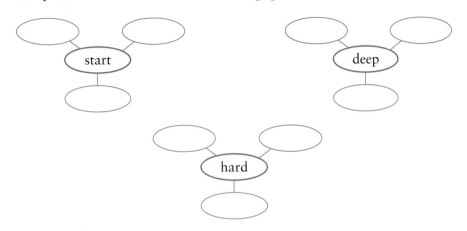

12.2 Write a collocation that means the opposite of each expression.

1. tell a lie *tell the truth*
2. a light sleep
3. speech with no accent
4. very likely

5. a hard time
6. a light rain
7. catch the bus
8. stop a computer program

12.3 Complete the sentences with collocations from page 24.

1. I had a hard .....*time*......... in my classes this year, but I still got .... A's.
2. A good comedian knows how to .... a joke with a straight ....
3. It was extremely cold last night. I couldn't .... the car this morning.
4. Michael's sister .... the company, even though Michael owns it.
5. I think they want to get married and .... a family.
6. He .... the same story about his trip to anyone who will listen.
7. A person who .... a crime should be punished.
8. You think I'll do your homework for you? That's .... ridiculous!
9. He has a .... accent. It's often hard to understand what he says.
10. The child was .... injured when he fell down the steps.

12.4 Write five sentences about yourself using collocations with the following words. Some words may be used more than once.

terribly	highly	virtually	utterly	heavy	hard

....

....

....

....

....

Idioms and fixed expressions

A What is an idiom?

An idiom is a group of words (or a compound) with a meaning that is different from the individual words, and often difficult to understand from the individual words. Many of the phrasal verbs in Units 22 and 23 are idiomatic. Here are some common idioms.

The teacher told us to **get a move on**. [hurry; be quick]
My wife and I **take turns** cooking. [I cook one day, she cooks the next, etc.]
I don't know the answer **offhand**. [without looking it up or asking someone]
I'm not very good at **small talk**. [social talk; not about serious things]
I'm sorry I can't **make it** on Friday. [come]
I asked her to **keep an eye on** my suitcase while I went to the bathroom. [watch]

B Fixed expressions

There are also expressions in English where the meaning is easy to understand, but the same idea in your language may need a completely different expression. If you translate each word from your language, you may say something in English that is completely wrong. For this reason, you need to learn certain fixed expressions as idioms. For example:

A: What was wrong with the hotel?
B: Well, **for starters**, it was next to a freeway and very noisy. And **to make matters worse**, there was a factory across the street, which stayed open 24 hours.

It's a good **short-term** (temporary, for now) solution, but **in the long run** (over a longer period of time) we will need to think about it.

C Using idioms

Idioms are important to know, but they can be difficult to use correctly. With many idioms, if you make just a small mistake, it can sound strange, funny, or completely wrong. For example: get the move on, offhands, small talks, put an eye on.

Idioms often have special features: They may be informal or funny or ironic; they may be used by certain people (e.g., young children, teenagers, or elderly people); they may appear only in limited contexts; they may have special grammar. For these reasons, you can sometimes "learn" the meaning of an idiom but then use it incorrectly. For example, "I was sorry to hear that your father **kicked the bucket**." This idiom means "died," but it is used humorously, never in a serious situation. It would be completely inappropriate when offering sympathy.

D Some easy idioms to use

Some idiomatic expressions are used alone, or with just one or two other words.

A: Can I borrow your dictionary?
B: Sure, **go ahead**. [it's OK; do it]

A: I don't know which one to choose.
B: Well, **make up your mind**. [decide]

A: **What's up?** [What's new/wrong?]
B: Nothing.

A: Are you coming?
B: Yeah, **right away**. [very soon]

Exercises

13.1 It can be difficult to guess the meaning of an idiom. Look at these examples (they are not presented on page 26).
1. I **feel like** having a soft drink.
2. They're gone **for good**.
3. I **changed my mind**.
4. I'm **tied up** all afternoon.
5. I can **make do** with what I'm getting.

Here is a fuller context for each idiom. Can you guess the meaning now?
1. A: Are you hungry?
   B: No, but I'm thirsty. I feel like having a soft drink.
2. A: Do you think they'll ever come back?
   B: No, they're gone for good.
3. A: You want to go out? You just said you wanted to stay home.
   B: I changed my mind.
4. A: Do you have a lot of clients to see?
   B: Yes, I'm tied up all afternoon.
5. A: Are you going to ask for a raise in salary?
   B: No, because I know I won't get it. I can make do with what I'm getting.

13.2 Replace the underlined words with idioms from the opposite page. (But try to do the exercise before looking at page 26.) Can you think of similar expressions in your language?
1. A: Could I borrow this for a minute?
   B: Yes, <u>take it</u>. *go ahead*
2. A: Sorry I can't <u>come</u> on Thursday.
   B: Don't worry. It's OK.
3. A: <u>What's the matter</u>?
   B: Nothing. Why?
4. A: Do we have to leave now?
   B: Yes, <u>hurry</u>, or we'll be late.
5. A: You'll have to <u>decide</u> soon.
   B: Yes, I know, but it's very difficult.
6. A: Would you <u>watch</u> my things for a minute?
   B: Yeah, sure.

13.3 Complete the expressions in these sentences.
1. It wasn't a very successful vacation. For ...*starters*......, the beach was a long way from our hotel; then to **make** .... **worse**, the car broke down on the third day and we had to walk to the beach for the rest of our stay.
2. We **take** .... walking the dog.
3. She asked me about the train schedule, but I couldn't tell her **off** ....
4. I don't enjoy parties where you just stand around and make .... **talk** with lots of people you don't know.
5. We can probably **make** .... with a one-bedroom apartment for now, but **in the long** .... we will have to move into a bigger place.

13.4 Find at least three idioms below. What do they mean?

I went to stay with my cousin last week. We are the same age but have very little in common: He loves sports and I hate them; I'm crazy about music and he's not interested in it. As you can imagine, we didn't have a very good time together, and by about Thursday we were really getting on each other's nerves, so I decided to go home.

Verb or adjective + preposition

A Verb + preposition

Some verbs are usually followed by a particular preposition. Pay special attention to any that are different in your language.

I **listen to** my MP3 player while I'm riding the bus.
My brother never **agrees with** me. [He never has the same view/opinion as me.]
I may go to the beach; it **depends on** the weather. [The weather will decide for me.]
She **suffers from** [feels sick because of] frequent headaches.
He **got married to** a woman he met in Brazil.
I'm going to **apologize for** [say I'm sorry for] the mistakes we made.
She has **applied for** a new job. [made a written request]
They were **waiting for** me when I arrived.
Don't **worry about** [be nervous about] your exam; it'll be OK.
She **complained to** the waiter **about** the food. [She said she was not satisfied.]
He **spends** a lot of money **on** new video games.
That camera **belongs to** Maria.

B Changes in meaning

Sometimes a different preposition changes the meaning of the verb:

Hey, Luisa!

How could you do that?

He **shouted to** me.
[said something loudly from a distance]

He **shouted at** me.
[He was angry with me and spoke loudly.]

She **threw** the ball **to** me. [for me to catch it]

She **threw** the ball **at** me. [in order to hit me; maybe she was angry]

We **searched** the lake **with** our boats. [We used boats to find things.]

We **searched** the lake **for** our missing boats. [We tried to find our boats.

C Adjective + preposition

I was never very **good at** math.
He is **afraid of** flying.
I'm **crazy about** cats. [I like cats very much.]
She is **similar to** [almost the same as] her sister, but very **different from** her brother.
He's very **interested in** electronic games.
I was **surprised at** (or **by**) his reaction. I thought he'd be happy to hear the news.
I think she is a**ware of** the problems in her class. [knows about]
I'm **tired of** studying foreign languages. [I've had enough and I want to stop.]
The streets are **full of** trash.
There is something **wrong with** this TV. [The TV is not working properly.]

Exercises

14.1 Complete these questions with the correct prepositions; then write a short answer for each one.

1. A: What is she worried ..*about*.......... ? B: ..*Her exams, I think.*..........
2. A: Who is she waiting .... ? B: ....
3. A: How much did you spend .... that bike? B: ....
4. A: What program is she listening .... ? B: ....
5. A: What did you apologize .... ? B: ....
6. A: Does this car belong .... her? B: ....
7. A: Who were you shouting .... ? B: ....
8. A: What's wrong .... the car? B: ....
9. A: What will the decision depend .... ? B: ....
10. A: What are you searching .... ? B: ....

14.2 Draw a line to match a phrase from the left column with one from the right.

1. He suffers
2. She wasn't aware
3. I was very surprised
4. He complained
5. That suit is similar
6. She applied
7. He threw a book
8. He said it depends
9. The suitcase was full
10. She said she agrees

a. at me, but it missed.
b. from a rare illness.
c. for a job in Puerto Rico.
d. on me.
e. with our boss's decision.
f. at his choice.
g. of clothes.
h. to the one my dad is wearing.
i. about the bad service.
j. of her mistakes.

14.3 Complete these sentences with your own ideas.

1. My steak was overcooked, so I complained ..*about it to the waiter.*...................
2. I work hard, but I'm not very good ....
3. I want to work in the travel business, so I've applied ....
4. Mel threw the basketball ....
5. I'm not crazy ...., but I'll go with you and listen.
6. I've always been interested ....
7. A lot of people are afraid ....
8. People in New York are very different ....
9. She's really tired ....
10. There's nothing wrong ....

14.4 Use a dictionary to find the prepositions that often follow the words below.

fond (adj.)　　　concentrate (v.)　　　responsible (adj.)　　　rely (v.)

Preposition + noun

A Common patterns

Some expressions are formed by a preposition + noun.

A play **by** Shakespeare, a movie **by** Ang Lee, a song **by** the school choir
You can go **for** a walk, **for** a drive, **for** a run, **for** a swim.
You can go **in** the morning, **in** the afternoon, **in** the evening (but **at night / at noon**).
You can travel **by** car, **by** plane, **by** bus, **by** train, **by** taxi (but **on foot**).
You can reach me **by** e-mail, **by** phone, **by** mail, **by** fax, **by** text message.
I heard it **on** the radio; I saw it **on** TV; I spoke to her **on** the phone (but I read it **in** the newspaper, **in** a magazine).
It was the man **in** the dark suit [wearing the dark suit]; the woman **in** the red dress / **in** red.

B Fixed expressions

Learn these phrases as fixed expressions. Notice that they do not contain *a/an* or *the*.

I took your pen **by mistake**. [an error; I didn't intend to take it.]
I did all the work **by myself**. [alone; without help from others]
The workers are **on strike**. [refuse to work unless their pay, hours, etc., improve]
I met them **by chance**. [It wasn't planned; it was luck.]
We're **on vacation**. [taking time away from work, school, etc.]
There were **at least** fifty people at the party. [a minimum of fifty]

He broke it **by accident**.
[It was a mistake.]

He broke it **on purpose**.
[He intended to do it.]

C Same noun, different preposition

When a different preposition is used with the same noun, it creates a different meaning.

We got home **in time for / in time to see** the soccer game on TV. [early enough]
Class begins at 8:30 and I always arrive **on time**. [at 8:30] (*not* on time to/for)

In the end, we went home. [finally, after a long period]
At the end of the book, they get married. [in the last part, the conclusion]

The two people are **in business**. [They are businesspeople.]
The two people are in Mexico **on business**. [They are there for work, not on vacation.]

I'll see you **in a moment**. [very soon]
I can't speak to you **at the moment**. [right now]

Exercises

15.1 Complete each sentence with the correct preposition.

1. I saw it .... TV.
2. They came .... car.
3. They are all .... strike.
4. She is here .... business.
5. She went there .... herself.
6. It was written .... J.K. Rowling.
7. We went .... a walk.
8. I read it .... a magazine.
9. He's .... vacation this week.
10. She took it .... mistake.
11. I went .... the afternoon.
12. He came .... foot.
13. I reached her .... e-mail
14. She broke it .... accident.
15. He did it .... purpose.
16. I'll see you .... a moment.
17. I'm very busy .... the moment.
18. It's very quiet here .... night.
19. We met .... chance.
20. She's .... least 25 years old.

15.2 Replace the underlined words with a prepositional phrase.

1. The meeting was planned for 11 a.m. We got here at 11 a.m. *on time.*
2. Did you get to the theater before the movie started?
3. She's talking to him in a phone call.
4. I saw the advertisement when I was watching TV last night.
5. He opened her letter because he incorrectly thought it was addressed to him.
6. The project was difficult for everyone, but finally it all worked out.
7. She gets killed in the last scene of the movie.
8. I'm afraid I'm very busy right now.
9. I saw her yesterday, but I didn't plan to see her.

15.3 Respond with a negative answer and a prepositional phrase from this unit.

1. A: Was it the woman wearing the blue blouse?
   B: *No, the woman in the white blouse.* ....

2. A: Did she hit him on purpose?
   B: ....

3. A: Did they go by car?
   B: ....

4. A: Are they here on vacation?
   B: ....

5. A: Did you read about the accident in the newspaper?
   B: ....

6. A: Did anyone go with him?
   B: ....

7. A: Is this store open for business?
   B: ....

8. A: Is your appointment in the morning?
   B: ....

9. A: Can I reach you by phone?
   B: ....

Apologies, excuses, acceptances, and thanks

A Apologies

We can **apologize** [say we are sorry] in different ways in different situations.

Apology	*Situation*
(I'm) sorry.	a general apology, e.g., when you interrupt someone, touch someone by mistake
I'm really / terribly / so / very sorry.	a stronger apology, e.g., when you step on someone's foot
Sorry to bother you, but . . .	when you want to interrupt someone, e.g., to ask them a question
Sorry to keep you waiting.	when someone is waiting to see or talk to you
My mistake. / It's my fault.	when you accept you did something wrong

> **note**   In formal situations (especially in writing), we often use **apologize** and **apology**:
> I don't know how to **apologize for** making this mistake.
> Please **accept our apologies for** the very slow service.

B Excuses

If the situation is important, we may:

- Add an excuse after the apology. An excuse gives the reason for the mistake – but the excuse may not be true.
- Offer to **fix** a problem. [make things better]

Excuses	**Offers to fix a problem**
I'm sorry I'm late but . . .	I'm sorry . . .
. . . I was **stuck in traffic**.	. . . about the **mess**. I'll **clean it up**.
. . . my car **broke down**.	. . . I **forgot** to call. I'll call tomorrow instead.
. . . I **lost track of** the time. [was not aware what the time was]	. . . about the spelling mistake. **It won't happen again.**

C Accepting an apology

In the response to an apology, two expressions may be used together for emphasis.

A: I'm sorry I'm late.
B: **That's OK. Don't worry.** *or* **Never mind. It doesn't matter.**

D Thanks and replies

A: I'll mail those letters for you.	A: I'm glad you could come.	A: Here's your change.
B: Oh, **thank you. That's very kind/nice (of you).**	B: It was a great dinner. **Thanks for having me over.**	B: **Thanks a lot.**
A: **Not at all. / No problem.**	A: **My pleasure.**	A: **You're welcome.**

Exercises

16.1 Complete these conversations with expressions from page 32.

1. A: I'm ...*so / very / terribly, etc.*... sorry.
   B: That's OK.
2. A: I'm sorry .... late, but I got .... in traffic.
   B: That's OK. Never ....
3. A: Sorry to .... you waiting.
   B: That's OK. Don't ....
4. A: I'll carry your bags for you.
   B: Oh, thank you. That's very .... of you.
5. A: I have to .... for missing the meeting.
   B: That's OK. It doesn't ....
6. A: I'm really .... I .... of the time.
   B: It's OK. Don't ....

16.2 What could you say in these situations? (If it is an apology, add an explanation or excuse.)

1. You get on a bus at the same time as another person and he/she almost falls over.
   I'm terribly sorry. I should be more careful. ....
2. You arrange to meet some friends downtown, but you are 20 minutes late.
   ....
3. Your car has broken down, and you are pushing it. A stranger offers help.
   ....
4. A friend apologizes for losing a pen that you lent him. Respond.
   ....
5. You have had dinner at a friend's house. Thank the friend as you leave.
   ....
6. You work for a company that sells computer equipment. A customer has e-mailed
   you to say she has not yet received some information you promised to send. Respond
   to her e-mail.
   ....
   ....

16.3 On the lines of the speech bubbles, write what you think the person in each picture should say.

A Requests and replies

Expressions for making requests differ depending on:

- who we are talking to
- the "size" of the request ("big" or "small")

Requests to close friends or for small things can be short and direct. Some examples and replies:

A: **Could you** pass me the salt?
B: **Sure.**

A: **Could I** borrow your dictionary?
B: Yes, **of course.** *or* Yes, **help yourself.** [Yes, take it.] *or* **Go ahead.** [Yes]

Other requests are longer and less direct. Some examples and replies:

A: **(Is there) any chance you could** lend me five dollars? *or*
Would it be possible for me to borrow five dollars?

A: **I was wondering if I could** leave work half an hour early today? *or*
Would you mind if I left work . . . ?

B: Yes, **sure.** *or*
I wish I could, but I don't have any money on me at all. *or*
I'm sorry, but . . .

B: **No problem.** *or*
Well, **I'd rather you didn't** because . . . *or*
Actually, that probably **won't work out.**

B Invitations and replies

A: **Do you want to** go out this evening?
B: **Yeah, great / I'd love to.** *or*
I'm sorry, I can't.

A: We're going out to dinner **and we were wondering if you'd like to** come with us.
B: **I'd love to, but I** can't tonight. I have to finish this report.

C Suggestions and replies

Asking for / making suggestions	
What do you want to do tonight? **Where should we go** this evening?	**How about** (*or* **What about**) a movie / just staying home? (*Note:* an *-ing* form is possible) **We could** go to the student center. **Why don't we** try that new café downtown?
Replying	
Positive: Yeah, **great/fine/OK.** **That's a good idea.** **Sounds good/great.**	*Weakly positive:* Yeah, **I guess / if you like.** [The speaker does not really want to.] **I'll see.** [The speaker is thinking about it.]
Negative: **I don't know.** [I don't really want to.] I think **I'd rather** stay home and watch videos. [I'd prefer to]	

Exercises

17.1 Correct the underlined mistakes in this conversation.

1. A: <u>Do you like</u> to go out this evening? *Do you want*
2. B: <u>I wish I can</u>, but I don't have any money.
3. A: That's OK, I'll pay. <u>How about go</u> to a movie?
   B: Yeah, great.
4. A: Lots of new comedies are playing. Why <u>we don't go</u> see one?
5. B: Yeah, <u>I am guessing</u>.
   A: You don't sound like you really want to.
6. B: Well, I don't know. I think <u>I'd rather to see</u> an action movie.
7. A: Well, <u>what like</u> that disaster movie about earthquakes?
8. B: Great! <u>I'll love</u>.

17.2 Complete the conversations with words or phrases from page 34.

1. A: .... you open that window? It's very hot in here.
   B: Sure. No ....

2. A: Tom and Heather are here and we were .... if you'd like to come over and have some dinner.
   B: Sure. I'd ....

3. A: What .... we do this evening?
   B: I don't know. Any ideas?
   A: Why .... we go for a walk around the lake?
   B: Yeah, that's a ....

4. A: Where .... we go on Saturday?
   B: .... going to the beach if the weather is nice?
   A: Yeah. Or we .... play golf.
   B: Mmm. I think I'd .... go to the beach.
   A: OK, I'll ....

17.3 Respond, either positively or negatively, as fast as you can to each statement. If possible, do this activity with someone else: One person asks the questions, the other answers.

1. Could I borrow a pen? *Sure, go ahead. / I'm sorry, but I don't have one.*
2. Would you mind mailing a letter for me?
3. I was wondering if you have a suitcase you could lend me.
4. Would you like to go out this evening?
5. I've got tickets for a concert. I was wondering if you'd like to go with me.
6. How about going to a baseball game this weekend?
7. Why don't we meet this afternoon and practice our English for an hour?
8. We could invite some other people from our English class to meet us, too.

A Asking for someone's opinion

What do you **think of** his new book/car? [asking about a specific thing/person]
What do you **think about** the elections? [asking about a general topic]
How do you **feel about** working here? [asking for feelings as well as thoughts]
What's your (**honest**) **opinion of** that painting? [asking for personal reactions]

B Giving your opinion

(**Personally,**) **I think** Carla's idea is the best.
    (negative: I **don't think** Carla's idea is the best.
    not I think Carla's idea is not the best.)
In my opinion, we should sell the old car
    and buy a new one.
As far as I'm concerned, the whole evening was a waste of time.

C Agreeing with someone

To agree, you might repeat the other person's opinion in different words.

A: I think we should concentrate on this one project.
B: Yes, it's better to do one thing well than two things badly.

You could also use a direct "agreement" expression.

Yes, **I agree (with you).** (*Note:* **Agree** is a verb; *not* I am agree.)
Yes, (**I think**) **you're right.**

D Disagreeing with someone

A "disagreement" statement might begin with an "agreement" expression. Then the speaker says "but" and gives a different opinion. This is a more polite and indirect way to disagree.

I see/know what you mean,		I'm not sure that . . . / about . . .
I agree **to some degree/extent,**		then again . . .
(Yes,) maybe/possibly/perhaps,	but	don't you think . . . ?
(Yes,) **that's true,**		what about . . . ?
(Yes,) **you could be right,**		don't forget . . .

If you disagree strongly, you can say:

	I **totally/completely disagree** (with you/him/that).
(I'm) sorry, but	I **can't go along with that.**
	I **don't agree** (with you) **at all.**

Exercises

18.1 Complete these questions in at least three different ways to ask people their opinions.

1. .... the changes in our town this year?
2. .... the new building?
3. .... the subway system?
4. .... these shoes? Do they look OK?

18.2 Complete each sentence with one word from page 36.

1. A: What did you think .... the movie?
   B: Well, ..., I didn't like it very much.
2. In my ...., we should start right away.
3. I agree with her to a certain ....
4. As far as I'm ...., the plan will never work.
5. I'm sorry, but I .... disagree with you.
6. I see what you ...., but I'm not sure I agree with you.

18.3 Rewrite each sentence using the word or phrase on the right.

1. In my opinion, you can't learn a language in three months. *Personally, I don't think you can learn a language in three months.*	personally
2. You may be right, but what about the cost?	but then again
3. I totally disagree with you about that.	at all
4. I know what you mean, but don't you think the story was interesting?	that's true
5. I know you think the homework was easy, but I disagree,	I don't think
6. Yes, I see what you mean, but I'm not sure about that.	you could be right
7. You feel that Sara is lying. So do I.	agree
8. Don thinks the weather is too hot. I completely disagree.	go along with

18.4 Continue each conversation. Use vocabulary items from page 36.

1. A: The government should lower the speed limit on highways from 70 miles per hour (113 kilometers per hour) to 50 miles per hour (80 kilometers per hour).
   B: ....

2. A: Teenage drivers drive a lot more safely than older drivers do.
   B: ....

3. A: The law that says anyone born in this country is a citizen is a good law.
   B: ....

Likes, preferences, and interests

A What do you like?

Statement	Agree	Disagree
[+++] **I love** rock music.	So do I. / Me too.	Really? I don't.
[++] I really **like** dance music.	Yeah.	Oh, not me.
[+] **I don't mind** jazz.	Yeah, it's OK.	I can't stand it.
[0] I'm **not** really **interested in** folk music.	Me neither.	Oh, I am.
[---] I **can't stand** opera.	Neither can I.	Really? I like it **a lot**.
[---] I **hate** classical music.	So do I.	Not me. I like it.
[--] I **dislike** loud music. *(formal)*	Me too.	I like some kinds of it.

> **note** Love, hate, like, dislike, don't mind, and can't stand can be followed by an **-ing** verb: I love driv**ing**; I don't mind work**ing** on weekends.

B And things like that

After one or two examples of things we like / don't like, we might finish with a general phrase:

She likes poetry and drama and **that sort of thing**.
I try to eat healthy foods – pasta, and salads, and **stuff like that**.
My husband likes boxing and wrestling, but I hate **things like that**.
What **kinds of things / sort of stuff** do you like?

C Look forward to

I'm **looking forward to** going home. [am excited about going home]
I always **look forward to** my birthday. [am excited when it is going to happen]
I'm **not looking forward to** the exams because I haven't done much work.
I **look forward to hearing from you**. (a common way to end a formal letter)

D Which do you prefer?

In general
A: Which do you **prefer**, tea or coffee?
B: I **prefer** coffee **over / instead of / to** tea in the morning.

Specific occasion
A: We could go to a movie or go bowling. Which **would you prefer**?
B: **I'd prefer to** go bowling. *or* **I'd rather** go bowling.

> **note** I'd rather is the same as I'd prefer to, but is more common in spoken English.

E What are you interested in?

A: Are you **interested in** Latin music?
B: Yes, **very (much)**. *or* No, **not really**. *or* No, it doesn't **interest** me (**at all**).

Exercises

19.1 Write a correction for each underlined mistake.

1. A: I love modern art.   B: Yes, <u>so I do</u>.   *so do I.*
2. A: Do you like this?   B: Yes, <u>I like very much</u>.
3. A: Would you like to go out?   B: No, <u>I'd prefer stay here</u>.
4. A: I'll be there next week.   B: I'm <u>looking forward to see you</u>.
5. A: Do you like tea?   B: Yes, but I prefer coffee <u>than tea</u>.
6. A: Does he like football?   B: No, he's not <u>interesting</u> in sports.
7. A: I don't like this kind of music.   B: No, <u>me too</u>.
8. A: Can you help them?   B: Yes. I don't mind <u>to help</u> them.

19.2 Complete the phrases in bold in these sentences.

1. My sister loves country-western music, but **I can't** ....*stand*............ it.
2. He likes windsurfing and waterskiing and **that sort of** ....
3. They're not very **interested** .... sightseeing.
4. Do you really enjoy **things** .... **that**?
5. **Are you looking** .... **to your holiday**?
6. I love the cinema, but this particular film **doesn't** .... **me at all**.
7. Carole .... modern art **a lot**. Personally, I hate it.
8. (*formal letter*) **We look forward to** .... **from you**.

19.3 Rewrite each sentence using a word from the box. Use each word only once.

mind	rather	interest	interested	stand	things

1. I hate these new shoes. ...*I can't stand these new shoes*.............................
2. They'd prefer to go home. ....
3. I don't like his books. ....
4. I don't like art and stuff like that. ....
5. I find art history very interesting. ....
6. I think this new building is OK. ....

19.4 Agree with each of these sentences using "so" or "neither" and the correct verb.

1. I love this ice cream.   *So do I.*
2. I like strawberries.
3. I don't like cold tea.
4. I can't work with music on.
5. I'm single.
6. I'm not married.

Now write "me too" or "me neither" next to each of your answers.

Greetings, farewells, and getting someone's attention

A Greetings

In North American English, truly formal greetings are almost never used.

Neutral greeting	*Neutral response*
Hi./Hello.	Hi./Hello.
How are you?	Fine (thank you). How are you? / How about you? And you?

Informal greeting	*Informal response*
Hi./Hey.	Hi./Hey.
How's it going? How're you?	Not bad. / Pretty good. / OK.
What's up?	Not much.

Formal greetings may be used when you meet someone new:

Pleased to meet you.
Nice to meet you.   Response: **Nice to meet you too.**
How do you do?

These greetings can be used at different times of day:

Good morning. (from sunrise until noon)
Good afternoon. (from noon until about 5:00 p.m.)
Most people do not use **Good evening** as a greeting. **Good night** is *not* used as a greeting.

B Farewells

Goodbye./Bye.
Good night. (used after about 9:00 at night or if one of you will soon go to bed)
Take care. / Take it easy. / So long. / See you. / See you later. (*informal*)
(It was) good/great/nice to see you (again). (to someone you already know)
Have a nice day/evening/weekend. (can be used after speaking with anyone, but is especially common to a customer in a store) Response: **You too.**
(It was) nice meeting / to meet you. (to say goodbye after you have met someone new)
    Responses: **Nice meeting you too. Nice meeting YOU.** (extra stress on "you") / **Same here.** (*informal*)

C Getting someone's attention

- To get someone's attention, e.g., "**Excuse me / Pardon me**, Dr. Post. Can I see you for a moment?"
- To get past someone who is in your way, e.g., "**Pardon me. / Excuse me.** Can I just get by you?"
- To get a server's attention in a restaurant: 1) Wait until the server is close; 2) Raise your hand slightly (no higher than your shoulders; 3) Say "**Excuse me. / Pardon me.**" Speak in a normal voice, not too loud.

Exercises

20.1 Complete the conversations.

1. A: Hi. *Good to see you.* ....
   B: Hey. Good to see you too.

2. A: ....
   B: I'm fine. How about you?

3. A: Thank you. Have a nice day.
   B: ....

4. A: ....
   B: OK. Good night. Sleep well.

5. A: Nice meeting you.
   B: ....

6. A: ....
   B: Yes. What would you like to ask?

7. A: Jim. Hi. What's up?
   B: .... How about you?

8. A: ....
   B: Yeah. See you.

20.2 Complete the conversations with your own ideas.

20.3 What would you say in these situations?

1. You are in a meeting. Someone comes in to say you have an urgent telephone call.
   What do you say as you leave? *Excuse me. I'll be right back.*
2. You are in a meeting. Your cell phone rings. What do you say to the people in the room
   as you turn it off?
3. Someone says something to you, but you don't hear all of it.
4. You are on a crowded bus. It is your stop and you want to get off. What do you say to
   the other passengers as you move past them?
5. You are staying with friends. You leave the room in the evening to go to bed.
6. You met a new business client for the first time an hour ago. Now you are both
   leaving.
7. While shopping, you meet an old friend (by chance), who you haven't seen in ages.
8. You are at a restaurant. You need to ask the waiter for some more coffee.

Common responses

A Short responses

Questions	Short responses
Are you going to the party tonight?	I think so. *or* I don't think so. / I doubt it.
Is Tom going to meet us?	Yes, I hope so. [I don't know, but I want it to happen.]
Is it going to rain?	I hope not. (*not* I don't hope so.)
Are you working this weekend?	I'm afraid so. [Unfortunately, I am.]
Can you come to the game?	I'm afraid not. [I'm sorry, but no, I can't.]

B Responding with interest and enthusiasm [a strong feeling of interest]

She finally got her visa to travel.	Really? That's great/fantastic/wonderful.
We're going camping in Greece.	That sounds wonderful / cool / like fun.
I'm going to meet some actors.	Really? That sounds interesting/unusual.
They're having a baby.	That's great news! That's nice.

C Responding to statements about problems

I can't go to the party this evening.	Oh, that's too bad.
Sam isn't feeling well, so he's staying here.	Oh, what a shame / that's a shame.
I think it's going to rain for our picnic.	Oh, what a nuisance/pain. [indicates strong disappointment/anger]
I dropped my cell phone in the lake.	That's not good.
I can't play. I hurt my leg in the last game.	Oh, that's awful / bad news / terrible.

D Weak agreement

We can agree to something, but not very strongly, with these statements.

When should we go?	Whenever you like. / Whenever.
What do you want to do?	Whatever you like. / Whatever.
Where should we put these chairs?	Wherever you like. / Wherever.
Do you want to go out?	I wouldn't mind.
How about playing some tennis?	Yeah, I guess.
Should we take a taxi?	Sure, if you like. [That's OK with me.]

E Remember to respond!

These short expressions can show you are listening. Say them occasionally while another person is talking.

mmm	OK	right
uh-huh	I know	I see [I understand]
yeah	sure	

Exercises

21.1 Practice saying these phrases. Check the pronunciation online or in your dictionary.

I doubt it.   Oh, what a nuisance.
I'm afraid so.   That sounds awful.

21.2 Complete each conversation. Practice them with a partner if possible.

1. A: Can we still get tickets?
   B: I hope ..*so*....................

2. A: Are you working tomorrow?
   B: Yes, I'm afraid ....

3. A: Is the price going up?
   B: Well, it's already expensive, so I hope ....

4. A: Are you going?
   B: I doubt ....

5. A: Are there any left?
   B: I don't think ....

6. A: Have you got any change for the coffee machine?
   B: I'm afraid ....

21.3 Write the letter of the best response for each question or statement.

....*c*.... 1. Tom can't come because he's working.

.... 2. We're staying in a very expensive hotel.

.... 3. Do you want to watch the end of the film?

.... 4. Does he often get angry like this?

.... 5. We can't get in. Joe's got the key.

.... 6. What time do you want to start?

a. Whenever you like.

b. I'm afraid so.

c. Oh, that's too bad.

d. That's a pain.

e. Yeah, if you like.

f. That sounds great.

21.4 Replace the underlined word or phrase with another word or phrase that has the same meaning.

1. A: She's ill.
   B: Oh, that's <u>a shame</u>   *too bad.*

2. A: Do you want to go?
   B: Yeah, <u>I wouldn't mind</u>.

3. A: We're going to take a cruise through the islands.
   B: Oh, <u>that's exciting</u>.

4. A: Is it still busy at this time of year?
   B: No, I <u>don't think so</u>.

5. A: What do you want to do?
   B: I don't know. <u>Whatever</u>.

6. A: He fell off his bike and broke his arm.
   B: Oh, <u>that's awful</u>.

21.5 Respond to these statements in a suitable way. Practice with someone else if possible.

1. I'm going to spend three weeks in Australia. ...*That's great. / That sounds like fun*.........
2. Alex lost your watch. ....
3. Do you want to finish this later? ....
4. Where shall we go? ....
5. I just won $1,000. ....
6. I can't go tomorrow. I have to work. ....
7. Peter lost his wallet with all his credit cards. ....
8. I wanted to speak to Karen, but she's out all day. ....

Phrasal verbs (1): form and meaning

A Formation

A phrasal verb contains a verb + an adverb and/or a preposition. The adverb or preposition part of a phrasal verb is called a particle.

The price of coffee may **go up** again next week. [increase]
He **fell down** as he was running for the bus. [fell to the ground]
She promised to **find out** more about the new project. [learn/discover]
If you don't understand the word, you can **look** it **up** online. [find the meaning]
He can't **get along with** his parents. [have a good relationship with]

B Particles that don't change meaning

Sometimes the adverb or preposition doesn't change the meaning, but makes it sound more natural.

I didn't **wake up** until 7 o'clock.   I'm **saving up** for a new computer.
Hurry up or we'll be late.   She **stood up** and walked to the door.
Sit down and be quiet.   The doctor told me to **lie down**.

C Particles with a core meaning

Particles can sometimes change the meaning of the verb but in a similar way.

back usually means to return something or return somewhere, e.g., **put back**, **go back**, **give something back**, **take** something **back**, **call** someone **back**.
up can suggest completing something, e.g., **use up** [use all of something], **finish up**, **drink up**, **eat up**.
on can indicate continuation of something, e.g., **go on**, **carry on**, **keep on**. [doing something]
off can mean separation or leaving, e.g., **take off**, **cut** something **off**, **see** someone **off**. [take someone to the airport, station, etc.]

D Multiple meanings

Many phrasal verbs have more than one meaning.

Meaning 1	*Meaning 2*
It was hot, so I **took off** my jacket. [removed]	I get nervous when the plane **takes off**. [leaves the ground]
I **picked up** the trash and put it in the garbage can. [lifted it]	I went to the store to **pick up** my pictures. [get/collect]
The bomb could **go off** at any minute. [explode]	My alarm clock didn't **go off** this morning. [ring]
They want to **bring up** their children in a peaceful environment. [raise]	Whenever you **bring up** the subject of food, I get hungry. [introduce a topic]
I **put** some food **out** for the birds. [placed outside]	I **put** the fire **out**. [stopped it burning]
His constant questions **put** me **off**. [make me angry/annoyed]	Don't **put off** your homework. [delay]

Exercises

22.1 Fill in the blanks to complete the phrasal verbs.

1. We went around the neighborhood and .....*picked*.......... **up** all the trash.
2. The police never .... **out** how the prisoner escaped.
3. I .... you **back** and left a message on your answering machine.
4. They didn't use to like each other, but they're .... **along** very well now.
5. The price of gold has .... **up** by 50% this year.
6. If you are not sure how to pronounce a word, ... it **up** in the dictionary.
7. Didn't your alarm clock .... **off** this morning?
8. I had .... **up** all the paper, so I couldn't print out my homework.
9. I was .... **down** when the phone rang. I .... **up** and answered it.
10. .... down in that chair, and I will tell you a story.
11. Write your essay now. If you .... it **off**, it will never get done.
12. We all went to the airport to .... him **off**.

22.2 Complete these sentences with your own ideas.

1. It will take him a long time to get over ..*his soccer team's loss.*.............................
2. To get to school on time, I have to wake up ....
3. Even though ...., she carried on and finished the race.
4. Before he stepped into the lake, he took off ....
5. I won't buy any more butter until we use up ....
6. Come on. Hurry up. I don't want ....
7. We're out of time. Finish up what you're writing and ....
8. If you're not careful walking .... you might fall down.

22.3 Look at the dictionary entry for *pick up*, and match the meanings with the sentences below.

> **pick up** *phrasal verb*
> 1 ▶LIFT UP◀ [T pick sb/sth ↔ **up**] to hold someone or something and lift him, her, or it from a surface: *The kids were **picking up** shells at the beach.*
> 2 ▶GO GET SB/ST◀ [T pick sb/sth ↔ **up**] to go somewhere, usually in a vehicle, in order to get someone or something: *What time should we **pick** you **up** at the airport?*
> 3 ▶BUY◀ [T pick sth ↔ **up**] INFORMAL to buy something: *Will you **pick up** something for dinner on your way home?*
> 4 ▶GET BETTER◀ [I] to improve: *Sales should **pick up** before Christmas.*
> 5 ▶LEARN◀ [T pick sth ↔ **up**] to learn something without deliberately trying to: *Craig **picked up** the guitar from his dad.*

1. I said I would pick them up at the train station.   *definition 2*
2. Could you pick up some milk on the way home?
3. Where did he pick up that strange idea?
4. Business was bad at the beginning of the year, but it's picking up now.
5. I hurt my back when I tried to pick up that suitcase.

Unit 23

Phrasal verbs (2): grammar and style

Look at Unit 22 before you do this unit.

A Grammar: intransitive verbs

Some phrasal verbs are intransitive. They don't need a direct object.

The cost of school **goes up** every year. [increases]

Don't wait out there. Please **come in**. [enter]

I **grew up** in a small town. [changed from a child into an adult]

I **stayed up** late last night. [did not go to bed until late]

An adverb ending in *-ly* can be placed:

- before the verb (he <u>quickly</u> **stood up**);
- after the particle (he **stood up** <u>quickly</u>).

Other adverbs (those *not* ending in *-ly*), usually don't come between the main verb and the particle (e.g., "He **stood up** <u>fast</u>," *not* "He fast stood up").

B Grammar: transitive verbs

Many phrasal verbs are transitive. They need a direct object. You can usually put the object either between the main verb and the particle or after the phrasal verb.

Put on your shoes. **Put** your shoes **on**.	**Turn off** your cell phone. **Turn** your cell phone **off**.	**Write down** your number. **Write** your number **down**.

If the object is a pronoun, it *must* go in the middle.
Put them on. [*not* Put on them.] **Turn it off. Write it down.**

C In dictionaries

You can use a dictionary to check the grammar. Most dictionaries show it like this:

carry on, get by (intransitive phrasal verb)
I can **get by** in French. [I can manage in French, but I don't speak it well.]

turn sth ↔ up, pick sth ↔ out (transitive phrasal verb)
Did you **turn** the volume **up**? [make the sound louder]
Did you **turn up** the volume?

Get over sth, look after sth (verb + preposition + object)
Our team will **get over** the loss. Our team will **get over** it.

D Phrasal verbs and style

A phrasal verb can help create a relaxed or informal style in a statement.

I **write down** new vocabulary items I learn. [record]
We had to **make up** a story. [invent]
I can usually **get by** on about $500 a week. [manage]
The town **set up** a new parking system. [established]
I can't **work out** a way to solve the math problem. [discover]
I offered to cut Mr. Cain's grass, but he **turned down** my offer. [rejected]
The heater **broke down** during the cold weather. [stopped working]

Exercises

These exercises also practice and test some of the phrasal verbs from Unit 22.

23.1 **Complete these sentences with your own ideas.**

1. I'm not very good at making up ..*excuses/stories*..
2. I'm tired today because I stayed up ....
3. Would you please turn on .... ?
4. .... was set up beside a river.
5. Could you please write down .... ?
6. .... broke down before we reached the city.
7. .... we'll have to get by on the food we already have.
8. Put on a sweater or a jacket ....

23.2 **If the underlined part is incorrect, rewrite it correctly. If it has no mistake, write "OK."**

Examples: You can <u>come now in</u>.   *come in now*
                I found my gloves and <u>put them on</u>.   *OK*

1. The two sides tried to <u>work out an agreement</u>.
2. I told the children I'd <u>pick up them</u> after school.
3. When he heard the bell, he <u>stood fast up</u>.
4. No one could hear, so I <u>turned the volume up</u>.
5. Children <u>grow up very quickly</u> these days.
6. My brother <u>stayed late up</u> watching TV.
7. I was sad about my bad grade, but I eventually <u>got over it</u>.
8. My bicycle <u>broke yesterday down</u>.

23.3 **Make these statements sound less formal by changing the underlined verbs to phrasal verbs.**

1. The cost of living is <u>increasing</u> *going up* all the time. It's hard to <u>manage</u> on my salary.
2. Our air conditioner <u>failed</u> on the hottest day of the year. Unfortunately, we could not <u>discover</u> what was wrong with it. In the end, we tried to solve the problem with electric fans. We <u>established</u> a system of them around the house.
3. The teacher showed the students a picture and asked them to <u>invent</u> a story to go with it. Each student <u>recorded</u> whatever the picture brought to mind. The teacher asked one student to tell his story to the class. He <u>rejected</u> her offer because he was shy.

23.4 **There are many phrasal verbs in other units. Find three phrasal verbs in each of these units: 28, 29, 52, 60, and 80.**

Have and *have got*

A *Have* vs. *have got*

We use both *have* and *have got* (less formal) to talk about possessions, relationships, illnesses, problems, ideas, and many other situations.

I **have** a new **DVD player.**
She**'s got** two brothers.
Do you **have** the **time?** [What time is it?]
He**'s got** a **headache.**
I **have/'ve got** a **problem.** I'm going to be late for class.
I **have/'ve got** an **idea** for solving your problem.

DVD player

In negative sentences, use *don't have* or *haven't got*.
I *don't have* a car. / I *haven't got* a car. (*not* I haven't a car.)

I **had** a car when I was at college. (*not* I had got)

The verb form used in an answer is usually the same as in the question.
A: **Do** you **have** a car?   A: **Have** you **got** a car?
B: Yes, (I **do**).   B: Yes, (I **have**).

B *Have* + object

Things to eat or drink
What time do you **have breakfast/lunch/dinner?**
I **had steak,** but Paul just **had a sandwich.**
Let's **have a drink** before dinner.

Events / occurrences
have a party, e.g, "I'm **having a party** for my birthday."
have a nice / great / terrible / etc., time, e.g., "We **had a very nice time** in Singapore."
have a meeting / discussion / argument / debate, e.g., "We **had a meeting** at noon."

Instead of "take"
I **had a shower.** [I took a shower]
Let me **have a look.** [I'll take a look]
I'll **have the bill,** please. [I'll take the bill]

Health and physical conditions
She **had a baby** last month. [delivered a baby]
He **had a heart attack.** [experienced a bad heart problem]

> **note**   If **have** means "are supposed to have; are scheduled to have," then **have got** can replace it:
> We**'ve got** a meeting tomorrow. [are scheduled to have a meeting]
> We**'ve got** dinner at 6:00. [are supposed to have dinner]

Exercises

24.1   Change the verbs from *have* to *have got* or from *have got* to *have*.

    1. I have an old computer. *I've got an old computer.* ....

    2. I don't have a job at the moment. ....

    3. Has he got any change for the machine? ....

    4. She hasn't got much money. ....

    5. We don't have wireless Internet at school. ....

    6. A: Do you have an English dictionary? ....

       B: Yes, I do. ....

24.2   Where possible, change *have* to *have got*. (Make other changes as necessary, too).
If the verb cannot be changed, write "no change."

    1. Do you have a car?   *Have you got a car?*

    2. Have you seen her today?   *no change*

    3. We have a small garden.

    4. I think I have a cold.

    5. Do you have a cell phone?

    6. Someone told me she has a new boyfriend.

    7. We usually have lunch at about 12:30.

    8. When they see each other, they always have a big argument.

24.3   Complete each sentence with a suitable word/phrase.

    1. I've got a ..*problem*...................... with my car. It won't start.

    2. After we ride our bikes, I usually have .... to cool off and clean up.

    3. How should we solve this problem? .... any ideas?

    4. She's having her 21st birthday .... next week. Are you going?

    5. We've set up a time to talk about our plans. We .... a meeting at 3:00.

    6. The weather was terrible. We didn't have a very good ....

24.4   Express each idea using *have* + an object. Keep the meaning the same.

    1. Fred suddenly experienced a really bad heart problem.
       Fred had a heart attack. ....

    2. Mary is pregnant.
       ....

    3. Fred found it very difficult to work the video projector.
       ....

    4. Mary examined my bad shoulder.
       ....

    5. Fred really enjoyed himself in Japan.
       ....

    6. Mary told the waiter, "I'll take the bill."
       ....

Make, do, and take

A Things we make

a mistake	She **made** a few **mistakes** on the exam. [errors]
a meal	I had to **make** my own **dinner** last night. [prepare and cook something]
money	He **made** a lot of **money** when he worked in California. [earned money]
friends	It's not easy to **make friends** in a new place.
a decision	Should we take the red one or the green one? We have to **make a decision** now.
a difference	Each person can **make** a **difference** in this world. [have an effect on a situation]
(a) noise	If we **make noise** after 10 p.m., our neighbors get angry. Something in my car is **making a** loud **noise**.
progress	Her English is good now. She has **made** a lot of **progress**. [became better, improved]

B Things we do

homework	I forgot to **do** my math **homework** last night.
jobs [cleaning, shopping, etc.]	My father **did a** good **job** of painting our living room. I always **do the shopping** at a little store near our house.
research	She's **doing research** in genetics. [detailed study]
(someone) **a favor** [do something to help somebody]	Can you **do** me **a favor**? Can you get that newspaper for me?
something / anything / nothing	We have to **do something** to make Jack feel better. Those kids don't **do anything** all day. If we **do nothing**, rain will keep getting in through the roof.

C Things we take

a course	I **took a** one-week **course** in Web site design.
an exam/test	I **took** my final **exams** last week.
a picture	I don't have a camera, but I can **take pictures** with my cell phone.
a train/bus/taxi	You can **take a train** directly from Singapore to Malaysia.
a rest/break/nap [a short sleep]	You've been working hard. **Take a rest.** I'm going to **take a break** and then finish my homework later.
a shower (bath)	I always **take a shower/bath** at night.
the time / your (my, his, etc.) time	Don't rush. **Take the time** to do it right. **Take your time.**
an amount of time	My drive to work **takes 45 minutes**.

Exercises

25.1 Underline the correct verb in italics.

1. I <u>took</u>/*made* the train to Athens last night.
2. He's going to *take*/*do* a shower after the game.
3. Did he *do*/*make* many mistakes?
4. Studying for the test *made*/*did* a big difference in my grade.
5. Did you *make*/*take* many pictures on your trip?
6. When do you *take*/*make* your next exam?
7. They *did*/*made* a lot of noise during the party.
8. I want to *take*/*make* a course in English.
9. The boss *took*/*did* the time to speak to each worker personally.
10. He is *doing*/*making* research in chemistry.

25.2 Rewrite each sentence. Replace the underlined word(s) with a *make*, *take*, or *do* phrase from page 50.

1. Dan <u>just sat around</u> all day. *Dan did nothing all day.*
2. I <u>did not hurry</u> in doing my homework.
3. A good manager can <u>be paid very well</u>.
4. I'm going to <u>prepare</u> lunch for some friends tomorrow.
5. I <u>helped my neighbor by doing something special</u>: I watered his garden.
6. I'll <u>clean the house</u> on the weekend.
7. He thought a lot about which city to live in. In the end, he <u>decided on</u> Chicago.
8. I usually <u>arrive at school 20 minutes after I leave</u> my house.
9. He is definitely <u>improving</u>.
10. I usually <u>go to the store and buy my food</u> on Saturdays.

25.3 Use the parts to build a sentence in the past tense about each picture. Use verbs from page 50.

Maria / after dinner

Bill / after he cut the grass

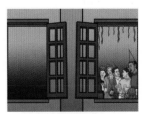
The neighbors / at their party

25.4 Test yourself. Without looking at page 50, write four things for each verb.

make ..*a mistake*............   do ....   take ....
....
....
....

Give, keep, break, and see

Learn these verbs with specific nouns as fixed expressions.

A Give

I'll **give** you **a call** this evening. [call you on the phone]
Could you **give** me **a hand**? [help me]
I'll **give** you **a ride** home. [take you home in my car]
Please **give my regards to** Paul. [say "hello" to him from me]
Give the situation **some thought** before you decide. [take time to consider it]

B Keep

Structure	Meaning	Examples
keep (+ noun/ pronoun) + adjective	make someone/something stay in a state/condition	The coat will **keep** you **warm**. The locked box will **keep** your jewelry **safe**. Please **keep quiet**.
keep + *-ing*	a) do something many times	I **keep leaving** my bike unlocked. Don **keeps getting** into trouble.
	b) continue to do an action despite some problem	The room was noisy, but I **kept working**.

Other **keep** expressions:

keep in touch. [stay in contact]
keep a record of something [write down information about it]

keep your **promise** [do what you have told other people you will do]

C Break

He **broke the** world speed **record**. [went faster than anyone else has ever gone]
If you **break the law,** you may get in trouble. [do something the law does not allow]
Politicians often **break** their **promises**. [don't do what they say they will do]
I hate to **break the news** to you, but our team just lost. [to tell you some bad news]

D See

A: Well, this tennis racket is useless.
B: Yes, **I see. / I see what you mean.** [I understand what you are saying.]

A: Do you think we should rent a car?
B: I don't know. **I'll see what the other guys say.** [I'll ask and find out.]

A: You should take a shower before the game.
B: I don't **see the point.** I'll just get dirty again.

A: **See you.** [*informal*; good-bye]
B: Right. **See you later.**

Exercises

26.1 Match each verb on the left with at least two nouns on the right to form common fixed expressions.

1. break
2. give
3. keep

someone a hand	quiet
a promise	someone a call
a record	the law

26.2 Complete the sentences with verbs from page 52.

1. A: This is a really bad storm.
   B: Yeah. I .... what you mean.
2. These boots should .... your feet warm and dry.
3. Please .... my regards to your mom when you see her.
4. Before we make a decision, let's .... what Antonio says.
5. A: .... you later.
   B: OK. ....
6. I don't .... the point in inviting Sue. She never comes anyway.
7. Tim .... getting lost because he's bad at reading maps.
8. A: Beth's party is canceled.
   B: Too bad. Did you .... the news to Al yet?

26.3 Complete the conversations using verb + noun combinations.

1. A: Do you think Tom will make dinner for you like he said?
   B: Yes. I'm pretty sure he'll ....

2. A: Why did you get a ticket from the police?
   B: I guess I .... by using my cell phone while I was driving.

3. A: It was nice talking to you. Let's ....
   B: Yeah. I'll .... in a week or so.

4. A: I can't organize the meeting all by myself. Can you .... ?
   B: I'd like to, but I'm not sure I can. I'll .... and let you know later.

26.4 Complete each sentence with an adjective or -*ing* form.

1. This sweater should keep you ....
2. She keeps .... her laptop in the library. She should be more careful about keeping it ....
3. Can you please keep .... ? The kids are trying to get to sleep.
4. Runners from East Africa keep .... speed records in races.
5. We keep .... our friends' birthdays. We should keep better records of them.
6. There's no need to keep .... you will help. Say it once and then keep your promise.

Unit 27

Leave, catch, and *let*

A Leave

leave home / the house / work / the office
[go away from it temporarily]
leave school / a job / a husband / a wife
[go away from it/him/her permanently]
leave (a person/thing) **somewhere** [put
something there while you are away]
leave (a thing) **somewhere** [forget it]

have / have got (an amount) **left**

leave a message

leave (someone) **alone** [go away so you
don't disturb him/her]

I always **leave home** before 8:00.

She **left her job** last year to have a baby.
No one knows why she **left her husband**.
You can **leave** your coats in my bedroom.

I wasn't thinking, and I **left** my books on
the bus.
I had $100 yesterday, and now **I've got**
only $20 **left**. [only $20 remains]
He wasn't in, so I **left a message** on his
voicemail.
Leave Tom **alone**. He's studying.

B Catch

catch a bus [get on a bus; travel by]
catch a criminal [find/arrest a criminal]
catch a cold / the flu [get sick
with a cold, etc.]
not catch [not hear; not understand]
catch (a ball, a stick, a falling leaf, etc.)

catch [see] (someone) doing something
[i.e., something wrong]

We can walk or **catch a bus**; I don't mind.
The police **caught the thief** near the bank.
I think I **caught a cold** from my friend.
I **didn't catch** what he said.
I'm sorry, I **didn't catch your name**.
He threw the ball hard; I had to run to
catch it.
My mother **caught** me taking an extra
cookie.

C Let

let [permit] **someone do something**
let someone know [inform him/her]

let's [I suggest that we]
let me see [give me time to think]
let me do something (for you)

My parents won't **let me drive** their new car.
I'll **let you know** tomorrow whether I can go
with you.
I have an idea. **Let's** hike to the river.
Where did I put my keys? **Let me see** . . .
Here. **Let me lift** that bag (for you).

Exercises

27.1 Complete each sentence or conversation with a form of *leave, catch,* or *let*.

1. We can walk to Main Street and then ..*catch*.............. a bus to the movie theater.
2. *(on the phone)* I'm afraid Paul's not here. Do you want to .... a message?
3. I asked Dad, but he won't .... me borrow the car.
4. The teacher .... them talking to each other in the exam. They are in trouble.
5. I put everything in my bag for school. Then I .... it on the kitchen table!
6. Is it OK if I .... my bike in front of the apartment?
7. A: I'm sorry, I didn't .... your name.
   B: It's Michael.
8. A: What should we do?
   B: Uh, ... me see. I know. .... go to the swimming pool.

27.2 Complete the phrases with an appropriate word.

1. Please leave me ....; I'm trying to finish this essay.
2. I'm sorry. I didn't quite .... what you said.
3. Here are your tickets. If you need more, just let me ....
4. A: How many people can fit on the bus?
   B: Oh . . . uh, let me .... About 30, I think.
5. We can't make an omelet. We haven't got any eggs .... in the refrigerator.
6. Do you want me to leave a .... on his voice mail?
7. After you .... the ball, throw it to someone else.
8. I caught a .... on vacation. I've still got it, and I feel terrible.

27.3 Match each sentence beginning (in the left column) with two possible endings. Write the letters in the blanks.

...*e, h*... 1. She left

.... 2. She let

.... 3. She caught

.... 4. Let me

a. me use her cell phone.
b. open the door for you.
c. the bus outside the supermarket.
d. know when you're ready to leave.
e. her job because it was boring.
f. us go home early today.
g. the man trying to steal her purse.
h. her bags at the station.

27.4 Would you let your best friend do these things? Explain. Ask somebody else the same questions if possible.

- borrow your bike or car for the weekend
- choose clothes for you in a shop
- take your child on a trip without you
- live in your home while you're away
- decide where you are both going for a holiday

Get: uses and expressions

A Meanings

Get is an extremely common word in English. Here are some of its basic meanings:

Meaning	get +	Examples
receive	get + noun	I **got** a letter this morning. You'll **get** a certificate at the end of the course.
find/obtain [sometimes "buy"]	get + noun	She's trying to **get** a new job. Where did you **get** those shoes?
become	get + adjective	It **gets** dark very early at this time of year. My hands are **getting** cold.
arrive	get + adverb	When did you **get** here? I'll call when I **get** home.
bring / pick up	get + noun	Could you **get** those books for me from that shelf? She went to **get** the children from school.

B *Get* + past participle

Many other verbs mean the same as *get* + a past participle:

get married [marry]	They **got married** in Canada.
get divorced [divorce]	They **got divorced** last year. [ended the marriage]
get dressed [dress]	I **got dressed** quickly and went out.
get lost [lose one's way]	I **got lost** on my way to the station.

C *Get* + adjectives

Get is part of many fixed expressions with adjectives. The meaning is "become."

It's getting	hot/cold	late		I'm getting	hot/cold	tired
	dark/light	crowded			ready	hungry
	better/worse				better/worse	

> **note** She had a cold but she's **getting better.** [becoming healthy again after an illness]
> A: We have to leave soon.
> B: Right. I'm **getting ready.** [preparing]

D Phrasal verbs and special expressions with *get*

I **get along** very well **with** my sister. [I have a very good relationship with her.]
Is it hard to **get to know** people in a foreign country? [meet them and make friends]
I want to **get rid of** my old CDs. [sell them, throw them away, etc.]
My alarm goes off at 7 a.m., but I don't usually **get up** until 7:15. [get out of bed]
I don't **get it.** [understand] Why do you let him **get on your nerves?** [annoy you]

Exercises

28.1 Write a synonym for each underlined word or phrase.

1. Where can I <u>get</u> something to eat around here?   *find /obtain*
2. Could you please <u>get</u> me some milk while you're in the kitchen?
3. What time did they <u>get here</u> last night?
4. He <u>got</u> very angry when I told him what you did with his CDs.
5. This noise really <u>gets on my nerves</u>.
6. We normally <u>get</u> five weeks' vacation.
7. This book is <u>getting</u> very interesting.
8. The movie stars <u>got divorced</u> soon after <u>getting married</u>.
9. I didn't <u>get</u> her letter until yesterday.
10. Mona had a bad cold, but she's <u>getting better.</u>

28.2 Complete each conversation. Use *I'm getting / it's getting* + adjective.

1. A: *It's getting cold in here.*
   B: Yes, it is. I'll turn on the heat.

2. A: ....
   B: Me too. Let's have something to eat.

3. A: ....
   B: I am too. I'll open the window.

4. A: ....
   B: Yes, it is. I think I'll go to bed.

5. A: ....
   B: Me too. I'm going to go to bed.

6. A: ....
   B: Well, I'll turn the lights on.

7. A: ....
   B: Yes, it is. A lot of people come here on the weekend.

28.3 Rewrite each of these sentences using an expression with *get*. The meaning must stay the same.

1. They're preparing to go out.
   They're *getting ready to go out.*
2. I had to put on my clothes very quickly.
   I had to ....
3. How do you meet people and make friends in this country?
   How do you .... ?
4. I have a good relationship with my boss.
   I ....
5. We're going to throw away most of these chairs.
   We're going to ....
6. You just don't understand, do you?
   You just don't .... ?

Go: uses and expressions

A *Come* vs. *go*

In general:

Go expresses a movement away from the speaker.

Come expresses a movement toward the speaker. Sometimes the speaker is in one place but imagines being in another place, e.g., a speaker in Chicago might say: "Would you like to **come** and visit me in Brazil next July?"

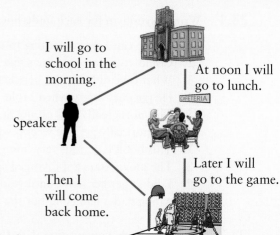

I will go to school in the morning.

At noon I will go to lunch.

Speaker

Later I will go to the game.

Then I will come back home.

B Different meanings of *go*

* Meaning: leave a place in order to do an activity

go + -*ing* form of a verb   **go (out) + for/on/to** + noun phrase

We could **go shopping**	They often **go (out) to** dinner.
Let's **go swimming**	We **went (out) for** a swim.
They all **went running**	I think they **went (out) on** a date.

* Meaning: describe a change in state expressed by an adjective, with the meaning of "become"

My father is **going bald**. [losing his hair]
The company **went bankrupt**. [lost all its money and had to stop operating]
My grandmother is **going blind**. [losing her ability to see]
He'll **go crazy/nuts** if you wear his jacket. [lose control of himself; get very angry]

* Meaning: be in its usual place; fit well (often with together)

Does this chair **go** in this room?
That shirt does not **go (together)** with those pants.

* Meaning: travel; lead to

Does this bus **go** to the National Gallery? [take me]
I don't think this road **goes** to the station. [leads]

C Very common expressions with *go*

Learn these everyday phrases as fixed expressions:

| A: **How's it going?** | A: **What's going on** here? [The speaker thinks something might be wrong.] |
| B: **It's going** OK. | B: Nothing. We're just watching TV. |

Exercises

29.1 Complete the conversation with correct forms of *come* or *go*.

A: What time are you (1) ....*going*........ to Jim's party tonight?

B: I'm not sure, because Chris is (2) .... here first, and then we'll
(3) .... together.

A: OK. And what are you doing tomorrow?

B: Well, I want to (4) .... shopping in the morning. Want to
(5) .... with me?

A: Yeah, sure. What time?

B: Oh, I don't know. Could you (6) .... over here before ten?

A: No problem.

29.2 Complete these sentences with an *-ing* noun (e.g., *riding*), or *for / on / to / at / with* + noun
(e.g., *for a walk*).

1. I went ....*shopping*......... yesterday and bought some books and clothes.
2. We didn't have any food in the house this morning, so we went out ....
3. Why don't we go .... at the new pool this weekend?
4. Last night I just felt like moving to some music. I wanted to go .... , but
everybody else wanted to go out .... at some cute little restaurant.
5. Tim asked Jan to go .... with him, but she had to say no. She already has
a boyfriend.
6. My brother just got a new motorcycle. I'm going .... with him this
weekend.

29.3 Complete these sentences. Use a dictionary to help you.

1. When she started going ....*blind*........ , she began learning how to read by touch.
2. If business doesn't improve, Don's company could go ....
3. The rain has kept me indoors for two days. If I can't get out soon, I'll go ....
4. Some men begin wearing caps when they start going ....
5. One of my neighbors goes .... whenever kids ride their bikes
on her lawn.
6. Those running shoes and that business suit do not really go ....

29.4 Replace the underlined words and expressions. The meaning must stay the same.

1. Hi Toshi. <u>How's it going</u>?
....

2. Excuse me. Does this road <u>go to</u> the bus station?
....

3. I think this bus <u>goes to</u> the shopping mall.
....

4. A: <u>What's going on</u> over there?
B: Nothing. Don't worry.
....

A The five basic senses

The five senses are: **sight, hearing, taste, touch,** and **smell.**

The following verbs are related to the five senses. They are followed by an adjective or a noun in these constructions. They do not usually take *-ing* forms.

Sight: It **looks** terrible. [from what I could see]
Hearing: He **sounds** Chinese. [from what I heard]
Taste: It **tastes** strange. [from tasting it]
Touch: It **feels** soft. [from touching it]
Smell: It **smells** wonderful. [from smelling it]

It **looks like** a wedding cake.
It **sounds like** a good idea.
This **tastes like** bread.
It **feels like** a blanket.
This **smells like** garlic.

We can also use the verbs as nouns. These are very common:

I didn't like **the look of** the fish.
I really like **the sound of** organ music.
I don't like **the taste of** olives.

I love **the feel of** silk.
I hate **the smell of** gasoline.

B *See, look (at),* and *watch*

See is the ability to use your eyes. (The verb is not usually used with the *-ing* form.) **Look (at)** often means to look carefully / pay attention to something that is not moving. **Watch** often means to pay attention to something that is moving.

I can't **see** a thing without my glasses. [I'm not able to see. / I am nearsighted.]
I can't find my keys, and I've **looked** everywhere. [searched/looked carefully]
The police have been **watching** the suspect for weeks. [watching secretly]
I **watched** the game and then went out with friends.
He ran into me because he wasn't **looking**. [paying attention; the speaker seems angry]
He ran into me because he didn't **see** me. [I wasn't visible; the speaker is not angry]
I **saw/watched** a great program last night. [on TV; we can use either verb here]
I **saw** a great movie last night. [at a movie theater; we cannot use **watch** here]

C *Hear* and *listen (to)*

Hear means "sense the sound of something." **Listen (to)** means "pay attention to something you hear."

I couldn't clearly **hear** what she said. [I wasn't able to clearly sense what she said.]
I don't know what she said because I wasn't **listening**. [I wasn't paying attention.]
I usually **listen to** the evening news on television. [I decide to listen.]
I was **listening to** the radio when I **heard** a loud noise outside.

Sometimes it is possible to use **hear** (but not with the *-ing* form) to mean "listen to":
I know he's dead – I **heard** it on the radio last night. [I heard it when I was listening.]

D *Touch*

Don't **touch** those wires – they're dangerous.
You have to **press** that button to start the machine.
I'm frightened. Could you **hold** my hand?

Exercises

30.1 Complete the sentences using words from the box. Use a dictionary to help you.

water	donkey	laundry detergent	silk	fresh
new	photo	ripe	doorbell	horrible	

1. After touching this peach, I decided not to eat it. It didn't feel ..*ripe*................ .
2. Those shoes look .... Did you just get them?
3. This milk smells .... I'll open another carton.
4. This coffee tastes like .... It's very weak.
5. I love the smell of .... bread.
6. That painting is so realistic that it looks like a ....
7. I know it's a horse, but it looks like a ....
8. I'm sure it's expensive perfume, but to me it smells like ....
9. Your telephone sounds just like a ....
10. This blouse was very cheap, but it feels like ....

30.2 Complete the sentence below each picture. Use *feels / looks / sounds / tastes* + adjective.

1. **This music**
   ..*sounds terrible* .
2. **That man**
   ....
3. **This pillow**
   ....
4. **This apple**
   ....

30.3 Circle the correct answer. Sometimes both answers are correct.

1. I was listening to / hearing the radio when I listened to / heard a terrible noise outside.
2. The city council is going to pass new laws against noisy neighbors – I listened to / heard it on the radio this morning.
3. She turned up the volume, but I still couldn't listen to / hear it.
4. They wanted to stay and watch / look at the TV program, but it was getting late.
5. I sensed that Tom was bored. He just wasn't hearing/listening when I spoke to him.
6. You have to touch/press the eject button if you want to get the video out.
7. Could you touch/hold this vase for a moment while I move the table?
8. If you watch/look carefully, you can look/see how he does the card trick.

30.4 Write one smell, sound, etc. that you like and one you don't like. If possible, compare your answers with someone else's.

I like the smell of ..*roses*....................   I don't like the smell of ....
I love the sound of ....   I don't like the sound of ....
I love the taste of ....   I don't like the taste of ....
I like the look of ....   I don't like the look of ....
I like the feel of ....   I don't like the feel of ....

Partitives (a bit of . . . , a piece of . . .)

Partitives are words that describe a part or quantity of something. They are usually followed by *of*.

A Containers and contents

a **box** of
chocolates

a **can**
of cola

a **cup** of
coffee

a **tube** of
toothpaste

a **bowl**
of sugar

a **carton** of
orange juice

a **glass**
of water

a **bottle** of
cough syrup

a **jar**
of jam

a **vase** of
flowers

B With uncountable nouns

When we use uncountable nouns (e.g., **advice**), we sometimes want to talk about *one* of something. We cannot say "an advice" or "one advice," but we can use certain words to make these nouns singular: **a piece of advice**, **a sheet of paper** [one piece of paper], **a slice of bread** [one piece of bread]. We can use the word **piece** with many nouns:

a piece of cake

a piece of wood

You can use **piece** with some abstract nouns, e.g., **a piece of information**.

A very common partitive is **a little bit** (or sometimes **a bit**), which usually means a small amount but can be fairly general. It can be used with the examples above and more: **a little bit of butter, a little bit of time, a bit of luck**, etc.

C *A pair of . . .*

Some nouns have two parts, e.g., pants (two legs) and shoes (left and right). You can use a **pair of**, e.g., **a pair of skis, two pairs of shoes, three pairs of gloves**.

D Groups of things

a **herd**
of cows

a **group**
of people

a **bunch**
of grapes

a **bunch** of
flowers

a **gang** of youths /
youngsters / kids /
teenagers

Gang has a negative meaning: It suggests a group of young people who cause trouble.

Exercises

31.1 Some of these containers do not look exactly the same as the ones on page 62, but the names are the same. Can you decide what the missing words are?

1. a ...*carton*......... of milk

5. a .... of mineral water

2. a .... of tea

6. a .... of orange juice

3. a .... of fruit

7. a .... of paint

4. a .... of matches

8. a .... of coffee

31.2 Contents come in different containers. Would you be surprised to see any of the following?

a glass of soup	a vase of coffee	a bowl of milk
a tube of milk	a can of tomatoes	a bag of soup
a jar of mustard	a bag of salt	a cup of toothpaste

31.3 Complete these sentences with a logical noun.

1. They gave her a big .....*bunch*...... of flowers for her birthday.
2. A .... of teenagers may be responsible for the damage.
3. I cut about six .... of bread for the sandwiches.
4. They own a large .... of land in the country.
5. She told us to take out a blank .... of paper, then write our names at the top.
6. A small .... of people gathered outside the embassy.
7. Have you seen that old .... of boots I use for hiking?
8. I have a little .... of time, so I can help you now if you like.

31.4 Circle the correct answer. Sometimes both answers are correct.

1. I ordered a piece / sheet of cake for dessert.
2. I asked her for a bit / piece of advice.
3. My lunch consisted of two slices / pieces of bread and a bunch / group of grapes.
4. I read a little piece / bit of a novel last night; then I fell asleep.
5. There's a herd / group of cows in the field.

Uncountable nouns and plural nouns

A Uncountable nouns

Uncountable nouns (e.g., information, advice, weather):

- cannot be used with **a/an**, e.g., **information** (*not* an information)
- cannot be made plural, e.g., **some advice** (*not* some advices)
- take a singular verb, e.g., "**The weather** is nice today." (*not* The weather are . . .)

> **note**   You can make many uncountable nouns singular by adding another noun
> + *of*: **a piece of** information, **a bit of** advice.

These uncountable nouns in English are often countable in other languages. Notice the underlined words that often go with these nouns.

We can <u>get</u> more **information** about the hotel through the Internet.
He <u>gave</u> me lots of **advice** about the best dictionary to buy.
We are going to sell all the **furniture**. [tables, chairs, sofas, etc.]
My **knowledge** of Korean is very <u>limited</u>.
You need a lot of **equipment** for camping. [tent, sleeping bag, cooking utensils, etc.]
She is <u>making</u> good **progress** in her English. [Her English is improving.]
What is the latest **news** <u>about</u> the storms?
We had fabulous **weather** in Mexico.
The teacher <u>gave</u> us a lot of **homework** last night.
I never take much **luggage** when I go on vacation. [bags and suitcases]

B In dictionaries

Many learner's dictionaries show countable nouns with a (C) and uncountable nouns with a (U). Some nouns are countable in one meaning and uncountable in another.

book (C): The books are on the table.   work (U): You'll get paid for your work.

hair (U): My hair is getting long.   hair (C): I found two hairs on my plate.

C Plural nouns

Plural nouns (e.g., pants, pajamas):

- have only a plural form and cannot be used with **a/an**, e.g., **pants** [*not* a pant *or* a pants]
- usually take a plural verb, e.g., "**These pants are** too long." [*not* "These pants is . . ."]
- can usually be made singular by using **a pair of**, e.g., **a pair of pants**

Here are some other nouns that are usually plural:

I bought a new pair of **jeans** when   When it's sunny, I wear **sunglasses**
I went shopping.   for driving.

The **headphones** for my MP3 player   These **shorts** don't fit me.
are great.

The **scissors** are on the table.   I put on my **pajamas** and went to bed.

Exercises

32.1 Correct the mistakes.

1. I need some informations. ...*I need some information.*.................................
2. We had a great weather. ....
3. I'm looking for a new jeans. ....
4. Your hairs are getting very long. ....
5. I can't find my sunglass. ....
6. We had a lot of homeworks yesterday. ....
7. Is she making a progress with her English? ....
8. These pajamas is too big for me. ....

32.2 Are these nouns typically countable (C) or uncountable (U)? Write sentences for each one on a separate sheet of paper. Use your dictionary for help.

butter ..*U*....   cup ....   paperwork ....   television ....   vocabulary ....

spaghetti ....   building ....   grape ....   work ....   people ....

32.3 Complete these conversations using a plural noun or an uncountable noun from page 64.

1. A: It's too hot for jeans.
   B: You need ..*a pair of shorts / some shorts.*..............

2. A: I have to cut this paper into three pieces.
   B: You need ....

3. A: I can't see because the sun is in my eyes.
   B: You need ....

4. A: I don't know what to do when I graduate.
   B: You need ....

5. A: My room looks so empty.
   B: You need ....

6. A: I can't play my music loud because my mother always complains.
   B: You need ....

7. A: My teacher said my English wasn't getting any better.
   B: Maybe you need to do more ....

32.4 In this report, find three uncountable nouns and two nouns that are always plural. These words are not on page 64. Then, summarize the report using words from page 64. Work with a partner if possible.

> Traffic has been heavy throughout the day because of construction on Pacific Coast Drive, on the outskirts of town, causing long delays for motorists heading into the city. The authorities are advising drivers to avoid the area if at all possible. We will keep you informed of the situation with the latest news every half hour, so don't go away.

Verb + *-ing* form or infinitive

A   Verb + *-ing* form

Some verbs are followed by an *-ing* form if the next word is a verb:

enjoy feel like	finish (don't) mind	imagine can't stand	admit give up	avoid deny

I stayed home last night, but I **feel like** go**ing** out tonight.
At the police station, he **admitted** steal**ing** her money but **denied** tak**ing** the camera.
I've lived in Texas all my life. I can't **imagine** liv**ing** anywhere else.
Some people **can't stand** [hate] work**ing** at night, but I **don't mind**. [for me it's OK]
I **don't mind** driv**ing** during rush hour, but I **avoid** tak**ing** crowded freeways.

B   Verb + infinitive

Some verbs are followed by an infinitive if the next word is a verb:

We <u>wanted</u> **to finish** before 6 p.m. After a lot of hard work, we <u>managed</u> **to do** it. [were able to finish]

I <u>offered</u> **to take** them home in my car, but they <u>decided</u> **to walk**.

A: Hey, you <u>forgot</u> **to call** me yesterday.
B: Oh, sorry. I <u>meant</u> **to do** it but I got too busy. [planned/intended to call]

A: Do you <u>promise</u> **to say** "hi" for me when you see Andy and Jen?
B: Sure, but I don't <u>expect</u> **to see** them soon.

I asked her to carry the suitcases, but she <u>refused</u> **to help**.

A: You <u>seem</u> **to be looking** for something.
B: Yes. I <u>need</u> **to find** an ATM.

C   Verb + *-ing* form or infinitive

Some verbs have almost similar meanings with either an *-ing* form or an infinitive, e.g., **love, like, hate, try,** and **prefer**:

I **like** go**ing** to the movies. / I **like to go** to the movies.
I **prefer to pay** by credit card. / I **prefer** pay**ing** by credit card.

Other verbs have different meanings with *-ing* than with the infinitive:

I **remembered to buy** a present for my brother. [I didn't forget to buy a present.]
I **remember** buy**ing** him a present. [I remember that it happened.]

D   Verb + infinitive without *to*

Two common verbs are followed by an object + infinitive without *to*: **make** someone do something, and **let** someone do something.

My parents **make** me **do** my homework before dinner. [They **force** me **to do** it first.]
My parents **let** me **go** out on weekends. [They **allow/permit** me **to go** out.]

Exercises

33.1 Underline the correct answer(s). In some sentences, both choices are correct.

1. We decided (<u>to work</u> / working) during our vacation.
2. She promised (to help / helping) us.
3. I don't feel like (to go / going) for a walk right now.
4. Don't you hate (to drive / driving) when it's wet?
5. We need (to make / making) plans for the holidays.
6. Most of the time she prefers (to work / working) at home.
7. I don't remember (to go / going) to the zoo when we visited San Diego.
8. I tried (to study / studying) with music, but I couldn't concentrate.

33.2 Add a third possible way (c) to complete each statement. Use the *-ing* form or infinitive of a verb.

1. Most people want:
   a) to be rich.
   b) to get married.
   c) *to be happy.*
2. A lot of people can't stand:
   a) getting wet.
   b) getting up early.
   c) ....
3. Many people enjoy:
   a) going to parties.
   b) lying on a beach.
   c) ....
4. Most people expect:
   a) to be happy.
   b) to find a job they will like.
   c) ....
5. Some people don't mind:
   a) washing dishes.
   b) ironing clothes.
   c) ....
6. Some parents make their teenage children:
   a) wear certain clothes.
   b) do housework.
   c) ....
7. Other parents let their teenage children:
   a) wear what they like.
   b) stay out all night.
   c) ....

33.3 Read the story and answer the questions below.

> When Julie was 17, her father said she could go on vacation with two school friends. He would lend her the money for a hotel, but she would have to pay for the airfare and her entertainment herself. Julie was happy and said she would bring him back a great present and pay him back in six months. First she and her friends had to decide where to go. They looked at lots of brochures and finally agreed on a two-week trip to Hawaii. They had a great time, but Julie spent all her money and forgot to buy a present for her father.

1. What did Julie's father let her do when she was 17? ...He let her go on vacation with two friends...........
2. And what did he offer to do? ....
3. But what did he refuse to do? ....
4. In return, what did Julie promise? ....
5. What did the three friends decide? ....
6. What did Julie forget? ....

Verb patterns

A Verb + object

Subject	Verb	Object	
She	**proposed** [*formal*; suggested]	the plan	at the meeting.
The travel agent	**confirmed** [said it was sure]	my reservation.	
They	**discussed** [talked about]	the movie	for hours.

B Verb + indirect object + object

Subject	Verb	Indirect object	Object
I	**told**	them	a story.
She	**sent**	me	a long e-mail.

C Verb + indirect object + question word

Subject	Verb	Indirect object	Question word
I	**told**	them	where to find it.
She	**asked**	us	why we wanted it.

> **note** There is no indirect object after **explain**; not "He explained me what to do."

D Verb + object + infinitive

Subject	Verb	Object	Infinitive	
She	**asked**	everyone	to leave.	
They	**told**	us	to wait	outside.
The doctor	**advised**	him	to stay	in bed.
I	**wanted**	the others	to help	us.
He	**persuaded**	me	to go	to the party.
She	**warned**	them	to be	careful.

persuade [get someone to do or believe something by giving good reasons; **convince**]
warn [tell someone of a possible danger or problem]

E Verb + (that) clause

Subject	Verb	(that) Clause
He	**said**	(that) it was good.
She	**suggested**	(that) we go together.
He	**mentioned**	(that) the meeting started at 12:00.

mention [say or write something in normal speech, without stressing it much]
We can also use *-ing* after **suggest**, e.g., "She **suggested** going there together."

F Verb + (object / *to* phrase) + preposition

They **blamed** me **for** the accident. [said I was responsible / said it was my **fault**]
She **complained** (to the manager) **about** the bad service. [said she was not happy]
The manager **apologized** (to the customer) **for** the bad service. [said he was sorry]
He **insisted on** paying the bill. (Notice the *-ing* form of the verb after the preposition.)

Exercises

34.1 Rewrite these sentences to correct the mistakes

1. She said me the movie was terrible. ..*She said the movie was terrible.*.....................
2. He told it was not possible. ....
3. Can you explain me what to do? ....
4. He suggested us to go home. ....
5. I want that he leaves. ....
6. I need to confirm me the flight. ....
7. I apologized my mistake. ....
8. She advised me buy a dictionary. ....

34.2 Complete each sentence with a verb.

1. They watched the movie together; then they .....*discussed*.... it in small groups.
2. Her room was very noisy, so she called the hotel manager to ....
3. She said something that made him feel bad, but she refused to ....
4. He knew it was dangerous, but he didn't .... me.
5. I didn't want to go at first, but she .... me to go.
6. She advised them not to leave, but they .... on going.
7. This e-mail .... a flight that I booked online.
8. It wasn't his fault, but they still .... him.

34.3 Complete the sentences with your own ideas.

1. Some of us were getting hungry, so I suggested ..*that we go out to eat.*.......... .
2. They could not agree about what to do, so I proposed ....
3. She went to that new Chinese restaurant and said ....
4. When you e-mail him, could you send ....
5. The streets are dangerous at night, so I insisted ....
6. It was only a few minutes to the beach, but I still couldn't persuade ....
7. He wasn't feeling very well, and the teacher advised ....
8. The whole team played badly, but most of the newspapers blamed ....
9. We realized we were neighbors when I mentioned ....
10. If you don't understand the instructions, someone will explain ....

34.4 Complete the chart. Follow the example. Use your dictionary for help.

ask	+ indirect object + question word	*I asked her who was coming to the party.*
	+ object + infinitive	....
	....	*Lee asked the waiter for a glass of water.*
order	....	*Our table ordered a pizza.*
	+ indirect object + object	....
	+ object + infinitive	....
	....	*The boss ordered that the meeting should start early.*

Unit 35 Adjectives

A Degrees of adjectives

Many adjectives (e.g., **good, bad, hard**) can go with different adverbs of degree (**very, a little, not so**, etc.).

extremely bad	very bad	**a little / sort of** bad	**not so / not very** bad	not bad **at all**
extremely hard	very hard	a little / sort of hard	not so / not very hard	not hard at all

> *note*   Most of these "degree" adjectives do not occur with **absolutely** in written English; *not* "an absolutely bad idea; an absolutely hard test."

B Extreme adjectives

Other adjectives such as **freezing** or **enormous** are "extreme." They describe a very strong characteristic. e.g., **freezing** is an extreme adjective for **cold**; **great** is an extreme adjective for **good**.

The adverb **absolutely** is common with extreme adjectives, but other adverbs of degree are not. Things are *not* usually "very freezing" or "somewhat enormous."

"Degree" adjective	*Extreme adjective*	*"Degree" adjective*	*Extreme adjective*
small	tiny	happy	delighted
big	enormous	cold	freezing
tired	exhausted	hot	boiling
interesting	fascinating	hungry	starving
good	great	frightened	terrified

C Adjectives (ending in -*ing* and -*ed*)

Some adjectives are based on verbs. The -*ing* ending on an adjective usually indicates what a person, thing, or situation does. The -*ed* ending may indicate the effect of that action on someone/something else.

The party bores me. It is a **boring** party. I am **bored**.
The movie could frighten people. I didn't think it was very **frightening**. Some **frightened** children had to leave early.
The instructions were not very clear. I think the students were **confused** because the instructions were so **confusing**.

Other examples of common adjectives ending in -*ing* and -*ed* include:

astonishing/astonished   exhausting/exhausted
terrifying/terrified   surprising/surprised
disappointing/disappointed   interesting/interested
embarrassing/embarrassed   exciting/excited

Exercises

35.1 Complete the conversations with an adjective from page 70.

1. A: Was that story interesting?   B: Yes, it was absolutely ..*fascinating*......
2. A: That car is tiny!   B: Well, it's a little .... , but not really "tiny."

3. A: Maria said it was a frightening film.   B: Yes, it was absolutely ....
4. A: That test seemed difficult.   B: Not really. It wasn't ....
5. A: Was the weather cold?   B: I thought it was sort of .... , but Tom thought it was absolutely ....

35.2 Use adjectives from page 70 to complete the descriptions. Add adverbs of degree as appropriate.

1. Josh and Aya walked 10 miles in the morning. In the afternoon they cut the lawn.
   Josh and Aya were absolutely ..*exhausted*....... . Their day was ....
2. The tourists expected a big, beautiful hotel on the beach. They found only a small, dirty hotel miles from the ocean.
   The hotel was .... The tourists were ....
3. The girls wore jeans to the party. Everyone else was dressed in formal clothes.
   The girls were .... The situation at the party was ....
4. One person told the Smiths to turn left, another told them to turn right, and a third said to go straight. At first the Smiths couldn't understand, but then they figured it out.
   The directions were .... The Smiths were ....
5. She spent $1 on a lottery ticket. The next week, she won $1 million in the lottery!
   She was .... Her luck was ....
6. The show was not interesting at all. Many people in the audience almost fell asleep.
   The audience was .... The show was ....

35.3 Rewrite this postcard. Replace the underlined words with different adjective phrases.

Dear Sandy,
                                            starving
   Arrived Sunday evening. We were <u>hungry</u> and had dinner right away. We are <u>happy</u> with our hotel. We have <u>a big</u> room and the food is <u>good</u>. It's been <u>hot</u> every day so far, so we've spent most of the time on the beach. But the water is actually <u>cold</u> – that's because it's the Pacific coast, I suppose. Tomorrow we're going to walk to a <u>very small</u> town about three miles from here – I'm sure I'll be <u>tired</u> by the time we get back, but it sounds like an <u>interesting</u> place and I'm looking forward to it. It's so small that I was <u>surprised</u> to find it on a map! I'll write again in a couple of days and tell you about it.
   Benita

Prepositions: place

A At, on, in

at a point/place	I met her **at** the bus stop. He is **at work** / **at home** / **at school.**	She lives **at** 43 Lake Drive. They are **at** a party tonight.
on a surface	The book is **on** the desk	We sat **on** the floor.
in an area or space	Ghana is a country **in** Africa. She lives **in** Taipei.	He is **in** the kitchen. The key is **in** my pocket. Put it **in** the box.

B Opposites

up ↑   down ↓   into ⌐↓   out of ⌐↗

The picture is **over/above** the shelf.   The bus is **in front of** the car.
The wastebasket is **under/below** the shelf.   The car is **behind** / **in back of** the bus.

> *note*   **Over/above** and **under/below** usually mean the same thing, but **over** and **under** sometimes suggest movement:
> When we flew **over** the city, we couldn't see much because we were **above** the clouds. **Below** us was the river, which ran **under** the bridge.

C Other common prepositions of place

We drove **along** the lake, **around** the top, **past** the old fort, and **through** the town.

We came **over** the bridge and parked **next to** the house, which was **opposite** the hotel.

The office is **between** two stores. There's a bus stop **near**: you just go **across** the street and walk **along** the other side **toward** the school.

Exercises

36.1 Fill in the blanks with *at, on,* or *in.*

1. The ice cream is .....*in*..... the freezer, where it won't melt.
2. We saw them .... the bus stop.
3. I met her .... a party.
4. She works .... Mexico City.
5. The dictionary is .... my desk, next to the telephone.
6. I left my briefcase .... work.
7. There was still a lot of snow .... the ground when I arrived.
8. He lives .... a very nice area.

36.2 Answer the questions using the opposite preposition.

1. Was he standing in front of the statue? No, *behind the statue.*....................................
2. Is his house up the hill? No, ...
3. Did you climb over the fence? No, ...
4. Did you see her get into the car? No, ...
5. Did you fly below the clouds? No, ...
6. Does she live in the apartment above you? No, ...
7. Do you keep most of your books in the desk? No, ...
8. Should we meet in back of the library? No, ...

36.3 Look at the map and complete the description of the route you took.

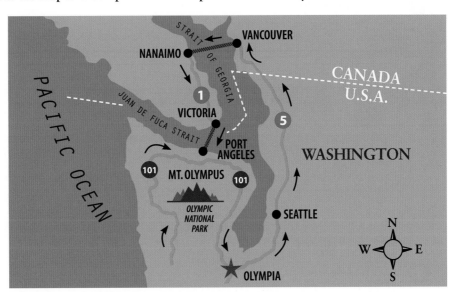

We took Route 101 (1) ....*around*....... Olympic National Park, which is
(2) .... Washington state. We drove (3) .... Port Angeles, without
stopping, and then south to Olympia, the state capital. From there, we headed north to
Seattle, then drove (4) .... the border, (5) .... Canada. We drove
all the way up to Vancouver, where we stayed overnight. The next morning, we took the
ferry (6) .... the strait to Nanaimo. From there, we drove
(7) .... the island's eastern shore to beautiful Victoria, where we went
sightseeing and stopped for tea (8) .... a charming tearoom. Later we took
another ferry (9) .... the strait to Port Angeles.

Adverbs: frequency and degree

A Frequency (how often)

100%   *0%*

	almost always	often	occasionally	seldom (formal)	
always	usually	regularly	sometimes	hardly ever	never
	generally	frequently		rarely	
				almost never	

Adverbs of frequency go before the main verb, except the verb *to be*:

I **rarely** see them.   They **hardly ever** go to the movies.
She is **often** late these days.   I've **never** tried Korean food.

Sometimes and **occasionally** can go at the beginning (perhaps with a comma) or end of a sentence:

My parents give me money **sometimes**.   I play tennis **occasionally**.
Sometimes, my parents give me money.   **Occasionally**, I work on weekends.

B Degree (how much)

less   *more*

a (little) bit	kind of	fairly	quite	extremely
a little	sort of	pretty	very	
slightly	somewhat	rather *(formal)*	really	

Kind of, **sort of**, and **pretty** are used more in spoken English than in written English:

I'm **sort of / kind of** disappointed that they couldn't come. [in some ways]
The food was **pretty** good. [almost "very" good]

Quite can mean "very" and is also used more in spoken than in written English, e.g., "It's **quite** warm [very warm] outside."

C *Almost / nearly / just about*

It's **almost / nearly / just about** five o'clock. [It is a minute or so before five.]
We **almost / nearly / just about** lost the game. [We won, but only by a small amount.]

D *Hardly*

Hardly + a positive often has the same meaning as **almost** + a negative:

I **hardly** had **anything** to eat for lunch. [I had almost nothing.]
She could **hardly** walk after her operation. [She almost couldn't walk.]
We **hardly ever** go to the beach. [We almost never go to the beach.]

Exercises

37.1 Make sentences from these scrambled words.

1. brother / often / us / Sundays / visits / on / my *My brother often visits us on Sundays.*
2. me / ever / calls / she / hardly ....
3. visit / saw / I / hardly / his / him / during ....
4. get / occasionally / I / early / up ....
5. have / ridden / never / I / motorcycle / a ....

37.2 Replace the underlined word/phrase with an adverb that has a similar meaning.

1. She <u>seldom</u> goes to conferences. *almost never*
2. I can <u>not</u> remember <u>very well</u> the first house we lived in. ....
3. There were <u>almost</u> fifty people at the party. ....
4. I thought the play was <u>kind of</u> disappointing, didn't you? ....
5. I'm sorry, but I'm <u>extremely</u> busy next week. ....

37.3 Change the underlined adverbs. Change the meaning according to the directions in brackets.

1. John said the apartment was <u>very</u> small. [Make the apartment seem slightly bigger.]
   John said the apartment was a bit small.
2. They said it was <u>fairly</u> boring. [Make it seem less boring.]
3. The clothes were <u>very</u> expensive. [Make them seem slightly less expensive.]
4. I felt <u>kind of</u> happy at the wedding. [Make yourself seem much happier.]
5. He's been getting <u>pretty</u> good marks on his exams. [Make his marks seem better.]

37.4 Rewrite each sentence to make a true statement about yourself. Use a frequency adverb. Compare your answers with someone else's if possible.

1. I buy clothes I don't wear.   *I sometimes buy clothes I don't wear.*
2. I polish my shoes.
3. I remember my dreams.
4. I give money to people on the street if they ask me.
5. I speak to strangers on buses and trains.
6. I'm rude to people who are rude to me.

Now think about each of your answers to the above sentences (and if possible, your partner's) answers). Do you think they are:

a) very typical?   b) fairly typical?   c) slightly unusual?   d) extremely unusual?

37.5 Think of something you . . .

1. always do *I always wash my hands before meals.*
2. usually do in the morning ....
3. sometimes do in the evening ....
4. would never do ....
5. would like to do more often ....

Time and sequence

A When / as soon as

I'll call you **when** I get home.
When you've finished, you can leave.

As soon as I get home, I'll call you.
You can leave **as soon as** you've finished.

> **note** The meaning is almost the same, but **as soon as** suggests the second action is more immediate. **When** and **as soon as** can be followed by the present tense, the simple past, or the present perfect (but not **will**).

B Two things happening at the same time

Pat wrote letters **while** I cooked dinner. [two actions lasting the same amount of time]

The accident happened **while** I was on my way to work. [a shorter event "the accident happened" inside a longer one "on my way to work"; **when** or **as** could also be used]

I saw him (**just**) **as** I was coming out of the office. [two short actions happening at the same time]

> **note** Use **just** to emphasize "exactly at this point in time."

C One thing after another

We met them at the café, and **then/afterwards** we went to the concert.
After my visit to / **After** visiting New York, I decided to relax for a few days.
We had something to eat **before** we went out / **before** going out.

> **note** Before and after can be followed by an **-ing** form.

D A sequence of actions

We had a great vacation. **First (of all)**, we went to San Francisco. **Then / After that / Afterwards**, we drove to Los Angeles. **Finally**, we went to San Diego.

> **note** If something happened after a long time and/or many problems, you can use **eventually** or **in the end**, e.g., "I made several wrong turns, but **eventually** I got there."

E A sequence of reasons

SON: Why can't we go away this weekend?
DAD: **First / First of all**, because I'm busy this weekend. **Second(ly)**, you've got a lot of homework to do. And **third(ly)**, we're planning to go away next weekend.

Also possible:

To begin with / To start with, I'm busy this weekend . . .
For one thing I'm busy . . . **And for another (thing)**, you have a lot of homework.
I'm busy this weekend. **(And) Besides** or **Anyway**, you have a lot of homework.

Exercises

38.1 Circle the correct answer. Sometimes both answers are correct.

1. I'll give them your message as soon as I (get / will get) there.
2. Mary cleaned the kitchen (just as / while) I cleaned the bathroom.
3. I'd like to visit that gallery before (to leave / leaving) the city.
4. I had to complain a lot, but (eventually / finally) the store gave me a refund.
5. I did my homework. (After / After that), I went out.
6. We can have dinner (as soon as / when) I get home.

38.2 Complete the sentences with your own ideas.

1. We played tennis, and afterwards ...*we went for a swim.*...
2. I'll meet you as soon as ....
3. Remember to lock the back door before ....
4. My cell phone fell out of my pocket as ....
5. I searched the Internet for some topics while ....
6. We had to wait for hours, but eventually ....
7. I saw the burglar breaking the window just as ....

38.3 Complete each conversation. Add a sentence that starts with a linking word or phrase from page 76.

1. A: Why do you want to stay home? We could go to Karl's party.
   B: Well, for one thing, my ex-girlfriend will be there and I really don't
      want to see her. ....

2. A: What did you do on your trip?
   B: First of all, we spent a few days in Tokyo. ....
      ....

3. A: Why can't we send one of our staff members to the conference?
   B: Well, to begin with, I don't think we should send anyone. And ....
      ....

38.4 Imagine you had these problems at a restaurant: The food was not cooked properly, and the service was very slow. When you mentioned these things to the staff, they were very rude. You have decided to write a letter of complaint to the owner. Complete this letter.

> Ms. M. Watson
> Owner, Park Royal Restaurant
>
> Dear Ms. Watson:
>
> Last weekend, some friends and I had dinner at the Park
> Royal. I am writing to express my dissatisfaction with the
> food and service in your restaurant.

Addition and contrast

A *Also, as well, in addition,* etc.

Two ideas in a sentence may be joined with **and**, e.g., "The food is good **and** the prices are low." When this information goes in two sentences, these words/phrases can link them:

The restaurant has a reputation for excellent food. The prices are **also** reasonable.
The food is excellent. The prices are reasonable **as well / too.**
The food is excellent. **Furthermore / What's more,** the prices are reasonable.
The dinner special includes salad, steak, and dessert. **In addition,** you get a free beverage.

B *Although, despite, in spite of,* etc.

Use the following linking words/phrases if:

• Two pieces of information are contrasted in a single sentence;
• The second fact is surprising after the first.

They **still** went out **in spite of** the fact that it was raining hard / **in spite of** the rain.
  (*Note:* **Still** emphasizes that the second fact is a surprise.)
He failed the exam **despite** the fact that he'd studied hard / **despite** studying hard.
She still won the game, **although / though / even though** she had a bad knee.

After **although, though,** or **even though,** you must use a clause (subject + verb),
e.g., "**Although** she had a bad knee, . . . / **Although** her knee was bad, . . ."

The linking word(s) could also come first in the sentence, e.g., "**Although** she had a bad knee, she still won the game."

C *Whereas, on the other hand*

Whereas and **on the other hand** show that a fact is true of one thing but not of another. **Whereas** connects clauses within one sentence. **On the other hand** connects ideas in two sentences.

Pat is very careful, **whereas**
  Chris makes lots of mistakes.
Whereas the south is hot and dry,
  the north gets a lot of rain.

Pat is very careful. **On the other hand,**
  Chris makes lots of mistakes.
The south is hot and dry. The north,
  on the other hand, gets a lot of rain.

D *However*

However is very common to show general contrasts between sentences. It may come at the beginning of a sentence or elsewhere.

I don't agree with all of her methods. **However,** she is a good teacher.
We didn't like the hotel at all. We still enjoyed the vacation, **however.**

Exercises

39.1 Circle the correct answer. Sometimes both answers are correct.

1. **Although** / In spite of we left late, we still got there on time.
2. It was a fantastic evening <u>although / in spite of</u> the terrible food.
3. We decided to go <u>in spite of / despite</u> the cost of the tickets.
4. They enjoyed the course, <u>even though / whereas</u> it was very difficult.
5. I love the ocean, <u>furthermore / whereas</u> most of my friends prefer the mountains.
6. We found a lovely cabin near the lake that we can rent. <u>In addition, / However</u>, it has a boat.
7. We both told John the car was too expensive. <u>However, / On the other hand</u>, he still decided to buy it.
8. Most people we met tried to help us. They were very friendly <u>too / as well</u>.

39.2 Connect parts from each column to form five short sentences or groups of sentences.

A	B	C
He went to school today	even though	the pay isn't very good.
He always did his best at school,	in spite of	he's the most experienced.
He has the right qualifications.	However,	the help I gave him.
He didn't pass the exam	whereas	he didn't feel very well.
He decided to take the job.	What's more,	most of his classmates were very lazy.

39.3 Fill in the blanks with a linking word or phrase.

1. ....*Despite*........ having a map, they still got lost.
2. It took me two hours to do it, ... the others finished in less than an hour.
3. The hotel has a good reputation. .... , it is reasonably priced.
4. She managed to get there .... she had a broken ankle.
5. It's not the best dictionary; .... , it's better than nothing.
6. She's smarter than the others, and she's better trained than them ....

39.4 Complete the sentences with your own ideas.

1. I was able to follow what she said even though ..*she spoke very quickly*................
2. I was able to follow what she was saying, whereas ....
3. We enjoyed the vacation in spite of ....
4. If you buy a season ticket, you can go as often as you like. Furthermore, ...
   ....
5. The exam was very difficult. However, ...
6. Although it was a very long movie, ...

Similarities, differences, exceptions, and conditions

A Similarities

Joe is **similar to / like** his brother in many ways. They are very **similar**. Joe and his brother are (**very much**) **alike**.

Sue and Pat both passed their exams. [Sue passed and Pat passed.] But **neither (one)** wants to go to college. [Sue doesn't want to go, and Pat doesn't want to go either.]

The two boys **have a lot in common**. [They have many things, e.g., hobbies, interests, beliefs, that are the same or very similar.]

B Differences

Paula is **not at all like / (quite/totally) unlike** her sister Pam. [very different from]

They **have nothing in common**. They **are nothing like** each other. [no interests, beliefs, etc., that are the same]

His early movies are (**quite/really/totally**) **different from** his later ones.

C Using *compare*

When we **compare** things we can see similarities and differences.

The study **made a comparison** between the U.S. and Canada.

Our new home is very big **compared with/to** our old one.

If you **compare** this one **with** the others, I'm sure you'll see a difference.

D Exceptions

To say that a fact applies to a general group but *not* to (an)other thing(s), we use these words/phrases:

It snowed everywhere **except** on the west coast.

The two girls are very similar, **except** that Marie has slightly longer hair.

The museum is open every day **except** (**for**) / **apart from** Sunday(s).

> *note*   **Except for** and **apart from** are followed by noun phrases.

E Conditions with *unless, otherwise,* etc.

We will be late **unless** we hurry. [We will be late if we don't hurry.]

I have to go now. **Otherwise** I'll miss the last bus. [if I don't go now]

You can borrow it **as long as** you return it by Thursday. [**on** (**the**) **condition that**]

Take your umbrella **in case** it rains. [because it may rain later]

> *note*   **As long as** is similar to **if**, but it emphasizes that the condition is very important to the speaker.

Exercises

40.1 Complete the sentences using the words/phrases from page 80.

MICHAEL . . .	PHILIPPE . . .	PAUL . . .
is 21 and lives with his parents. He works in a store. He is shy, hardworking, and very good at sports. He would like to become the manager of a sports shop.	is 22 and lives alone. He is in college. He is smart but lazy and spends most of his time at parties. He has no plans for the future.	is 18 and lives with his parents. He is a trainee in a bank, but he would like to be the manager someday. He is very good at golf.

1. Michael and Paul are very ...*similar*.................................
2. Philippe is quite .... the other two.
3. Paul and Michael have ....
4. Paul and Philippe have almost nothing ....
5. Paul and Michael both ....
6. Neither of them ....

40.2 Rewrite the sentences using the word in brackets. Keep the meaning the same.

1. She's a lot like the others.
   She's ...*very similar to the others*..... [similar]
2. Hong is not at all like her sister.
   Hong is very .... [different]
3. When you see the houses, you realize that the apartments are a very good value.
   The apartments are a very good value .... [compare]
4. In her class, only Carla failed the exam.
   Everyone passed .... [except]
5. The two boys have completely different interests.
   They have .... [common]

40.3 Fill each blank with a word/phrase that indicates a condition.

1. You'd better write these words down; ....*otherwise*..... you might forget them.
2. I've got extra party food, ... more people come than we expect.
3. I can meet you for dinner tonight .... I have to work late at the office.
4. I agreed to buy my son a dog .... he takes it for a walk every day.
5. We'd better leave early .... we'll be stuck in traffic.

40.4 Complete the sentences with your own ideas.

1. You can't go into that club unless you ...*are a member*...
2. I want to finish this report today; otherwise I'll ....
3. You can borrow the money as long as you ....
4. I cleaned the guest room and made the bed in case ....
5. I'm not going to work overtime unless ....

Reason, purpose, and result

A Reason

We go there **because** the scenery is great. [**because** + clause (clause = subject + verb)]
We go there **because of** the great scenery. [**because of** + (adjective) + noun]

Since/As often comes at the beginning of the sentence, e.g., "**Since/As** I was feeling tired, I left early."

Due to means the same as **because of,** and it is often used to explain the reason for a problem. **Due to** can be used to explain a whole clause, mostly in speech or informal writing, e.g., "The plane was late **due to** bad weather." *or* "**Due to** bad weather, it was late."

In more formal writing, **due to** is used mostly immediately after the verb *to be*, e.g., "The plane's delay was **due to** bad weather."

B Purpose

A "purpose" is an intention, an aim, or a reason for doing something, e.g., "The **purpose of** buying this book **is** to improve my English."

You can introduce a purpose using **so (that)** or **in order to:**

I bought this book **so (that)** I can improve my English.
We moved to this neighborhood **so (that)** we could send our kids to this school.
They went home early **in order to** beat the traffic.

> **note** A modal verb (e.g., **can** or **could**) can occur in a clause after **so that** as in the examples above.

C Cause and result

Sentences that show cause:

The bus driver **caused / was responsible for** the accident. [made it happen]
The company's growth will **lead to / result in** an increase in jobs. [make it happen]

Sentences that show result:

I left my ticket at home, **so** I had to buy another one.
The manager was out sick. **As a result,** there was no one to make decisions.
I forgot to send an e-mail. **Consequently,** people didn't know about the game.
She worked extremely hard. **Therefore,** she deserved the promotion.

As a result, therefore, and **consequently** usually connect ideas in two separate sentences and are more common in written English.

Cause and result verbs sometimes appear together:

A cigarette **caused** the fire. This **resulted in** the building's destruction.

Exercises

41.1 Combine the two sentences using *so, so that, because, as,* or *since*.

1. I didn't call. It was very late. *I didn't call because it was very late.*
2. I turned up the radio in the living room. I could hear it in the kitchen.
3. The restaurant was full. We went to the coffee shop next door.
4. The company has poor management. There has been a drop in profits.
5. It is a very large city. You have to use public transportation a lot.
6. I learned to drive. My mother didn't have to take me to school every day.

41.2 Rewrite the sentences with *because of* or *due to*.

1. He couldn't play soccer because he had an injured shoulder.
   He couldn't play soccer because of his injured shoulder.
2. She was successful in her job because her training was excellent.
3. The weather was awful, so we couldn't eat outside.
4. She could not go to work because she had a broken ankle.
5. The flowers died because the weather was so dry.
6. The traffic was heavy. I was half an hour late.
7. It started raining, so the referee had to stop the game.

41.3 Complete this memo. Use words from page 82.

> **To:** All Staff   **Date:** August 9
> **From:** The Manager   **Subject:** Temporary road work
>
> Starting next Monday (and continuing all week), there will be construction on the
> major roads leading to the factory. (1) .... *Since* .... this will
> (2) .... delays, please try to leave home a few minutes earlier in the
> morning (3) .... everyone arrives on time. The construction could
> also (4) .... severe traffic congestion. (5) .... , you
> may want to consider using public transportation instead of driving.
>
> Thank you for your cooperation.

41.4 These sentences are about learning English. Complete them with your own ideas.

1. I want to improve my English because ..*I will need it in my job very soon.*.......
2. I bought myself an MP3 player so that ....
3. I study English on weekends since ....
4. I always write words down in my notebook in order to ....
5. I don't get many opportunities to practice my English. Consequently, ...
   ....
6. My brother has a lot of American and Canadian friends. As a result, ...
   ....

The physical world

A The solar system

The **Earth revolves** around **the sun**. The Earth's path through **space** is its **orbit**.
London and New York are in different **time zones**. London's time is five or six hours
ahead of New York's.

B Physical features

Continents: Asia, Europe	**Rivers:** the Yangtze, the Mississippi
Countries: Thailand, Hungary, Brazil	**Waterfalls:** Niagara Falls, Angel Falls
Islands: Sicily, Manhattan, Borneo	**Mountains:** Mount Everest, Mount Fuji
Island groups: the Bahamas, the West Indies	**Mountain ranges:** the Andes, the Rockies
Oceans: the Atlantic Ocean, the Pacific Ocean	**Jungles:** the Amazon (also called the Amazon Rain Forest)
Seas: the Adriatic Sea, the Red Sea	**Deserts:** the Sahara, the Gobi
Lakes: Lake Michigan, Lake Titicaca	

note Sometimes you need the definite article [**the**] e.g., **the** Atlantic Ocean,
the Andes; sometimes no article is used, e.g., Mount Everest and Lake
Titicaca.

C Natural disasters

A **disaster** is when something terrible happens, which often results in death, destruction,
and suffering. A **natural disaster** is caused by nature, not by humans.

| volcano / volcanic eruption | earthquake | flood | hurricane |

The **earthquake destroyed** many homes.
The **weather forecast** says the **hurricane** could **hit/strike** [hit with great force] Florida.
The **floods** have been terrible. Many people have **drowned**. [died from being underwater]

Exercises

42.1 Match the items in the box with the descriptions below.

Earth	the moon	planets	stars
the equator	the North Pole	the South Pole	the sun

1. Mars, Jupiter, and Venus are all *planets*..............
2. It revolves around the Earth. ....
3. The Earth revolves around it. ....
4. The Big Dipper is a group of ....
5. It divides the Earth into northern and southern halves. ....
6. It's the most northern point on the surface of the Earth. ....
7. It's the most southern point on the surface of the Earth. ....
8. It rotates around the sun every 365 days. ....

42.2 Complete the sentences.

1. The Nile is ..*a river*........... .
2. The Atlantic is ....
3. The Alps are ....
4. Japan is ....
5. The Sahara is ....
6. The Amazon is ....
7. The Mediterranean is ....
8. The West Indies are ....
9. Africa is ....
10. Everest is the highest .... in the world.

42.3 Complete the paragraph with *the* if necessary or Ø if no article is necessary.

My trip took me across (1) .....*the*..... Atlantic Ocean from (2) .... Europe to (3) .... South America. I traveled through (4) .... Amazon Rain Forest and down through the interior of (5) .... Brazil, and then into (6) .... Paraguay. From there I headed north again, through Bolivia, around (7) .... Lake Titicaca, and up to Cuzco. Then I crossed (8) .... Andes and finally arrived in Lima. For the last part of the journey I flew to (9) .... Jamaica in (10) .... West Indies.

42.4 What kind of disaster is described in each of these sentences?

1. Its strong winds bent the trees and knocked over some telephone poles.
2. It was about six feet (183 centimeters) deep. We watched as our furniture just floated away.
3. The walls began to move visibly, and large cracks opened up in the ground.
4. We saw the lava slowly advancing toward the town just 10 miles (16 kilometers) away.

Unit 43 Weather

A Weather conditions

Statements about weather often start with "It . . . / The weather is . . ."; e.g., "The **weather** is **hot**. / It is hot."

Here are some common weather words. You can often form adjectives by adding -*y*.

Noun	Adjective	Noun	Adjective
sun	sunny	wind	windy
cloud	cloudy	ice	icy
fog	foggy	rain	rainy
heat	hot	humidity	humid

B Rain

A light rain, which comes down in fine drops, is a **drizzle**. A rain that lasts only a short time is a **shower** (e.g., "We had a few **showers** yesterday."). When it is raining a lot (or **raining hard**), we often say it's **pouring**. A **drought** is a long period without rain.

C Temperature

freezing   cold/chilly   pleasant/warm   hot   boiling
(= very cold)   (= very hot)

A: How cold does **it get** in the winter?
B. It can **go down** to 0 **degrees Fahrenheit**. [about 18 degrees **below zero Celsius**]

A: How hot does **it get** in summer?
B. It can **get up to** 95°. [95 degrees **Fahrenheit** (about 35 degrees Celsius)]

D Wind

a **breeze**   a **wind**   a **strong wind**   a **gale**   a **hurricane**

A **breeze** is a gentle and pleasant wind; a **gale** has winds between around 32 and 63 miles per hour (51 and 102 kilometers per hour); a **hurricane** has violent winds over around 74 miles (119 kilometers) per hour.

It was a hot day, but there was a nice **breeze**.
The **wind** blew my hat off.
A gale caused serious damage in Puerto Rico, but the **hurricane** that hit Cuba was worse.

E Thunderstorms

A spell [period] of very hot weather often ends with a **thunderstorm**. The air may be very **hot** and **humid** [wet air]. Then you get **thunder** [loud noises during a storm] **and lightning** [flashes of light during a storm], and finally, very **heavy rain**. Afterwards, the air usually feels **cooler** (**cool**) and **fresher** (**fresh**).

Exercises

43.1 Identify the weather conditions in these pictures.

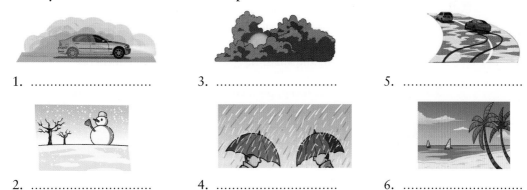

1. ....

3. ....

5. ....

2. ....

4. ....

6. ....

43.2 Mark each sentence *true* or *false*. If a sentence is *false*, make it true.

1. It frequently pours in the desert. *false: It hardly ever pours in the desert.*
2. It can get very chilly in the desert at night.
3. Thunder makes a noise.
4. Lightning can kill people.
5. A shower is a light breeze.
6. A spell of hot weather may end in a thunderstorm.
7. When it is humid, the air is very dry.
8. At 32°F / 0°C, water turns to ice.
9. Drought is a long period of rain.
10. When it's foggy, you need sunglasses.

43.3 Complete these scales.

(1) .... → wind → strong wind → (2) .... → hurricane

(3) .... → cold → not very warm → warm → hot → (4) ....

43.4 Complete the paragraph with words from the box.

blows	heavy	hot	humid	snows	spell	winds

The single greatest influence on Japanese weather is the wind. During the summer it (1) ....*blows*........ from the Pacific, causing (2) .... and humid weather. In winter, however, the northwesterly (3) .... from Siberia are very cold, and it (4) .... heavily in the central mountain ranges. Areas along the Pacific coast receive cold dry air. Between June and mid-July, there is a (5) .... of wet weather when the rice fields get the water they need for growth. After that, there is less (6) .... rain, but the air is still (7) .... Autumn, however, is drier, and usually very pleasant.

43.5 Write a paragraph about the weather in some place where you once lived.

Animals, insects, and other creatures

A   Pets and farm animals

Many people keep **pets** [animals that live with people]. In the U.S. and Canada, the most common pets are **dogs** and **cats**. Some people keep birds, such as **parakeets** [small **parrots**]; fish, such as **goldfish;** and small furry animals, such as **hamsters.**

Farm animals include: **sheep, pigs, cows, horses, chickens,** and **goats.**

> *note*   The word **sheep** is both the singular and plural form, i.e., a sheep or two sheep.
> A young sheep is called a **lamb.**

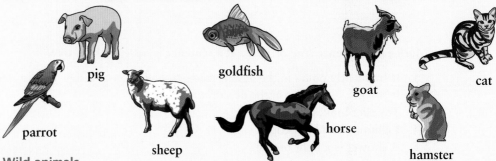

parrot

pig

goldfish

goat

cat

sheep

horse

hamster

B   Wild animals

In a zoo or **in the wild** [in a natural area, outside human control], you may find these wild animals.

giraffe

camel

bear

gorilla

elephant

monkey

lion

leopard

tiger

zebra

C   Common insects and other small creatures

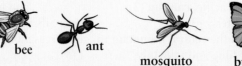

bee   ant

mosquito   butterfly

fly

spider

D   In the water, in the air, and on the ground

Here are some **creatures** [living things, e.g., animals, birds, fish] that swim, fly, or move along the ground.

shark

eagle

snail

snake

whale

Exercises

44.1 Look at the underlined letters in each pair of words. Is the pronunciation the same or different?

Examples: wh<u>a</u>le <u>a</u>nimal *different*   <u>c</u>at <u>c</u>amel *same*

1. l<u>i</u>on t<u>i</u>ger   5. sp<u>i</u>der w<u>i</u>ld
2. b<u>ea</u>r <u>ea</u>gle   6. m<u>o</u>nkey b<u>u</u>tterfly
3. g<u>oa</u>t mosquit<u>o</u>   7. c<u>a</u>mel sn<u>a</u>ke
4. <u>g</u>orilla <u>g</u>iraffe   8. leop<u>ar</u>d sh<u>ar</u>k

44.2 Arrange the words into three groups: farm animals, wild animals, and insects.

monkey	tiger	fly	gorilla	elephant	bear
butterfly	goat	sheep	cow	leopard	mosquito
horse	bee	lion	ant	pig	chicken

44.3 Start each sentence with a creature from page 88.

1. ....*Eagles*........ can fly at great heights.
2. .... can swim very long distances.
3. .... can understand lots of human commands.
4. .... can run very fast.
5. .... can travel through the desert for long distances without water.
6. .... can be as long as 100 feet (about 30 meters).
7. .... can eat fruit from tall trees.
8. .... change their skin several times a year.
9. .... can pick things up with their trunk.
10. .... provide us with wool.

44.4 Complete the sentences.

1. They have lots of pets: two dogs, four cats, and a ...*hamster.*..............................
2. Their farm animals include cows, sheep, and ....
3. The children love to see the "big cats" at the zoo, such as lions, tigers, and ....
4. I hate most insects, but especially mosquitoes and ....
5. We saw some really large wild animals at the zoo: elephants, giraffes, and ....

44.5 Match each animal with its maximum speed. Search online if necessary.

lion	spider	40 mph (64 kph)	0.03 mph (0.05 kph)
rabbit	pig	35 mph (56 kph)	25 mph (40 kph)
shark	golden eagle	168 mph (270 kph)	1.17 mph (1.88 kph)
elephant	snail	50 mph (80 kph)	11 mph (17.7 kph)

Note: mph = miles per hour; kph = kilometers per hour

A Who speaks what and where?

Country	Nationality	Language
Argentina	Argentinean	Spanish
Australia	Australian	English
Brazil	Brazilian	Portuguese
Canada	Canadian	English / French
Chile	Chilean	Spanish
China	Chinese	Mandarin Chinese / Cantonese
Colombia	Colombian	Spanish
Egypt	Egyptian	Arabic
France	French	French
Great Britain	British	English
Indonesia	Indonesian	Indonesian
Iraq	Iraqi	Arabic/Kurdish
Israel	Israeli	Hebrew
Italy	Italian	Italian
Japan	Japanese	Japanese
South Korea	South Korean	Korean
Mexico	Mexican	Spanish
the Philippines	Philippine/Filipino	Tagalog/English
Russia	Russian	Russian
Saudi Arabia	Saudi Arabian	Arabic
Spain	Spanish/Spaniard	Spanish
Thailand	Thai	Thai
Turkey	Turkish/Turk	Turkish
the United States	American	English
Vietnam	Vietnamese	Vietnamese

B Regions

Some common words for regions [areas of more than one country]:

Europe [e.g., Spain, Poland, the U.K.] **the Mediterranean** [e.g., Spain, Italy, Lebanon]
East Asia [e.g., China, South Korea, Japan] **the Middle East** [e.g., Egypt, U.A.E., Jordan]
the Caribbean [e.g., Jamaica, Trinidad] **Latin America** [e.g., Panama, Chile, Peru]

C The people

The plural word for people of a certain nationality may or may not end in an -s.
Most Russians means "most Russian people." **The Japanese** means "Japanese people in general." You can always add "people" after the nationality.

Most	Brazilians	Mexicans	Chinese	Japanese	like to eat . . .
	South Koreans	Canadians	French	Vietnamese	
	Italians	Iraqis	Spanish	British	
	Brazilian people	Mexican people	Chinese people	Japanese people	

Exercises

45.1 **Answer these questions without looking at page 90.**

1. Name at least four countries where the national language is English.
2. What language is spoken in Brazil?
3. What are people from Israel called?
4. What language is spoken in Egypt?
5. What nationality are people from Thailand?
6. What language is spoken in Argentina?
7. What are people from South Korea called?
8. Where do people speak Mandarin Chinese?
9. Name at least three countries where Spanish is spoken.
10. What are the people of Turkey called?

45.2 **Mark the main stress in these words and practice saying them.**

Example: I<u>ta</u>lian

Japan	Japanese	Brazilian	Egyptian	Arabic
Chinese	Australia	Indonesia	Indonesian	Vietnamese

Which syllable is stressed in the words ending in _-ian_? Those ending in _-ese_?

45.3 **Complete each sentence with the name of the people from a country or region on page 90.**

1. I've worked with many ...<u>Russians</u>..........
2. .... usually eat dinner late, sometimes after 10 p.m.
3. Many .... speak or understand both French and English.
4. .... are well known for their classic cuisine.
5. On my visit to Mexico City, I found .... very warm and welcoming.
6. .... have a healthy diet. They eat a lot of fish, rice, and vegetables.
7. Some people say that .... are very friendly.
8. I met a lot of .... on my trip to Rio de Janeiro.

45.4 **Complete the sentences.**

1. Bangkok is the capital of ...<u>Thailand</u>...........
2. Buenos Aires is the capital of ....
3. Ankara is the capital of ....
4. Seoul is the capital of ....
5. Canberra is the capital of ....
6. Washington, D.C. is the capital of ....
7. Moscow is the capital of ....
8. The island of Jamaica is in ....
9. Madrid is the capital of ....
10. Tokyo is the capital of ....

45.5 **Have you ever met anyone from the countries on page 90? Go through the list and check the people you have met.**

The body and what it can do

A Parts of the body

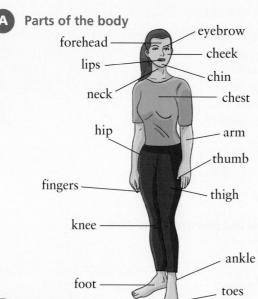

forehead
eyebrow
lips
cheek
chin
neck
chest
hip
arm
thumb
fingers
thigh
knee
ankle
foot
toes

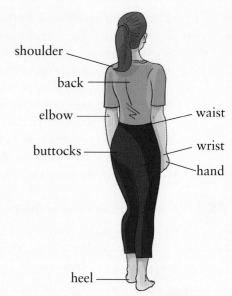

shoulder
back
elbow
waist
buttocks
wrist
hand
heel

B Physical actions

You can **breathe** through your nose or your mouth.
People **smile** when they're happy or think something is funny,
or to be polite. They **laugh** at something very funny; they may **cry**
when they're sad; they **yawn** when they're tired or bored.

Many people **nod** their head (up and down) to mean "yes"
and **shake** their head (side to side) when they mean "no."

When you pick up something heavy, you should **bend**
your knees and keep your back straight.

C Common phrases

shake hands

fold your arms

comb your hair

bite your nails

blow your nose

Exercises

46.1 How much of the picture can you label without looking at page 92?

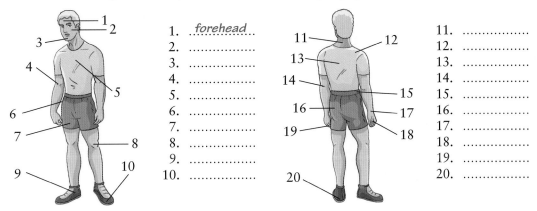

1. _forehead_	11. ....
2.	12. ....
3.	13. ....
4.	14. ....
5.	15. ....
6.	16. ....
7.	17. ....
8.	18. ....
9.	19. ....
10.	20. ....

46.2 Match the verbs on the left with a part of the body on the right to form common phrases. Use each verb and body part only once.

1. blow —————————— your knees
2. nod ————————————— your nose
3. comb   your nails
4. fold   your head
5. bend   your arms
6. shake   your hair
7. bite   hands

46.3 What do these actions often mean? (There may be lots of possible answers.)

1. People often smile when ..they're happy or think something is funny.......................
2. They often breathe quickly after ....
3. They laugh when ....
4. They may bite their nails when ....
5. They shake their head when ....
6. And nod their head when ....
7. They yawn when ....

46.4 There are fourteen words describing parts of the body, either across or down, in this word square. Can you find them?

C	E	L	B	O	W	A
H	T	I	A	E	N	R
I	O	P	C	Y	A	M
N	E	C	K	E	I	H
I	H	A	N	K	L	E
K	C	H	E	S	T	E
C	H	E	E	K	A	L

Describing people's appearance

A General description

Positive: **Beautiful** is generally used to describe women; **handsome** is often used to describe men. **Good-looking** and **attractive** are used for both men and women. **Pretty** is another positive word to describe a woman (often a girl) meaning "pleasing to look at."

note	Ugly is a very negative word. **Not very good-looking** is less negative.

B Height and build

tall and slim   medium height and **build**   short and fat   muscular

note	**Slim** is positive. **Thin** is less positive. **Skinny** is usually negative. **Fat** is not polite. **Overweight** is less rude.

C Hair

gray   blond   red   light brown   dark brown   black   straight   wavy   curly

D Special features

The man on the left has **pale skin** [very light skin]. He has **blue eyes**. He also has **broad shoulders**, with a **scar** on his forehead. The other man has **darker skin / a darker complexion**. He also has a **beard** and a **mustache**. His eyes are **brown**.

E Asking questions about a person's appearance

Q: What does she **look like**?   A: She's fairly tall, with short, blond hair.
Q: **How tall** is she?   A: **About** 5 foot 9 (175 centimeters).
Q: **How much** does she **weigh**?   A: **Roughly** 140 pounds (63 kilograms).

Exercises

47.1 Complete these sentences. (More than one answer may be possible.)

1. She has blond ..*hair*...............
2. He has very pale ....
3. They both have .... hair.
4. I would say he has a .... build.
5. Her brother has very broad ....
6. She exercises a lot, so she has a .... build.
7. Last time I saw him he had grown a ....
8. She once got a deep cut on her arm, so now she has a ....
9. Both men had .... eyes.
10. All of them have dark ....

47.2 Replace the underlined word in each sentence with a word that is either more appropriate or more polite.

1. He told me he'd met a <u>handsome</u> woman at the club last night.
2. She's beautiful, but her younger sister is <u>really ugly</u>.
3. Peter should get some exercise; he's getting <u>fat</u>.
4. Most people want to stay slim, but not as <u>skinny</u> as that woman over there.
5. I think she's hoping she'll meet a few <u>beautiful</u> men at the tennis club.

47.3 You want to know about someone's:

      general appearance   height   weight

What questions do you need to ask? Complete these questions.

1. What .... ?
2. How .... ?
3. How much .... ?

47.4 Now answer these questions about yourself. If possible, ask another person these questions too.

1. About how tall are you?
2. How would you describe your build?
3. What color are your eyes?
4. What kind of hair do you have?
5. What color is it?
6. Would you like your hair to look different? If so, in what way?
7. Do you think you have any special features?
8. Are there any special features you would like to have?
9. Do you like beards?
10. Can you think of a famous woman you would describe as beautiful? A famous man you would describe as handsome?

Describing character

A Opposites

Positive	Negative
warm and **friendly**	**cold** and **unfriendly**
kind [good to others]	**unkind, mean**
nice, pleasant	**unpleasant**
generous [likes to give/share]	**stingy** [does not often give to others]
optimistic [thinks positively]	**pessimistic** [thinks negatively]
cheerful [happy and smiling]	**grumpy, gloomy** [always seems unhappy]
relaxed, easygoing	**tense** [nervous, anxious, not calm]
strong	**weak**
sensitive [aware of others' feelings]	**insensitive**
honest [tells the truth]	**dishonest**

Sandra is **tense** now because of her exams, but she's usually **relaxed** and **easygoing**.
When the weather's nice I feel **cheerful** and **optimistic**. When it's rainy I'm **grumpy**.
He seemed **unfriendly** at first. Later, I realized he's really very **warm** and **kind**.
She called the student's work "boring." She was just trying to be **honest**, but that was an
   insensitive thing to say.

B Describing character in work situations

Positive	Negative
hardworking	**lazy** [doesn't want to work]
punctual [always on time]	not very punctual; often late
reliable, dependable [someone who can be trusted]	**unreliable, undependable**
intelligent, smart, bright	**stupid, dumb** *(informal)*
flexible [able to change or to try new ways]	**inflexible**
organized [having a clear system/schedule for getting things done]	**disorganized**

C Other phrases to describe character

She **takes the initiative** to solve problems. [She takes necessary actions without waiting
   for orders from anyone else.]
That boy has **no common sense**. [He does stupid things without thinking.] His sister, on
   the other hand, is very **sensible**. [thinks before taking action]
Paul **is a character**; he is a lot of fun to be around. [He's an unusual, often humorous
   person.]

Exercises

48.1 Arrange these words into pairs of opposites. Write them in the columns.

| smart | stingy | nice | lazy | relaxed | hardworking |
| tense | cheerful | generous | unpleasant | stupid | gloomy |

Positive	Negative
...smart...	...stupid...
....	....
....	....
....	....
....	....
....	....

48.2 Write the opposite of each adjective, using one of these prefixes: *un-*, *in-*, or *dis-*.

Example: kind – *unkind*

| kind | organized | dependable | pleasant |
| reliable | flexible | sensitive | honest |

48.3 Use the words from page 96 to describe each person.

1. She locks the door but leaves the windows open.   *She has no common sense.*
2. He always promises to do things, but half the time he forgets.
3. I always have to tell him what to do. He does nothing without being told.
4. She is always here on time.
5. I don't think he's done any work since he started this job.
6. She isn't very tense. She seems not to worry too much.
7. He can work well in any department. It doesn't matter to him.
8. She is very aware of other people's feelings.

Write at least three sentences of your own to describe people's character.

48.4 What nouns can be formed from these adjectives? Use a dictionary.

1. kind *kindness*	5. organized	9. flexible
2. generous	6. strong	10. lazy
3. sensitive	7. reliable	11. weak
4. optimistic	8. stupid	12. friendly

48.5 1. Choose three words from page 96 that describe you.
2. Is there one quality you do not have but would like to have?
3. What, in your opinion, is the worst quality described on page 96?
   If possible, compare your answers with a friend.

Human feelings and actions

(A) Feelings / emotions

Noun	Adjective(s)
love [≠ hate]	loving [≠ hateful]
happiness [≠ sadness]	happy [≠ sad]
anger	angry
fear	afraid (of) / frightened (of)
pride	proud (of)
jealousy	jealous (of)
embarrassment	embarrassed/embarrassing (see Unit 35)

- **Pride** can be a positive feeling of satisfaction when you or someone close to you does something well, e.g., "He was **proud** of his wife when she became the first president of the organization."
- **Jealousy** is a feeling of anger and unhappiness you may have if: (a) someone you love shows interest in others, or (b) if someone has something you want but don't have.
  a) My girlfriend gets **jealous** when I talk to other girls.
  b) He is **jealous of** his sister because she is smarter.
- **Upset** means being unhappy or angry because something unpleasant has happened, e.g., "He was **upset** when we didn't invite him."; "She'll get **upset** if you shout at her."

(B) Ways of speaking, looking, and walking

whisper (v., n.) [speak very quietly]

shout (v., n.) [speak in a very loud voice]

glance (at) (v., n.) [look at someone or something quickly]

stare (v., n.) [look at someone/something in a fixed way for a long time]

stroll (v., n.) [walk in a slow and relaxed/casual way]

march (v., n.) [walk quickly and with a clear purpose, as in a parade]

(C) Things we do with our hands

clap

knock (on/at a door)

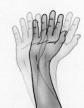

wave (goodbye)

point
(at something/someone)

press (a button)

push something

Exercises

49.1 **What nouns can you make from these adjectives?**

a. angry – *anger*   c. happy   e. jealous
b. sad   d. proud   f. embarrassed

49.2 **Connect the two parts of each sentence.**

1. He was very proud when
2. He was very jealous when
3. He was very embarrassed when
4. He was very angry when
5. He was very sad when

6. He was very frightened when

a. someone stole his money.
b. his aunt died.
c. his father won the tennis match.
d. he saw a group of dogs running toward him.
e. he wished her "happy birthday" on the wrong day.
f. his best friend went out with a woman he really liked.

49.3 **Answer these questions about yourself. If possible, ask someone else these questions too.**

1. How would you feel if you forgot your mother's or your father's birthday?
2. Have you ever been in a car that was going too fast? How did you feel?
3. How do you feel when others talk to you while you're trying to concentrate?
4. If you made a stupid mistake in English, how would you feel?
5. What are you very proud of?
6. Can you remember a situation when you felt embarrassed? What happened?

49.4 **What are these people doing? Describe their actions using words from page 98.**

1.    2.   3.    4.    5.

49.5 **Replace the underlined words with a one-word verb that has the same meaning.**

1. He stopped working and <u>looked quickly</u> at the clock.   *glanced*
2. Because we were in the library, he <u>spoke very quietly</u> in my ear.
3. We <u>walked casually</u> along the sidewalk and then stopped for coffee.
4. The soldiers <u>walked quickly</u> in the parade.
5. The man <u>looked</u> at Susan <u>steadily for a long time</u>, but she didn't seem to notice.

A Relatives [members of your family]

	Male	Female
Your parents' parents (your **grandparents**)	grandfather	grandmother
Your parents' brothers and sisters	uncles	aunts
Your aunt's/uncle's children	cousins	cousins
The father and mother of the person you marry	father-in-law	mother-in-law
The brother and sister of the person you marry	brother-in-law	sister-in-law
Your brother's/sister's children	nephews	nieces
If the person you marry dies, you are a . . .	widower	widow
If your mother or father **remarries**, you have a	stepfather	stepmother
The children of your children (your **grandchildren**)	grandson	granddaughter

note We ask "Are you **related to** him/her?" [Are you a relative / connected by a family relationship?] Also, you can say you are **related** to someone **by marriage**. [not by birth]

B Family background [family history]

My **paternal** grandfather [on my father's side] was a farmer in Ireland. He had **twin sons** [two children born at the same time] – my Uncle Bob and my father – who **inherited** his house and land [received the property after he died]. My dad didn't want to be a farmer, so he sold his share to my uncle. My **maternal grandmother** [on my mother's side] was also Irish. My parents met each other at college in Ireland. After my mom and dad graduated, they got married and moved to Boston. I **was born** two years later. They didn't have any more children, so I am an **only child**.

C Patterns for names

Robert	Patrick	O'Neill		Lee	Mei Shao		Harry	M.	Kitano
first name / given name	middle name	family name / surname		family name	personal name		first name	middle initial	family name

D Friends

an **old** friend [someone you have known for a long time]	a **close** friend [a very good friend]	**co-workers/colleagues** [people you work with]
your **best** friend [the one friend you feel closest to]	**classmates** [people in your class at school]	a **roommate** [someone you share a room or apartment with]

E *Ex-*

We use this for a husband / wife / boyfriend / girlfriend we had in the past, e.g., an **ex-husband** or an **ex-girlfriend**.

Exercises

50.1 Look at the family tree and complete the sentences below.

Don & Karen Graham

John + Susan   Jill + Paul   Barry + Vicki
                    (died 1997)

Rita   Ana   Michael   Tom

1. John is Jill's ..*brother-in-law.*..
2. Michael is Jill's ....
3. Rita and Ana are Michael's ....
4. Rita is Vicki's ....
5. Don Graham is Tom's ....
6. Barry is Rita's ....
7. Susan is Michael's ....
8. Paul died in 1997, making Jill a ....
9. Tom is Karen's ....
10. John and Vicki are related ....

50.2 Answer these questions about yourself.

1. What's your first name?
2. What's your last name?
3. Is that a common name in your country?
4. Do you have a middle name?
5. Are you an only child? If not, how many brothers and sisters do you have?
6. Do you have any brothers-in-law or sisters-in-law?
7. Who is your oldest friend?
8. Who is your closest friend?
9. Do you work? If so, how many of your co-workers are also your friends?
10. Do you have any ex-boyfriends or ex-girlfriends who speak English very well?

50.3 Write a short summary of your family background (as in B on page 100).

....
....
....
....
....
....
....

50.4 Draw your own family tree (as in Exercise 50.1 above). Are there any relationships you cannot describe in English?

Ages and stages

A Growing up and growing older

Age	Stage of life
0–1 approximately	a **baby**
1–3	a **toddler**
3–12 approximately	a **child** [This period is your **childhood**.]
13–19	a **teenager** [The **early teens** are 13–14.]
18+	an **adult** [In some places you are an adult at 21.]
20–29	**in your twenties** [The **mid-twenties** are 24–26.]
30–39	**in your thirties** [The **late thirties** are 38–39.]
45–65	**middle age** [A person at this age is **middle-aged**.]
65	People older than this are sometimes called **seniors / senior citizens**.
75+	**old age** [also **elderly**, e.g., "an **elderly** woman"]

note The period from about 13 to 17 is called **adolescence** [becoming an adult]. The person is an **adolescent**. A person who is **grown (up)** is **an adult**. The period after you stop working at your usual job is **retirement**. People can **retire** at almost any age, but most do it after 65.

B Childhood and adolescence

Sam (on the right) **was born** in Chicago, but when he was two, his father got a new job in Los Angeles. He **grew up** in southern California. He **went to college** at 18, where . . .

C Dating and romance

. . . he met Ann. He **went out with** her [she was his **girlfriend**; he was her **boyfriend**] for three years. Toward the end they had lots of **fights** [arguments], and they **split up** [**broke up / separated**]. In his **mid-twenties** he met Marie. They **fell in love** and . . .

D Marriage

. . . **got married** within six months. A year later she got **pregnant,** and they **had their first child,** a boy. But the marriage was not a success. Sam **left** after two years, and they **got divorced**. Four years later, Marie remarried. Now she is **expecting** a second baby [she is pregnant].

Exercises

51.1 In what stage of life are these people? Use expressions from page 102.

1. Paulo isn't three yet, so he's still ...*a toddler.*...................
2. Al was a bus driver for 40 years. He stopped working last year.
   Now he's ....
3. Susan is 25, so she is in her ....
4. Caroline will be 49 this year. She is now ....
5. Ron is 32 and his wife is 31. They are both in ....
6. Joan is 70, so she is ....
7. Kevin was born six months ago. He is ....
8. Leila will be 13 this year, so soon she will be ....
9. In most countries, you can't vote until you're ....
10. Fifteen is often a difficult age for boys going through ....

51.2 Are these sentences *true* or *false* about the people on page 102? If *false*, write a sentence that is more accurate.

1. Sam was born in Los Angeles.   *false: He was born in Chicago.*
2. He grew up in southern California.
3. He went out with Ann for three years.
4. They split up because Sam went to live in Japan.
5. Sam fell in love with Marie.
6. Marie got pregnant six months after they got married.
7. Marie is now expecting her third child.
8. Marie left Sam.

51.3 Connect the two parts of each sentence to build a story about Marta's life.

Beginnings	Endings
1. Marta was born	a. was a boy she met in high school.
2. She grew up	b. in her mid-twenties.
3. Her first boyfriend	c. in a small town.
4. She went out with him	d. after high school, when she was in her late teens.
5. She went to college	e. in a small local hospital 30 years ago.
6. She fell in love	f. for six months.
7. They got married	g. with another student, who was studying law.
8. She had a baby	h. when she graduated, in her early twenties.

51.4 Use as many of the sentence beginnings (from 51.3) as possible to tell about your own life.

Unit 52

Daily routines

A Sleep

During the week, I **wake up** at about 6:30 a.m. Sometimes I **lie in bed** for a few minutes, but then I have to **get up** [get out of bed] and **get dressed**. Most nights, I **go to bed** at about 11:30 p.m. I usually **fall asleep** right away, but sometimes I can't **get to sleep** [succeed in sleeping]. I might finally **fall asleep** at about 3 a.m., and then I **oversleep** [sleep too long] in the morning. If I **stay up late** [go to bed very late], I try to **take a nap** [a short sleep, e.g., 30 minutes] in the afternoon. On the **weekends** [Saturday and Sunday], I **sleep in** [sleep later than usual] until 10 or 10:30 a.m.

B Food

During the week, I **have breakfast** at 7:30 a.m., **lunch** at 1:00 p.m., and **dinner** around 7 p.m. I also have one or two **snacks** [small amounts of food, e.g., cookies or fruit] during the day at work. I live **alone / by myself** [not with anyone else], so I have to **make my own meals** [prepare them for myself]. I also have to **feed** [give food to] my two cats twice a day.

C Staying clean

In the morning, I **take a shower**, and I usually **wash my hair** at the same time. I usually **shave** after I **wash my face**, and then I **brush my teeth**. Sometimes I **take a bath** in the evening if I want to relax.

D Work

I **leave for work / leave home / leave the house** at about 8 a.m. and **get to work** [arrive at work] by 9 a.m. I have lunch at about 1 p.m., and I **take** a couple of **coffee breaks** [short times off work] during the day. I **leave work / get off work** around 5 p.m. and **get home** by 6 p.m.

E Evenings

On weeknights, I **stay home** and **watch TV** or just **relax**. On weekends, I often **go out** with friends and **stay out** late [come home late at night]. Sometimes I **have friends over** for dinner [invite friends to my home]. Sometimes my friends **come over** [visit my house] to **watch videos** or **play cards**.

F Housework

I **do the shopping** [buy groceries] on Saturdays. I also **do the laundry** [wash clothes] and **ironing** on weekends. I **do the dishes** [wash the dishes] every evening and **take out the garbage / trash** every other day. I guess I don't **do the vacuuming** [clean carpets with a vacuum cleaner] as often as I should.

Exercises

52.1 Combine each verb with a noun from page 104.

have ..*breakfast*..........	take ....*a nap*............	do ...*the dishes*..........
have	take	do ....
have	take	do ....
have	take	do ....

52.2 Match the verbs on the left with the words on the right.

1. brush   a. home
2. do   b. my teeth
3. stay   c. the dog
4. fall   d. early
5. get up   e. the shopping
6. feed   f. asleep

52.3 Answer these questions about yourself. If possible, compare your answers with someone else's.

1. What time did you get home yesterday / last night?
2. Did you go out last night or stay home?
3. Do you have trouble getting to sleep at night?
4. How often do you have friends over for dinner?
5. Have you ever fallen asleep in class? If so, when?
6. When was the last time you overslept?

52.4 Find three facts from page 104 that are the same in your routine and three that are different.

Same   *Different*
Example: *I go to bed around 11:30 p.m.*   *I never do any ironing.*

1. ....
2. ....
3. ....

52.5 Describe what each person is doing in the pictures below.

1.
2.
3.

4.
5.

Homes and buildings

A Houses

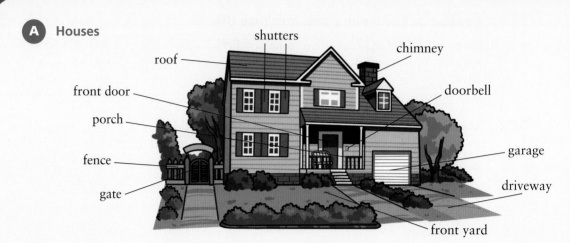

roof · shutters · chimney · front door · doorbell · porch · fence · gate · garage · driveway · front yard

B Apartments

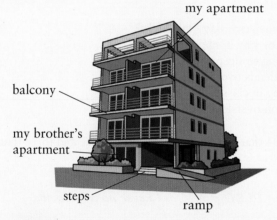

my apartment

balcony

my brother's apartment

steps · ramp

I live in an apartment building. My brother lives **on the first floor / ground floor**, and I have an apartment **on the fourth floor**. Of course, the building has an **elevator**, but I like to **climb** [go up / walk up] the three **flights of stairs** for the exercise. I have a **balcony** with a wonderful **view** of the park opposite the building.

note   **Steps** are usually outside a building or inside a public building; they are often stone or wooden. **Stairs** (plural) connect floors inside a building.

C Buying and renting

Many people **rent** a house or an apartment. [They pay money every month to the owner.] The money is called **the rent**. The person who owns the house or apartment is the **landlord / landlady**.

Other people **buy** a house or an apartment or a **condominium** (**condo**) [an apartment in a building in which the apartments are not rented]. They **own** it. It **belongs** to them. They usually borrow money from a bank to pay for the home. This money (called a **mortgage**) is usually paid back over a period of many years.

D Describing an apartment or a house

My home is very **bright** [≠ **dark**] and **sunny** because it has lots of windows. Sometimes it gets **noisy** [≠ **quiet**] because it is near the street and the traffic. Overall, it is **in good condition** [doesn't need to be repaired (≠ **in bad condition**)], and the rooms and **closets** are **huge/enormous** [very big]. The front yard is tiny [very small].

Exercises

53.1 What can you remember about the house and apartment building on page 106?
Answer these questions without looking. Then check your answers.

1. Does the house have a garage?
2. Does it have a fence around the front yard?
3. Is there any furniture on the porch?
4. Is the gate open or shut?
5. Are there any steps in front of the apartment building?
6. Do some apartments have a balcony?
7. Does the brother live on the second floor?
8. Do the apartments have a view of the mountains?

53.2 Fill each blank with a noun or verb.

1. I walked up to the ....*front door*..... and rang the ....
2. We had to .... six flights of stairs to get to her apartment because the
.... wasn't working.
3. I've got a great .... from my balcony.
4. Do you own the apartment or do you .... it?
5. I live in a house that actually .... to my brother. He bought it two years
ago. It was in bad .... then, but he has fixed it up.
6. It took years to pay off the .... , but now we own our house.

53.3 Write three positive and three negative things about a house / an apartment / a room.

Positive	*Negative*
It's bright and sunny.	It's very dark.

1. ....
2. ....
3. ....

Which positive features are the most important to you? Which negative features do you
dislike the most?

53.4 Answer these questions about your home.

1. Do you live in a house or an apartment?
2. If you live in an apartment, what floor is it on?
3. If you live in a house, do you have a front or backyard?
4. Does the house/apartment belong to you (or your family), or do you rent it?
5. Do you have your own garage or personal parking space?
6. Would you describe your house/apartment as dark or bright?
7. Is it noisy or quiet?
8. Are the rooms and closets big enough?

Around the home (1)

A Rooms

The **living room** [where you sit, relax, talk, and watch TV]; the **family room** [similar to a living room but less formal]; the **dining room** [where you eat meals]; the **kitchen**; the **bedroom(s)**; the **bathroom(s)**.

Some people also have a **home office / study** [a room with a desk where you work]; a **spare room** [a room you don't use every day, sometimes used by guests]; a **guest room**; and possibly a **playroom** for small children, sometimes located in the **basement** [a room or an area under the house, often used for storage or a play area].

B The living room / the family room

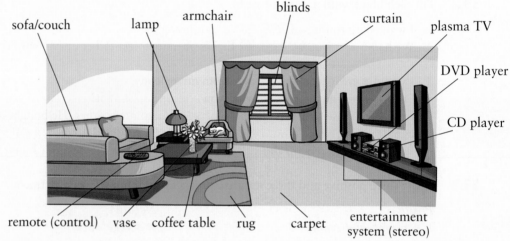

While the cat was asleep **in the armchair**, I sat **on the sofa** and **looked at/through** the newspaper. Then I **turned on** the TV and went to get a snack.

C The kitchen

I **put** the roast **in the oven**, put the dirty dishes **in the dishwasher**, **made the coffee**, and **put** the milk **back** in the refrigerator.

Exercises

54.1 Complete the descriptions.

1. The bathroom is where you take a ......*bath*............ or a ....
2. The bedroom is where you ....
3. The kitchen is where you do the ....
4. The living room is where you .... and ....
5. The dining room is where you ....
6. A spare room is often where ....
7. A study is usually where you ....
8. A basement is located ....

54.2 You are in the kitchen. Where would you put these things?

1. milk   *in the refrigerator*
2. meat that you are going to cook
3. frozen food that you want to store
4. dirty cups and plates
5. clean cups and plates
6. cookies and a package of spaghetti
7. vegetables that you want to chop or slice
8. different juices for a drink that you are going to mix

54.3 Complete these sentences with the correct adverb or preposition.

1. He put the plates ......*in*...... the cabinet.
2. I took the chicken .... of the refrigerator, made some sandwiches, and then I put the rest of the chicken .... in the refrigerator.
3. I usually sit .... the sofa, and my husband sits .... an armchair.
4. I finished looking .... the newspaper, so I turned .... the television.
5. You usually bake it .... the oven for about 40 minutes.
6. I took the butter .... of the refrigerator and put it .... the table.

54.4 Imagine you have just moved into a new home, and for the first six months you can have only six of the following. Which would you choose and why?

sofa	carpets	TV	bed	coffee table
refrigerator	dishwasher	stove	entertainment system	coffeemaker
DVD player	blinds	blender	teakettle	frying pan

54.5 On a separate sheet of paper, write one or two sentences to describe:

1. how you make breakfast for yourself;
2. what your living room or family room looks like;
3. what your kitchen looks like.

Around the home (2)

A The bedroom

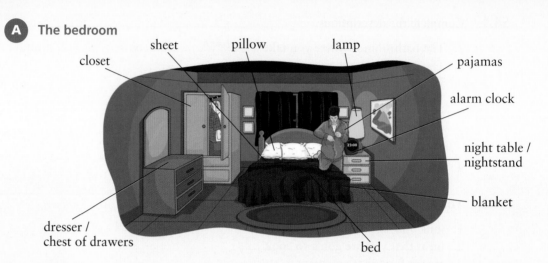

I **put on** my **pajamas, got into bed, set** the **alarm clock, turned out/off** the light, and **went to sleep.**

B The bathroom

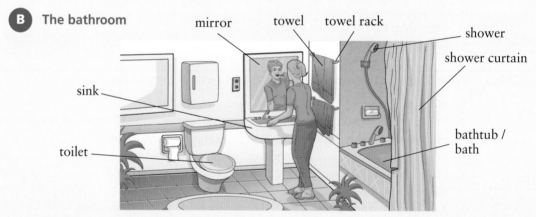

I didn't have time to **take a shower,** but **I washed my face, brushed my teeth,** and then I **went to school.**

C Housework

washing machine   iron   vacuum cleaner

My room is very **neat** and **clean** [everything in order]. I always **make my bed.** But my brother's room is very **messy** [not neat]; he is **sloppy** [not careful] and leaves his clothes all over the floor.

I **wash/do the dishes** every evening after dinner, and I usually **do the laundry** and **do the ironing / iron my clothes** on weekends when I have more free time. I also **vacuum** the carpets / **do the vacuuming** and **dust** the furniture once a week.

Exercises

55.1 Connect the two parts of each sentence. Then put the sentences in a logical order.

1. I brushed	the light.	Logical order: _5_ , ___ , ___ , ___ , ___ , ___ , ___
2. I went	into bed.	
3. I set	a shower.	
4. I turned out	my teeth.	
5. I took	to sleep.	
6. I put on	the alarm clock.	
7. I got	my pajamas.	

55.2 The pictures show six things the man did this morning. Complete the sentences below.

1.

3.

5.

2.

4.

6.

1. He _dusted the furniture._ ....
2. He ....
3. He ....
4. He ....
5. He ....
6. He ....

55.3 How often do you do the things in the pictures above? Write sentences.

1. I often ....
2. I sometimes ....
3. I occasionally ....
4. I never ....
5. I ....
6. I ....

55.4 Answer these questions about you and your home. Use a separate sheet of paper.

1. What things are near the sink in your bathroom?
2. How do you make sure you get up at the right time in the morning?
3. After you get up in the morning, how do you wash in the bathroom?
4. What is the hardest part about the housework you do?
5. What furniture do you have in your bedroom?

Everyday problems

A There's something wrong with . . .

If there is a problem with a machine or something that we use, e.g., TV, light, washing machine, computer, pen, etc., we can say:

There's something wrong with the TV. [There is a problem with it.]
The light **is not working**. [not functioning / there is no light]
The washing machine is **out of order**. [not functioning]

> **note** The phrase **out of order** is used when a public machine or piece of equipment isn't working, e.g., an office copier, a parking meter, vending machine.
> If the machine or equipment is at home, we usually say **it isn't working**.

B In the home

Yesterday morning, Paul had a lot of problems.

He **dropped** a cup,      and it **broke**.

He got another cup, made some coffee and then **spilled** it.      It **ruined** [spoiled] his shirt by making a large **stain** on it.

He decided to make some toast, but he **burned** the first piece. [If you **burn** something, you damage it with heat or fire.] Then he realized he had **run out of** bread [there was no more bread]. He left home **in a bad mood** [feeling very unhappy; *opposite*: **a good mood**].

C Out and about

After Paul went out, things got worse. He left home with a 10-dollar bill in his pocket and walked to the bus stop. Unfortunately he was a few minutes late, so he **missed the bus**. While he waited for the next one, he took out his MP3 player, but the **batteries** had **run out**. [The batteries were dead.] When the bus arrived, he got on and put his hand in his pocket – no 10-dollar bill. (He had **lost his money**.) The driver told him to get off. He didn't want to be late for school, so he started running. Moments later, he **tripped over** a bump in the sidewalk and fell down. He got to his feet and continued on to school; then he realized he had **left** his bag on the bus.

> **note** Students often mistakenly say "He forgot his bag on the bus" in this situation. In English, we use the verb **leave** if we say where something is. For example: "I **forgot** my bag," but "I **left** my bag on the bus."

Exercises

56.1 Write the past tense and past participle of these verbs.

Infinitive	Past tense	Past participle
to burn	*burned*	*burned*
to break		
to forget		
to run		
to lose		
to leave		

56.2 Connect the two parts of each sentence.

1. I dropped the radio on the floor,
2. The batteries have run out,
3. Unfortunately I left
4. I spilled the drink,
5. I missed the bus
6. I forgot

a. and it made a stain on the carpet.
b. and had to wait ages for another one.
c. to bring my money.
d. and now I can't get it to work.
e. my money at home.
f. so I can't listen to my MP3 player.

56.3 This is what happened when Julia had a party at her house. Write a description of the damage.

1.  2. 3.

56.4 Write a response to each question using vocabulary from page 112.

1. How did you break that glass? *I dropped it.*
2. Why can't we watch TV? ....
3. What happened to the money I gave you? ....
4. Where's your homework? ....
5. Why can't you use the fax machine at the office? ....

56.5 How often do you do these things? Use *all the time / fairly often / sometimes / hardly ever / never.*

Example: *I drop things all the time.*

drop things?	break things?	burn things?
spill things?	lose things?	forget things?
trip over things?	leave things behind?	run out of things?

What kinds of things do you drop, burn, run out of, etc.?

Money

A Bills and coins

Here are some examples of money used in the United States. The **currency** [the type of money used in a country] is called **the dollar**.

Bills	Coins			
10 **dollars** a 10-dollar bill	25 **cents** a **quarter**	10 cents a **dime**	5 cents a **nickel**	1 cent a **penny**

B Common verbs

spend (an amount) on . . .	Last week I **spent** $100 **on** food and $20 **on** books.
pay for . . .	I **paid** $200 **for** my new desk. [It cost me $200.]
cost	My new desk **cost** (me) $200. [I paid $200.]
charge	The mechanic **charged** $75 to repair my car. [asked me to pay $75 for the service]
lend/borrow	Could you **lend me** some money? [give me money that I will return] *or* Could **I borrow** some money? [receive money that I will return]
waste	Parents often think their children **waste** money on things they don't need. [use the money badly]
save (up)	I'm **saving (up)** for a new bike. [keeping my money when I receive it]

C Adjectives

free   cheap   inexpensive   reasonable   pretty expensive   very expensive

– $ $ $ $ $

> **note** Sometimes **cheap** is used to indicate "of low quality." **Inexpensive** does not have this possible meaning.

D Words and phrases about money

I **can't afford** to take a vacation this year. [I don't have enough money.]
A: How much is that watch **worth**? [What is the **value**?]
B: It is **worth** about $50.
The **cost of living** [how much people pay for things] is high in Japan, but most people still have a good **standard of living** [the level of money and comfort people have].
His house **cost a fortune** [was very expensive], but he can afford it because he's **well-off** [rich/wealthy].

Exercises

57.1 Complete the sentences with the past tense of verbs from the box. Some verbs are irregular.

spend	be worth	pay	cost
charge	save up	borrow	waste

1. It took me a whole year, but I finally .... enough money to buy a new car.
2. I was upset when I lost my watch at the gym. It was a present from my wife, and it .... her a lot of money.
3. I .... more than $2,000 for my computer two years ago. It .... a lot more than that now.
4. I .... $50 from my dad last week, and I .... most of it on a concert ticket.
5. The Copy Center made photocopies for me. They .... 10 cents a page.
6. I .... a lot of money on a new video-game system. It isn't any better than my old one.

57.2 Complete the sentences with words from page 114.

1. You want to tell a friend that a restaurant wasn't cheap.
   The restaurant ...*was pretty expensive.*..
2. You want to know the value of your friend's laptop computer.
   How much is .... ?
3. A friend wants to go to an expensive restaurant, but you don't have enough money.
   I'm sorry, but I can't ....
4. You want to borrow $10 from a friend.
   Could you please .... ?
5. You want to know how much a friend paid for her dictionary.
   How much .... ?

57.3 Answer these questions as quickly as you can with *yes* or *no*. Write down answers to all of them in one minute. Then go back and check.

1. Is a nickel worth 10 cents?
2. Is a quarter worth more than 50 cents?
3. If you lend something to someone, do they borrow it?
4. If you waste money, do you use it well?
5. Is the dollar a currency?
6. If you can't afford something, are you well-off?
7. Does cost of living mean the same as "standard of living"?
8. If someone tells you a hotel is reasonable, is it very expensive?

57.4 Write down the approximate price of six things you buy often, e.g., a daily newspaper, a short bus ride, a cup of coffee. Do you think each item is expensive, reasonably priced, or cheap? If possible, compare your answers with someone else's.

Health: illness and disease

A Common problems

She's **sneezing.**

She's **coughing.**

She **has a sore throat.**

She's **blowing her nose.**

She has a **temperature/fever.**

What's the matter?	How do you know? (the symptoms)	Cause of illness
I have a cold.	sneezing, a runny nose, a sore throat, a cough	a **virus**
I have **the flu.** [more serious than a cold]	symptoms for a cold + aching muscles and a temperature/fever	a virus
I have **allergies.** / I have **hay fever.**	sneezing, a runny nose, itchy eyes	allergic reaction to pollen from grass, trees, plants
I have **diarrhea.**	I have a stomachache and keep going to the bathroom.	often food, or a virus
I feel nauseous.	afraid I may **vomit / throw up**	food, a virus

note For some of these **illnesses,** you can see a doctor, who may give you a **prescription** [a paper with an order for medicine] that you take to a **pharmacy / drugstore.** Sometimes, you can buy an **over-the-counter medication.** [medicine that doesn't require a prescription]

B Aches and pains

Nouns: We use -ache with the following: I have a **toothache, a stomachache, a backache, an earache,** and a **headache.** For other parts of the body, we use **pain,** e.g., "I woke up during the night with a terrible **pain** in my chest."

Verbs: The verb **ache** is used in some situations, e.g., "My back **aches.**" The verb **hurt** is more common. It can be used [meaning "**injure**"] with a direct object:
She **hurt/injured** her foot when she jumped off the bus and fell down. *or*
She **hurt herself** when she jumped off the bus and fell down.
I hit my leg against the table, and now it really **hurts.** [gives me a terrible pain]

Adjectives: **Painful** [≠ **painless**] is a common adjective.
I got **a shot / an injection** yesterday and it was very **painful.**
A: Did it hurt when the **dentist** filled the **cavity** [small hole] in your tooth?
B: No, it was **painless.**

C Serious illnesses

Doctors believe smoking is a major cause of **lung cancer.**
He had a **heart attack** and died almost immediately.
Asthma is an illness in the lungs causing **breathing** problems.
Many people **suffer from** [have] it.

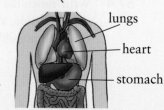
lungs
heart
stomach

Exercises

58.1 Cover page 116. What are the main symptoms of these conditions?

1. a cold: ...*sneezing, a runny nose, a sore throat, a cough*...........
2. the flu: ....
3. allergies / hay fever: ....
4. diarrhea: ....
5. asthma: ....

58.2 Look at the underlined letters in these pairs of words. Is the pronunciation the same or different?

1. ache   pain   *same* /eɪ/
2. shot   stomach   *different* /ɑ/, /ʌ/
3. disease   diarrhea
4. cough   fever

5. hurt   allergic
6. virus   illness
7. flu   pharmacy
8. cough   enough

58.3 Look at the pictures and write what happened. In your description, use the words in the box.

cavity	dentist	filling	injection	painful	painless

58.4 Complete the sentences with an appropriate word.

1. I hit my hand on the desk, and now it really ....*hurts.*........
2. They say she died of a heart ....
3. She had some apples that weren't ready to eat, and now she has a ....
4. I've got this terrible .... in my neck from sleeping in the wrong position.
5. He died of .... cancer, even though he never smoked a cigarette in his life.
6. I went to the doctor, and she gave me a .... for some medication.
7. Pollution makes his .... worse, and it's difficult for him to breathe.
8. I hurt .... when I fell off that chair.

58.5 Look at page 116 again. Have you had any of these illnesses recently? Have you had any aches or pains recently? Are there any other illnesses you have had or still have? If so, find the name for it/them in English. Write them below.

....
....
....
....

Health: injuries

A Common injuries

An **injury** is damage to part of your body, usually caused by an accident at home, in a car, or playing sports. Here are some common injuries:

1.  3.  5.

2.  4.  6.

What's the problem?	How did it happen?	Result	Treatment
1. **I cut** my finger.	using a knife	It's **bleeding**.	a Band-Aid®
2. I have a **concussion**.	playing soccer	I'm confused; I don't	rest
3. **I twisted my ankle**.	running for a bus	I can't walk on it.	rest + **bandage**
4. **I burned** my hand.	taking something out of a hot oven	It's very **painful**.	special cream
5. **I broke** my arm.	falling off my bike	I can't use it.	a **cast** and **sling**
6. I have a **bruise** on my arm.	hitting it on the side of my desk	It's **swollen** and **black-and-blue**.	ice pack

B Hospital treatment

Jane fell off a chair, hit her head on the floor, and **knocked herself out**. Her husband **called 911**. An **ambulance** came, and she was still **unconscious** when it arrived. She was **rushed** [taken very quickly] to the **emergency room** (**ER**). They kept her at the **hospital** for two days **for observation** [the hospital staff watched her to decide if anything was wrong].

I jumped for the ball and **collided** with another player. [We ran into / hit each other.] We both had **cuts** on our heads. I had to go to the hospital for eight **stitches**.

C Wounds and injuries

Wound (n., v.) and **injury** (n.) are both used to describe harm to the body. A **wound** is generally caused by a **weapon** (e.g., gun or knife) and is often intentional. (Note the pronunciation of **wound** /wuːnd/.)

The guard **shot** the man in the chest. [The man got a **bullet wound**, from a gun, in the chest.]
The attackers **stabbed** the police officer in the back. [He got a **knife wound** in the back.]
He **got into a fight** and **got beaten up**. He had a **black eye** and two **broken ribs**.

Exercises

59.1 Complete the table. Write the verb that belongs to the same word family as the noun. Use a dictionary if necessary.

Noun	Verb
cut	*cut*
bandage	
blood	
bruise	

Noun	Verb
injury	
shot	
treatment	
wound	

59.2 Match the injuries and the causes.

1. He burned his finger.
2. He twisted his ankle.
3. He cut his foot.
4. He has a bullet wound in his arm.
5. He has a concussion.

a. He fell down and hit his head.
b. He was shot during a robbery.
c. He touched a hot burner on the stove.
d. He walked barefoot on some glass.
e. He missed a step walking downstairs.

59.3 Look at the pictures and write the story.

59.4 Answer these questions about yourself. If possible, ask another person the same questions.

1. Have you ever broken your arm or leg?
2. Have you ever needed stitches?
3. Have you ever had a concussion?
4. Have you ever been unconscious?
5. Have you ever been in an ambulance?
6. Have you ever been in the hospital?

A Pockets, buttons, gloves, sleeves

earring
necklace
blouse / top
jacket
belt
skirt
purse / pocketbook
pantyhose / stockings
shoe
hat
scarf
button
glove
overcoat

V-neck
sleeve
pullover / sweater
pocket
jeans
cuff
boot
collar
shirt
necktie/tie
suit
pants

> **note** Some of these words are plural nouns, e.g., **jeans** and **pants**. (See Unit 32.)

B Verbs and phrases used with clothes

I got up at 7:30, took a shower, **got dressed**, and had breakfast. It was a cold morning, so I **put on** my coat and left home about 8:20. When I got to work, I **took off** my coat and **hung** it **up** behind the door. It was hot in the office, so I **took** my jacket **off**, too. During my lunch break I went shopping. I saw a nice **jacket** in a clothing store and **tried** it **on**, but it didn't **fit** me – it was **too small** and they didn't have a **larger size**. I usually **wear** an **extra large (XL)**.

> **note** Notice the different word order with the verbs **put on, take off, hang up,** and **try on**. See Unit 23 if you want to know the rule about this.

C *Too* + adjective and *(not)* + adjective + *enough*

The man is wearing a suit, but it doesn't **fit** him very well.
It's not the **right size**. The jacket is **too small** [**not big enough**], and the pants are **too short** [**not long enough**].

Exercises

60.1 Finish this sentence with different items of clothes.

I need a pair of ...*shoes.*..

....

....

....

....

....

60.2 Number the sentences in time order.

.... a. He took off his pants.
.... b. He put his shoes back on.
.... c. He tried on the suit.
....*1*.... d. He went into the fitting room.
.... e. He took it off.

.... f. He paid for the suit.
.... g. He took off his shoes.
.... h. He went back to the salesperson.
.... i. He put his pants on again.

60.3 What's different? Find five things that the woman has in the first picture but not in the second picture.

1. ...*a button*............................
2. ....
3. ....
4. ....
5. ....

60.4 Fill in the blanks. More than one answer may be possible.

1. She decided to wear a ....*skirt*......... and a .... instead of a dress.
2. I tried on a .... ; the jacket was fine, but the .... were too short.
3. It was hot in the office, so he took off his jacket and .... Then he rolled up the sleeves of his ....
4. I wanted to buy the jacket, but unfortunately the one I tried on wasn't big .... , and they didn't have it in a larger ....
5. I also wanted a new sweater. They had one in large, but that was .... big. They also had a small, but that wasn't big ....

60.5 Write down . . .

1. five things usually worn by women only.
2. five things worn by men and women.
3. a list of clothes you like and don't like wearing.

Shopping

A Stores and shopping

store: a place where you can buy things; a **shop** is usually a small store
salesperson: a person who helps customers in a store
store window: the window at the front of the store/shop
window shopping: looking at things in store windows without buying anything
shopping list: a list of things you plan to buy
shopping center: a group of stores built together and sharing a parking area
(shopping) mall: stores, restaurants, and movie theaters in a large, covered area
go shopping: go to a store or stores to buy food, clothes, etc.
do the shopping: buy food or other things you need
grocery shopping: buying food only, usually at a supermarket

B Types of stores and what they sell

Type of store	What it sells
department store	furniture, clothes, appliances (e.g., washing machines), electronics (e.g., TVs, music players, cell phones) toys, jewelry [Most do not sell food.]
supermarket	a large store for food and household goods (e.g., cleaning products)
office-supply store	paper, pens, pencils, staplers, paper clips, files, folders, tape, stationery (e.g., writing paper, cards, envelopes)
newsstand	(often outdoors) newspapers and magazines, candy, lottery tickets
butcher shop	meat and poultry (e.g., chicken, turkey) [Note: Supermarkets have meat departments too.]
grocery store	fruit and vegetables; other food items [smaller than a supermarket]
pharmacy / drugstore	medicine [both prescription and nonprescription], baby products, shampoo, soap, toothpaste, etc.

note Many stores are called by the name of the main product sold + store (camera store, shoe store, etc.).

C Useful words and expressions

SALESPERSON: Can I help you? or May I help you?
CUSTOMER: I'm **looking for** a skirt. or No, **I'm just looking**, thanks. [I don't need any help.] or I'm **already being helped**, thanks. [Another salesperson is already helping me.]

CUSTOMER: Where's the **fitting room**? [the room where you try on clothes] I want to see if this size (e.g., medium, large, 12) fits me.
SALESPERSON: It's over there on the right.

CUSTOMER: Excuse me. Where do I pay for this/these?
SALESPERSON: At the **cashier / checkout counter**.
CUSTOMER: And can I **pay by** check / credit card?
SALESPERSON: Yes, of course.

Cashier

Exercises

61.1 What "general" words on page 122 describe the groups of items below?

1. ...._fruit_........... apples, oranges, peaches
2. .... shoes, a blouse, a jacket
3. .... a sofa, an armchair, a table
4. .... a washing machine, a refrigerator, a stove
5. .... detergent, soap, toilet paper
6. .... stuffed animals, dolls, electric train set
7. .... writing paper, envelopes, cards
8. .... a DVD player, a cell phone, a TV

61.2 Where would you buy each of the items below? Choose from the stores in the box.

| butcher shop | department store | grocery store | pharmacy | office-supply store |

Can you think of two more things you could buy in each store?

61.3 What word or phrase is being defined?

1. a person who works in a store _salesperson or salesclerk_
2. the place where you can try on clothes in a store
3. the place where you pay for things in a store
4. a large indoor area where you can shop, eat, and go to a movie
5. looking in store windows without going inside to buy
6. the place where you buy newspapers, lottery tickets, and candy

61.4 Complete these conversations about shopping.

1. SALESPERSON: Can I help you?
   CUSTOMER: Yes, I'm (1) .... a sweater like this, but in blue.
   SALESPERSON: And what (2) .... are you looking for?
   CUSTOMER: Extra large.
   SALESPERSON: Here's an extra large one in blue.
   CUSTOMER: Great! I'll buy it. Can I (3) .... check?
   SALESPERSON: Yes, of course.

2. SALESPERSON: Can I help you?
   CUSTOMER: No, it's OK, I'm just (4) ...., thanks.

Food

A **Fruit**

orange

pineapple

grapes

apple

pear

banana

lemon   raspberry   plum   strawberry

peach   cherries   melon

B **Vegetables**

potato   green beans   peas   carrot   cauliflower   pepper

cabbage   eggplant   mushrooms   zucchini   broccoli   garlic

I **peeled** the potatoes and **sliced** the zucchini [cut them into thin pieces]. I **chopped (up)** the carrots.

C **Salad**

A green **salad** is a mixture of uncooked vegetables. The main ingredient in a salad is usually **lettuce**. It may also contain **tomatoes, cucumbers, onions,** and other things.

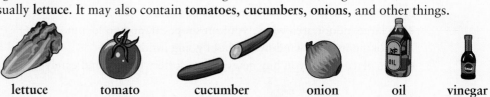

lettuce   tomato   cucumber   onion   oil   vinegar

We often put **salad dressing** [a mixture of **oil** and **vinegar** or lemon juice] on the salad.

D **Meat (from land animals), fish, and shellfish**

Animal:	cow	calf [a young cow]	lamb [a young sheep]	pig	chicken
Meat:	beef	veal	lamb		pork	chicken

> | note | A person who does not eat meat is a **vegetarian**. |

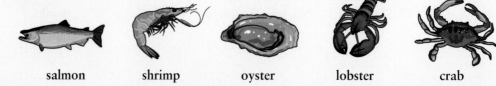

salmon   shrimp   oyster   lobster   crab

Exercises

62.1 Write the name of a vegetable and a fruit . . .

	Vegetable	Fruit
1. beginning with the letter **p**:	....	....
2. beginning with the letter **b**:	....	....
3. beginning with the letter **g**:	....	....
4. beginning with the letter **c**:	....	....
5. beginning with the letter **l**:	....	....

62.2 Match words in the two boxes where the underlined letters are pronounced the same.

Example: *b<u>a</u>nana - watermel<u>o</u>n* /ə/

b<u>a</u>nana	<u>o</u>nion	l<u>e</u>mon	l<u>a</u>mb
p<u>ea</u>ch	s<u>a</u>lmon	<u>oi</u>l	m<u>u</u>shroom
p<u>e</u>pper	<u>oy</u>sters	zucch<u>i</u>ni	watermel<u>o</u>n

62.3 Which is the odd one out in each group, and why?

1. pork   veal   salmon   beef
   Salmon is the only fish; the others are types of meat.
2. chicken   shrimp   oyster   lobster
3. lettuce   eggplant   tomato   cucumber
4. peach   onion   mushroom   zucchini
5. pork   lamb   oyster   beef

62.4 Do you eat the skin [the outside] of these fruits always, sometimes, or never? Make three lists.

apples	pineapples	cherries	grapes
pears	bananas	peaches	mangoes
oranges	lemons	watermelons	strawberries

62.5 Use words from page 124 to complete these sentences about yourself and your country. If possible, compare your answers with someone else's.

1. In my country, ... is/are more common than ....
2. In my country, ... is/are more expensive than ....
3. In my country, a green salad usually contains ....
4. We don't often eat ....
5. When I prepare .... for dinner, I .... them/it.
6. Personally, I prefer .... to ....
7. I love .... , but I don't really like ....
8. My favorite meat (or fish or vegetable or fruit) is ....

Cooking and restaurants

A Ways of cooking food

boil: in water, e.g., potatoes
fry: in oil or butter above the heat, e.g., eggs
broil: under high heat, one side at a time, e.g., chicken
grill: on a metal frame, over the heat, e.g., steak
bake: in the oven without fat or liquid, e.g., cakes, potatoes
roast: in the oven, usually with fat or oil [especially meat], e.g., meat, chicken
microwave: cook in a microwave oven

microwave (oven)

boil

roast / bake

fry

broil

note   Food that is not cooked is **raw**.

B Cooking meat

rare [cooked very quickly and still red on the inside]	**medium** [cooked a bit more and pink in the middle]
medium-rare [cooked a bit longer and a little red in the middle]	**well-done** [cooked even longer and not pink at all]

C Describing food

How does food **taste**?

tasty: has lots of flavor [a positive word]; **tasteless:** has no taste [a negative word]
bland: without a strong taste, neutral in flavor [sometimes negative], e.g., boiled rice
sweet: lots of sugar; **bitter** (e.g., strong black coffee); **sour** (e.g., lemons)
salty: lots of salt; **hot/spicy:** lots of spice (e.g., curry, salsa)

Other food adjectives:

fresh: recently produced or picked, e.g., fresh bread, fresh fruit
tender: easy to cut; a positive word used to describe meat [≠ **tough**]
fatty: has a lot of fat, especially meat [≠ **lean**]
fattening: food that makes you **put on weight** (e.g., cake) [≠ **low-calorie, low-fat**]

D Eating in restaurants

Courses: an **appetizer** (e.g., soup), a **main course / entrée** (e.g., chicken), and a **dessert** (e.g., ice cream). You **pay the check** [money for the meal]. You might also **leave a tip** [extra money] for the server. If the restaurant is popular, you should **make a reservation** [call to reserve a table] **in advance** [before you go].

E A menu

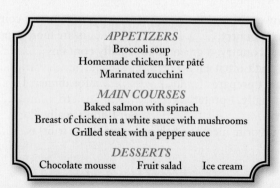

APPETIZERS
Broccoli soup
Homemade chicken liver pâté
Marinated zucchini

MAIN COURSES
Baked salmon with spinach
Breast of chicken in a white sauce with mushrooms
Grilled steak with a pepper sauce

DESSERTS
Chocolate mousse   Fruit salad   Ice cream

Exercises

63.1 Do you often eat the following foods in your native country? If so, do you eat them in the same way?

Example: *People in my country eat fish, but not usually raw fish.*

raw fish	fried rice
fried eggs	fried chicken
baked potatoes	roast beef
raw spinach	roasted peppers
fried bread	boiled eggs
grilled cheese	baked bananas

63.2 Choose a possible adjective from page 126 to describe each of these foods.

	Adjective		*Adjective*
lemon	..sour....................	ice cream	....
chicken	....	steak	....
honey	....	chili peppers	....
bacon	....	avocado	....

63.3 Answer these questions about the menu on page 126.

1. Which appetizer doesn't contain vegetables? *homemade chicken liver pâté*
2. What is another name for the main course?
3. Which dish may be rare or well-done?
4. Which dish is definitely cooked in the oven?
5. Which dish will probably be spicy?
6. Which main dishes do not contain beef?
7. Which meat may be fatty or tough if you are unlucky?
8. Which dessert(s) will be very sweet?
9. Which dessert should be very fresh?
10. Imagine you are trying to lose weight and you want to have a low-fat meal. Which would probably be the best dish to choose for each course?

63.4 Answer these questions about restaurants in your native country and about your own taste in food. If possible, ask another person the same questions.

1. Do you usually make a reservation at a restaurant?
2. Is it common to give the server a tip? If so, how much?
3. Do servers normally leave fresh bread on the table?
4. How many courses are common in a restaurant?
5. What is your favorite food in a restaurant?
6. Do you like steak? If so, how do you like it cooked?
7. Do you like very spicy food? If so, what kind?
8. Which of your favorite foods is most fattening? How often do you eat it?

A Cities

Here are some of the things you will find in or near most cities.

business district / downtown: an area with lots of banks, stores, and offices

shopping center: a place with many stores, either indoors or outdoors

(shopping) mall: a group of stores, restaurants, and movie theaters in a large, covered area

parking lot / parking garage: a place to leave cars

factory: a building or group of buildings where people make/manufacture things, e.g., cars

public library: a place where you can borrow books

resident: someone who lives in a certain place

neighborhood: a part of a city where people live [not an area mostly for shopping or business]

night life: places to go at night for entertainment, e.g., theaters, dance clubs, bars.

B Transportation and traffic

In many cities, **traffic** [the amount of cars, trucks, etc., moving on the roads] is a problem. The roads can get **congested** [too full of cars], especially during the morning and evening **rush hours** [roughly, 7 to 9 a.m. and 4 to 6 p.m.]. Traffic moves slowly, and people are always **in a hurry** [want to get somewhere else quickly]. Also, it may be hard to find a place to **park**. In some cities, **public transportation** systems are a good way to **commute** [travel to and from work]. A metro area includes a big city and its **suburbs** [area outside the town where people live]. There is usually a **railroad** (train) **system** and a **bus system**. Some **urban** [city] areas also have **subways** [train systems that are entirely or partly underground].

C Advantages and disadvantages

The best things about living in a city are that:

There's **plenty to do.** [a lot of activities you could be part of]
The **nightlife** is good.
You can find a **wide range** of shops. [many different types of places to shop]
There are lots of **cultural activities.** [plays, concerts, art shows, etc.]
The population is really **diverse.** [from many different backgrounds]
There are a lot of **job opportunities.** [chances / possible places to get a job]

The worst things about living in a city are that:

It's very **crowded.** [full of people]
People can be **aggressive** [trying too hard to get what they want] and **rude.** [not polite]
It can be **noisy** [not quiet] and **dangerous.** [not safe]
Some cities have high **crime rates.** [a lot of stealing, etc.]
The air can be very **polluted.** [full of smoke, dirt, etc.]
The **cost of living** can be higher than in smaller towns. [what you pay for housing, food, etc.]

Exercises

64.1 Draw lines to make common compound words/phrases.

1. rush
2. public
3. night
4. cost
5. crime
6. shopping
7. job
8. bus

a. system
b. opportunity
c. rate
d. hour
e. mall
f. transportation
g. of living
h. life

64.2 Complete each sentence to replace the underlined phrase.

1. I've met all the <u>people who live in</u> the building.
   I've met all the ..... *residents of* ..... the building.
2. I usually <u>travel to and from work</u> by bus.
   I usually .... by bus.
3. She lives in a <u>metro area outside the city</u> called Elmdale.
   She lives in a .... called Elmdale.
4. The mall has <u>many different kinds</u> of shops.
   The mall has .... of shops.
5. The houses in my <u>section of the city</u> are small.
   The houses in my .... are small.
6. The residents of the city <u>are from many different backgrounds</u>.
   The residents of the city are ....

64.3 Think of your trip to work or school. Put a check mark ☑ next to each of the following that you see or pass.

☐ a parking lot   ☐ a factory   ☐ a library
☐ congested roads   ☐ trains   ☐ a business district
☐ rude people   ☐ polluted air   ☐ a suburb

64.4 Do you live in a big metro area / city? If so, answer questions 1a and 1b. If not, answer 2a and 2b.

1a. What are the things you like best about living in a big metro area / city?
   ....

1b. What are the things you don't like about living in a big metro area / city?
   ....

2a. What are the best things about not living in a big metro area / city?
   ....

2b. What are the worst things about not living in a big metro area / city?
   ....

A Surrounded by nature

I **grew up** [spent my childhood] in a **rural** area [an area in the country]. Most of the **surrounding** area [area all around] was farmland. We used to see **deer** and other **wildlife** in the **fields**. There were some **woods** [an area of trees, a small forest] near our house. A **river flowed** out of the **hills**, through a **valley**, and into a **lake**.

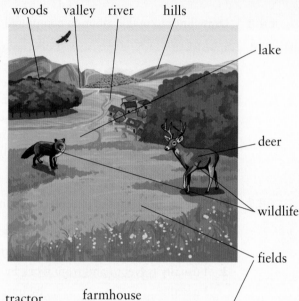

woods valley river hills

lake

deer

wildlife

fields

B Farms and fields

We lived in a **farmhouse** on a small **farm**. Next to our house we had a **barn** with a **silo** [a place to keep food for farm animals]. We **kept cows** in the barn and we **milked** them every day. We **grew crops** [e.g., corn, carrots, potatoes], and we had a little apple **orchard** [area for fruit trees]. Every **spring**, my father **tilled** the **soil** [prepared the earth for planting] with a **tractor** and **planted seeds** [things that plants grow from]. In the fall, we used a machine to **harvest** [collect] the crops, and we picked our apples by hand.

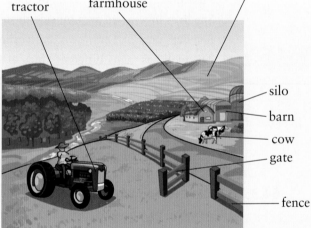

tractor farmhouse

silo

barn

cow

gate

fence

C Advantages and disadvantages

The best things about living in the country are that:

You get **peace and quiet**. [a place that is quiet and calm]
You learn to **appreciate** nature. [understand the good things about nature]
You are **in touch with** the **seasons**. [able to see changes that happen during the four seasons: spring, summer, fall, and winter]
The **pace of life** is slower than in the city. [the number and speed of things that happen to you and around you]

The worst things about living in the country are that:

There is not much **nightlife**.
Shopping centers are **far away**.
You don't **meet** new people very often.
You have to travel **large distances**. [go very far to get from one place to another]

Exercises

65.1 Draw lines to match each verb on the left with a word/phrase on the right. Match each verb only once.

1. live in	a. a valley
2. pick	b. apples
3. flow through	c. the soil
4. milk	d. crops
5. harvest	e. large distances
6. plant	f. a farmhouse
7. till	g. seeds
8. travel	h. cows

65.2 Circle the best word/phrase to complete each sentence.

1. People in the country live in a (rural / surrounding) area.
2. We (grow / grow up) corn in fields on our farm.
3. We keep (deer / cows) in the barn.
4. A (hill / river) can flow.
5. We keep harvested crops in our (silos / tractors).
6. (Woods / Wildlife) and orchards both contain trees.
7. Spring is the season to (harvest crops / plant seeds).
8. Using a tractor to harvest crops is faster than (picking / tilling) them by hand.

65.3 Fill each blank with a suitable word from page 130.

One good (1) ....*thing*........ about living in the country is that you can
(2) .... nature and the seasons. You also learn how to do important work, like
(3) .... seeds in the spring. You learn how to take care of
(4) .... while they grow. And finally, you learn to (5) .... crops
in the fall. Some people who like to live in cities think differently. They think there is too
much peace and (6) .... in the country. It's hard to (7) .... very
many new people, because not very many people live there. There are not many theaters or
restaurants, so there is not much (8) ....

65.4 Answer each question about a country or community you know well.

1. Do most of the people live in rural areas? Explain.
2. What are the main crops grown on farms?
3. Are people in the country more in touch with nature? Explain.
4. Do a lot of country people move to the cities? If so, why?

On the road

A Road features

traffic light /
traffic signal

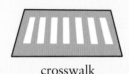

intersection

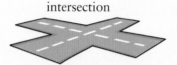

crosswalk

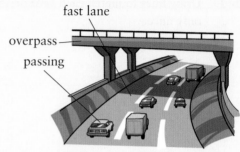

highway/freeway/expressway
[a wide road where cars travel at high speed]

road signs

left only   pedestrians   construction

B An accident

There was a serious car **accident** this morning. A **truck broke down**
in the middle of the road, and the driver couldn't move it. It was
8:00, the height of the **rush hour**, so it quickly caused a major
traffic jam. Drivers got very angry, and one driver tried to go around
the truck. Unfortunately another car was coming **in the opposite
direction**. The driver **braked** hard and tried to stop but couldn't
prevent the accident – the cars **crashed into** each other. Both drivers
were **badly injured**, and both cars were very **badly damaged**.

> *note* People are **injured**; things are **damaged**.

C Giving directions

Go straight, turn right onto the main road,
then **take the first left**. **Keep going**, and
you'll see a bank **on your left**. When you
get to the bank, **turn left** again.

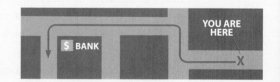

D Important words and phrases

Taxis and cars use the road; **pedestrians** [people who walk] use the **sidewalk**.
I was **doing** [traveling at] the **speed limit**, which on this road is
  55 miles per hour (mph). [55 mph = 88 kilometers per hour]
This **gas station** has both **self-service** and **full-service**.
Get in the car and remember to **fasten/buckle** your
  seat belt.
If you **slam on the brakes** [suddenly brake hard]
  on a wet, **slippery** road, your car might **skid**.

A car skidding

Exercises

66.1 Complete the directions to the bank, using the map.

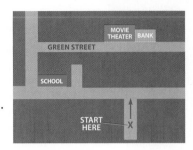

Go ... *straight* .... and .... at the intersection.
Then you keep .... and .... right
when you .... to the .... Then
.... again at .... Street, and
the bank is .... left, just after the ....

66.2 Fill in the blanks.

1. Don't forget to ... *fasten/buckle* .. your .... *seat* .... belt when you get in the car.
2. There was a bad accident last night. One driver was killed, the other driver was badly .... , and both cars were badly ....
3. In the morning, ... starts at about 7:00 and goes on until at least 9:00. Then it starts again about 4:00 in the afternoon.
4. It was raining, so when I .... , the car didn't stop quickly enough, and I .... into the rear of the car ahead.
5. The bicycle hit me just as I stepped into the .... to cross the street.
6. The car .... on the highway, so I called a garage and they sent someone to repair it.
7. There was a terrible .... on the highway. There were just too many cars going in the same direction.
8. I was doing about 55 mph on the freeway, and suddenly a car .... me in the fast .... , doing about 90 mph.

66.3 What do these road signs mean?

1. You can't .... 3. traffic .... ahead 5. .... ahead

2. .... road 4. 55 mph is the .... limit 6. ....

(See also Unit 98.)

66.4 Describe the following:

1. Directions from the place where you live to the nearest post office
2. Traffic conditions in the nearest city
3. Your most frightening experience in a car

Transportation

A Vehicles

Vehicle is the general word for all types of road transportation.

SUV [Sport Utility Vehicle]

A: How did you get here?
B: I took the **bus**.
A: And the others?
B: Sue and John came **by car**.
A: And Paul?
B: He missed the bus, so he had to take a **taxi**.

bicycle/bike

bus

motorcycle/motorbike

truck

B Catch a bus, take a taxi

Bus	Train	Plane	Taxi / Cab	Bicycle	Car
driver	engineer	pilot	taxidriver	cyclist/rider	driver
drives	drives	flies	drives	rides	drives
fare ($)	fare ($)	airfare ($)	fare ($)	–	–
catch/take	catch/take	catch/take	catch/take	–	go by
get on/off	get on/off	get on/off	get in / out of	get on/off	get in / out of
bus station	train station	airport	taxi stand	–	–
bus stop	platform	gate	–	–	–

C Buses

Sometimes buses are not **on time** [they don't arrive when they should]. The bus I usually take should run [come] every 10 minutes, but sometimes I **wait** at the **bus stop** [a place where buses stop for people] for half an hour or more. When the bus finally comes, it is almost **full** [does not have much room] so not many passengers can get on. Other times the bus is early and I **miss** it [I don't catch it; *not* I lost the bus].

D Announcements at a train station

The 7:30 train **to** Washington, D.C., is now **boarding** [passengers are getting on] on **track** number 10. This is the **final call** [last announcement] for the 7:30 train **departing** [leaving] for Washington, D.C., making stops at Newark, Philadelphia, Wilmington, and Baltimore. Now arriving, the 7:25 train from Toronto, on track number 4. The 7:45 train from Chicago is **running** [operating or going] 10 minutes late **due to** [because of] operating difficulties. We apologize for the **delay** [late arrival].

Exercises

67.1 Circle the best word in each sentence.

1. It's not a good idea to (ride)/ drive a bicycle without a helmet.
2. She told him to get in / get on the car and fasten his seat belt.
3. Buses to the airport ride / run every half hour.
4. The pilot couldn't drive / fly the plane in such bad weather.
5. We were late, so we had to take / drive a taxi.
6. I left my house a little late and I lost / missed the bus.

67.2 Write two different words or phrases that combine with each item below.

1. ..*the bus*..   3. ....   5. ....
   miss ....   get in ....   get on ....

2. ....   4. ....   6. ....
.... station   .... driver   .... fare

67.3 Identify these vehicles without looking at page 134.

1. ....   2. ....   3. ....   4. ....   5. ....

67.4 Complete the sentences.

1. I waited at the ......*bus stop*..... for 10 minutes, and then two buses arrived.
2. Our train leaves from .... number 7.
3. I couldn't get on the first bus because it was ....
4. The train was half an hour late. The announcer said the .... was due .... bad weather.
5. The bus to my house is often not .... I wait and wait, but it doesn't come.
6. When I got to the bus stop, there were other .... waiting there.
7. I came here .... car, but John .... a taxi.
8. The train .... for Chicago makes a few .... before arriving in Chicago.

67.5 Are these statements *true* or *false* in your experience? Why?

1. Trains are more reliable than buses.
2. The easiest way to travel is by car.
3. Traveling by plane is unpleasant and uncomfortable.
4. You get to the place you are going faster by taxi than by bus.

Unit 68 Work: responsibilities, conditions, and pay

A What do you do?

People may ask you about your job. They can ask and you can respond in different ways.

What do you do? / What's your job?	I'm a banker / an engineer / a teacher. (be + a(n) + name of job)
What kind of work do you do?	I work in marketing / a bank. (work in + place or general area)
What do you do for a living?	I work for IBM/Toyota. (work for + name of company)

note — Work [n., when it means employment] is usually uncountable. You cannot say "I have a work." However, you can say "a job," e.g., "She doesn't have a job."

B What does that involve?

Question: "What does your job involve?" [What do you do in your job?]
You can answer by describing your responsibilities [what you have to do] or your daily routine [what you do every day/week].

Main responsibilities	*Daily routines*
• I'm in charge of all the shipments out of the factory. [responsible for] • I have to deal with any complaints. [take all necessary action if there are complaints] • I run the restaurant in the museum. [I manage it.]	• I have to go to / attend (*formal*) a lot of meetings. • I meet with / visit / see clients. [people I do business with, who pay for my service] • It involves doing a lot of paperwork. [routine work that involves paper, e.g., writing letters, filling in forms] (*Note* the -ing form after involve.)

C Pay

Most workers are paid regularly, e.g., every week or month. [They receive money.] This pay is called a salary. They earn or make an amount of money, e.g., "I earn/make $60,000 a year." [My salary is $60,000 a year.] Some people are paid for the hours they work. They earn an hourly wage, an amount of money per hour, e.g., "In my state, the minimum wage [lowest pay the law allows] is $8 per hour." The total amount of money you receive from your job(s) is called your income. You usually have to pay part of your income to the government. The amount you pay is called income tax.

D Working hours

For many people in the United States and Canada, working hours are 9:00 a.m. to 5:00 p.m.; any job with regular working hours may be called a nine-to-five job. Some people have flextime [they can start work earlier or finish later]. In a large workplace, different people may work different shifts [periods when they are scheduled to work], e.g., the night shift or day shift. Some people also work overtime [work extra hours]. Most people get two days off each week [when they don't have to go to work]. They usually also get holidays (e.g., New Year's Day) off.

Exercises

68.1 Match the verbs on the left with the words on the right. Use each word or phrase only once.

1. earn
2. work
3. pay
4. attend
5. see
6. run

a. overtime
b. meetings
c. a store
d. clients
e. a salary
f. income tax

68.2 Rewrite each sentence using vocabulary from page 136. Keep the basic meaning the same.

1. I'm a banker.
   I work in ...*a bank.*...
2. What kind of work do you do?
   What do ....?
3. I earn $35,000 a year at my job.
   My ....
4. I make $40,000 from my teaching job and another $10,000 from writing.
   My .... is $50,000.
5. I'm an engineer.
   I work for ....
6. I'm responsible for one of the smaller departments.
   I'm in ....

68.3 This is part of a conversation with a teacher about her job. Write the missing questions.

1. A: ...*What hours do you work?*..
   B: I usually start at nine and finish at four.

2. A: ....?
   B: Yes. Sometimes I teach evening courses, and then I get paid extra.

3. A: ....?
   B: No, they don't. That's one of the disadvantages of being a teacher. But I suppose money isn't everything.

68.4 Answer these questions about work in a country you know well.

1. What are normal working hours for most office jobs?
2. What are three jobs that are paid very high salaries?
3. Do most workers pay taxes on their salary or wages?
4. What jobs often involve working in shifts? (Give at least two examples.)
5. Is flextime common in companies?

Jobs

A Manual jobs

Manual jobs are jobs in which you work with your hands. All the examples below are skilled jobs [need a lot of training].

| **bricklayer** [builds walls with bricks] | **carpenter** [makes things using wood] | **plumber** [installs and fixes water pipes, etc.] | **electrician** [installs and fixes electrical things] | **mechanic** [fixes cars] |

B Professions

Job	Definition
architect	designs buildings
lawyer	advises people on legal problems
engineer	plans the building of roads, bridges, machines, etc.
accountant	keeps and examines financial records of people and companies
professor	teaches in a university
stockbroker (stock market)	buys and sells stocks and bonds

C The medical profession

These people **treat** [give medical help] and **take care of** [care for] others: **doctor, nurse, surgeon** [a specialist doctor who **operates on** people in a hospital], **dentist,** and **veterinarian** [animal doctor; **vet** for short].

D The armed forces and emergency services

| **soldier** (in the army) | **sailor** (in the navy) | **pilot** (in the air force) | **police officer** (in the police force) | **firefighter** (in the fire department) |

Exercises

69.1 Write down at least one job from page 138 that would probably be impossible for these people.

1. Someone who doesn't have a college education.   *a doctor*
2. Someone who cannot see very well.
3. Someone who is always seasick on a boat.
4. Someone who does not understand about cars.
5. Someone who will not work in the evening or on weekends.
6. Someone who is afraid of dogs.
7. Someone who is afraid of heights and high places.
8. Someone who is terrible at numbers and math.
9. Someone who can't stand the sight of blood.
10. Someone who is against war.

69.2 Complete these definitions without looking at page 138.

1. An architect *..designs buildings.*...
2. A professor ....
3. An accountant ....
4. A veterinarian ....
5. A lawyer ....
6. An engineer ....
7. A bricklayer ....
8. A stockbroker ....
9. A mechanic ....
10. A surgeon ....

69.3 Respond to the statements below, as in the example.

1. A: He's a police officer.
   B: *..Really? When did he join the police force?*...

2. A: She's a soldier.
   B: ....?

3. A: He's a sailor.
   B: ....?

4. A: He's a fighter pilot.
   B: ....?

5. A: She's a firefighter.
   B: ....?

69.4 Imagine you just bought a piece of land and you are planning to build a house on it.
Write down at least six people from page 138 that you may need to help you.
What would you need their help for?

Example: *a bricklayer to build the walls*

69.5 Write a list of at least four friends, relatives, and neighbors who have jobs. What does each person do?

Example: *My uncle Jim is an engineer. His wife is an accountant.*

A Getting a job

During his last year of college, Ray was an **intern** / had an **internship** [an unpaid job for a short time] to gain **experience** [skill or knowledge you get from doing a job] at a local company. Before he graduated, he **applied for** [wrote an official request for] a job in the accounting department of the same company. He got a job as a **trainee** [a very junior person in a company]. He didn't earn much money, but they gave him a lot of **training** [help and advice in learning the job].

> *note* **Training** is an uncountable noun, so you cannot say "a training."
> **Experience** is uncountable when it means skill or knowledge.

B Moving up

Ray worked hard and his **prospects** [future possibilities in the job] looked good. After his first year he got a **raise** [more money], and after two years he was **promoted** [given a higher position with a higher salary and more responsibility]. After five years he was **in charge of** / **responsible for** [the boss of] the accounting department. He had five other **employees** [workers] **under him** [managed by him].

C Leaving the company

By the time Ray was 30, however, he decided he wanted a **new challenge** [a new, exciting situation]. He was interested in working **abroad** [in foreign countries], so he **resigned from** / **quit** the company [officially told the company he was leaving his job]. He started looking for a new job with a bigger company. He found a job with an international company, which **involved** [included] a lot of foreign travel. He was excited about the new job and at first he really enjoyed the traveling, but things soon changed.

D Hard times

After about six months, Ray started to **dislike** moving around constantly, and after a year he hated it. He hated living in hotels, and he never really made any friends in the new company. Unfortunately his **job performance** [how well he did his job] was not satisfactory either. He **was fired** / **let go** / **dismissed** [told to leave the company] a year later.

We have to let you go.

After that, Ray was **unemployed** / **out of work** [without a job] for over a year. He had to sell his car and move to a smaller house. Things were looking bad, and finally Ray had to accept a **part-time** job [working only part of the day or part of the week] as a chef's assistant at a restaurant.

E Happier times

To his surprise, Ray loved working at the restaurant. He made lots of friends and enjoyed learning to cook. After two years he became chef, and two years later he **took over** [took control of] the restaurant. Later he opened a second restaurant, and after 10 years he had five restaurants. Ray **retired** [stopped working at his career] at the age of 60, a rich man.

Exercises

70.1 Write a synonym [word with the same meaning] for each word/phrase.

1. dismissed .....*fired*...........................
2. someone who does an unpaid job to gain experience ....
3. out of work ....
4. left the company ....
5. given a better position in the company ....
6. future possibilities in a job ....
7. stopped working at the end of a career ....
8. workers in a company ....
9. an increase in salary ....
10. in a foreign country ....

70.2 Find the best answer on the right for each question. Use each answer only once.

1. Why did they fire him?
2. Why did they promote him?
3. Why did he apply for the job?
4. Why did he retire?
5. Why did he resign?

a. Because he was nearly 65.
b. Because he was late for work every day.
c. Because he didn't like his boss.
d. Because he was out of work.
e. Because he was the best person in the department.

70.3 Complete the sentences.

1. I don't want a full-time job. I'd prefer to work ..*part-time*................
2. She just started her first job and needs a lot of ....
3. I'm bored with my job. I need a new ....
4. She has more than a hundred workers under ....
5. I didn't know he was the new manager. When did he take .... ?

70.4 Complete the table. Use a dictionary to help you.

Verb	General noun	Person noun(s)
retire	.....*retirement*...............	.....*retiree*...................
promote	....	X
employ	....	....
resign	....	X
train	....	....

70.5 Answer the questions. If possible, ask another person the same questions.

1. Do you have a job? If so, what does it involve?
2. If you have a job: Are you responsible for anyone else? Explain.
3. If you have a job: Have you been promoted since you started? Explain.
4. If you have a job: Do you usually get a pay raise at the end of each year? Explain.
5. How do you feel about your future job prospects?

The office

A The work station

Larry works in a big **office**. He has his own **cubicle** [small working space separated from others by short walls]. This is his **workstation**.

bookshelf · cubicle · desk · calendar · bulletin board · monitor · wall / divider · screen · keyboard · filing cabinet · files · computer · drawer · fax machine / telephone · wastebasket

B Office work

Larry works for a company that **produces/manufactures** [makes] **furniture**. He works in an office, which is next to the **factory** where the furniture is made. This is how **he spends his time**:

He is **on his computer** most of the day. He **writes** memos and **reports**.
He **spends** much of **his day on the phone**. He answers many **calls** from **retailers** [stores that sell the factory's furniture] and **sends faxes** to them.
He **makes phone calls** to retailers and to the factory.
He gets a lot of **e-mail**. He **responds** to most of it.
He **does paperwork**, e.g., filing reports, writing memos, answering letters.
He **sends invoices** to customers. [paperwork showing the products sold and the money to pay]
He **arranges / schedules / sets up meetings**.
He **files reports** [puts them in a file / file cabinet] and other papers.

C In the office

There is a **receptionist** near the **elevators** on Larry's **floor**. [level of the building]
Larry's **co-workers/colleagues** work in cubicles around him.
There is a **copy room** (for making **photocopies**) just **down the hall**.
There is also a **break room** with a **coffeemaker**.
His **boss** has a **corner office**. [an office in the corner of the building, with windows on two walls]

Exercises

71.1 Cross out the word/phrase in brackets that *does not* fit well into the sentence.

1. Jim writes a lot of [~~phone calls~~ / reports / e-mail messages].
2. The company I work for [makes / arranges / produces] computers.
3. For much of my work day, I am on [a computer / the phone / the office].
4. [A receptionist / A retailer / One of my colleagues] sits at a desk near our elevator.
5. There is a desk in my [break room / workstation / cubicle].
6. You should quickly [answer / respond to / set up] every e-mail you get.
7. Ken spends a lot of his [time / paperwork / day] on the phone with retailers.
8. [The break room / My boss's office / Our floor] is just down the hall.

71.2 Fill in the blanks with compound nouns.

1. I make photocopies in the ..*copy room*......
2. There are lots of windows in the ....
3. His dictionary and other books are on his ....
4. He keeps file folders in a ....
5. People go to the .... to have a cup of coffee.
6. Pick up that piece of paper and throw it in the ....
7. When I use my computer, I type on a ....
8. There is a great view from the windows in my boss's ....

71.3 Which words from page 142 are being defined here?

1. someone you work with ..*co-worker*........
2. a machine to make coffee ....
3. someone who greets visitors to the office ....
4. your cubicle, desk, etc.; the place where you do your work ....
5. the person in charge of the work you and your co-workers do ....
6. a piece of paperwork showing how much a customer's order costs ....

71.4 Think of a job you have had – or someone you know well has had. How was each of the below involved in the job?

1. a computer
2. paperwork
3. phone calls
4. e-mail
5. meetings
6. co-workers

Business and finance

A Banks and businesses

Businesses sometimes borrow money from banks in order to **finance** [pay for] **investments** [things they need to spend money on, e.g., machines]. The money they borrow from the bank is called **a loan**, and they have to **pay interest** on it. For example, if you borrow $1,000 for a year and the **interest rate** is 10%, then you have to **pay back** the $1,000, plus $100 in interest at the end of the year.

B Profit and loss

One of the main **aims/objectives/goals** [things you hope to do/achieve] of a company is to **make a profit** [receive more money than it spends; ≠ **a loss**]. If a company does not make a profit or have a loss, it **breaks even**.

Companies receive money from selling their products or services. This money is called **income** or **revenue**. The money that they spend is called **expenses/expenditure(s)** *(formal)*. They spend money on these things: **raw materials** [natural materials used to make something else, e.g., the coal and oil used to make plastics]; **labor** [employees]; **overhead / overhead costs** [operating costs, e.g., rent and electricity].

C Rise and fall

These verbs describe **trends** [movements] in sales, prices, profit and loss, etc.

increase / rise / go up   rise slowly / gradually / steadily   increase sharply

fall / drop / go down   fall slowly / steadily   drop sharply

> **note** Increase, drop, fall, and rise can also be nouns: a steady **increase** in sales, a dramatic [sharp] **drop** in inflation, a sharp **fall** in profits, a slow **rise** in interest rates. Also possible: **be up/down**, e.g., Prices **are up** by 10%. Profits **are down**.

Notice the prepositions with these verbs:

by + size of change   Pre-tax profits rose **by** 11%.
from + previous level   Oil prices dropped **from** $140 **to** $129 a barrel.
to + new level

D Businesses and the economy

In order to **grow/expand** [get bigger] and **thrive/prosper** [do well / be successful], many companies want or need the following:

low inflation, so prices do not go up very much
low interest rates, so the company can borrow money without paying a lot of interest
economic and **political stability** [steady conditions with no sudden changes]
a **healthy/strong economy** [in good condition], not an economy **in recession** [in a period with no growth, a period with reduced and slow business activity]

Exercises

72.1 **What word or phrase is being defined?**

1. Money you borrow from a bank for your business. ...*a loan*...............
2. What you have to pay the bank if you borrow money. ....
3. A continuous increase in the price of things. ....
4. The things you hope to do/achieve within a period of time. ....
5. When a company does not make a profit or have a loss. ....
6. When an economy is in a period of reduced and slow business activity. ....

72.2 **Replace the underlined word(s) with another word that has a similar meaning.**

1. There has been a <u>slow</u> rise in sales. ...*gradual*...........
2. This comes after a <u>dramatic</u> fall last year. ....
3. Fortunately, the company is <u>doing well</u> now. ....
4. And it's <u>growing</u> very quickly. ....
5. This is one of their main <u>objectives</u>. ....
6. Profits have <u>risen</u> considerably. ....

72.3 **Look at the graph and complete the sentences. Fill each blank with one word.**

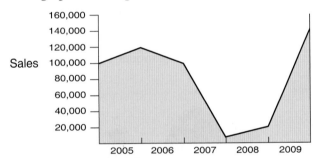

1. In 2005, sales ...*increased*......... .
2. The following year, they .... slightly.
3. In 2007, there was a sharp .... in sales.
4. In 2008, business improved, and there was a steady ....
5. And in 2009, sales increased ....
6. In the five-year period, sales .... by 40,000.

72.4 **Complete the compound words or common phrases.**

1. ...*break*................. even
2. .... stability
3. .... a profit
4. .... rate
5. raw ....
6. profit and ....

72.5 **Answer these questions about a country you know well. If you don't know the exact answers, take a guess.**

1. What is the current inflation rate?
2. If you borrowed $10,000 from your bank, what would the interest rate be?
3. What is the state of the economy right now? Is it strong? Is it in recession?
4. Are labor costs high, low, or about right?
5. Do you think businesses are optimistic about the future?

Hobbies

Hobbies are activities that we do in our **spare time**. [free time]

A Things people play

musical instruments

cards   board games   chess   guitar   saxophone

> *note*   Some people **join clubs** [become members] where they can **play** cards and chess.

B Things people collect

stamps   coins   antiques   shells   postcards

C Outdoor activities

hiking   camping   rock climbing   running/jogging

With these hobbies we often use the verb **go**, e.g., "I **go** **camping** in the summer." *or* "I **go** **jogging** every morning."

D Creative hobbies

Caroline **makes jewelry**.   Roberto likes **photography**.   Maria loves **carpentry**.

> *note*   When we start a hobby for the first time we often use the phrasal verb **take up**, and if we stop doing the hobby, we often use the phrasal verb **give up**, e.g., "I **took up** photography when I was 15, but I **gave** it **up** last year."

Exercises

73.1 **Without looking at page 146, write down . . .**

1. three things that people often play.
2. three things that people often collect.
3. three outdoor activities that include some physical exercise.

73.2 **Here are some people talking about their hobbies. Can you guess what each hobby is?**

1. I usually use color, but sometimes you get a better effect with black and white. It really depends on the subject. ..*photography*.................................
2. I really enjoy going to stores and markets looking for a bargain.
   ....
3. I try to practice every day, but sometimes it's difficult because I don't like to disturb my neighbors too much. And one neighbor gets very angry if I play the same thing over and over again. ....
4. The great thing is you can do it whenever you like. I usually do it three times a week – either early in the morning or after school. It really keeps me in good shape.
   ....
5. I enjoy stringing beads together to make different designs. My friends always compliment me on my earrings and necklaces. ....
6. I joined a club because I wanted to get better. It has helped me a lot, and I have a much better memory for all the different moves and strategies.
   ....
7. I love to work with wood, especially around the house. That's why I started, but now I think I do a better job than many professionals. ....
8. I go to the beach and find them in the sand. ....

73.3 **Complete these sentences with a verb from page 146.**

1. How often do you ....*go*.......... running?
2. She .... hiking because she wanted to get more exercise. Unfortunately she didn't like it, and she .... it .... about six months later.
3. She has always .... her own jewelry; it's much cheaper than buying it.
4. He .... old coins.
5. I like to .... rock climbing when I'm on vacation.
6. I learned to .... the guitar when I was in school.
7. I wanted to improve my chess, so I .... a chess club.
8. I don't really .... anything in my spare time.

73.4 **Answer these questions. If possible, ask another person the same questions.**

1. Do you have a hobby? If so, what is it?
2. How long have you had this hobby?
3. Is it an expensive hobby?
4. Why do you like it?
5. How much time do you spend on your hobby?
6. Is it a common hobby in your country?
7. Write down three other common hobbies in your country.

Sports

I **play** many sports – baseball, tennis, soccer, etc. (Use **play** with sports that are games.)
I also **do** some swimming, running, and hiking. (Use **do** with sports that aren't games.)
Someone who plays/does a sport often or professionally is an **athlete**.

A **Ball games and racquet sports**

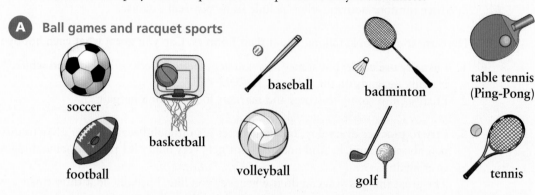

For tennis and badminton you need a **racquet**. For table tennis you use a **paddle**.
You hit a baseball with a **bat**. You catch the ball with a **glove**. For golf you need **golf clubs**.
In tennis, volleyball, and badminton there is a **net** across the middle of the **court**.
There is also a **net** around each **goal** in soccer.

B **Things you can do with a ball**

C **Places and people**

The playing area for soccer, football, and baseball is called a **field**. Tennis, volleyball,
basketball, and badminton are played on **courts**. For golf it is a **course**. The **spectators**
[people who watch a game] at a football game sit in the **stands** in a **stadium**. Most people
in the **crowd** [large number of people who watch a game; also called spectators] **cheer** for
the **home team**. Other people cheer for the **visitors**.

Sports like swimming or running can be **individual sports** [played by one person at a time]
or **team** sports [played by a group of people together]. Both **professional** sports teams
[who are paid] and **amateur** teams [who play without being paid] usually have **coaches**
[people who train and manage the team]. A **referee** (as in basketball or soccer) or an
umpire (as in tennis or baseball) makes sure players follow the **rules** during a game.

D **Winning and losing**

Mexico **beat** France 3–2. In other words, Mexico **defeated** France. Mexico **won** the game,
and France **lost**. It was **a victory** for Mexico and a **loss** for France.

The team with more points during a game **is leading / is ahead**. The team with fewer points
trails / is behind, e.g., "Brazil is **leading** Italy 2–1. Italy is **behind** by one point."

If both teams have the same **score** [number of goals or points] the game/score is **tied** or the
teams are tied, e.g., "The Lakers and the Pistons are **tied** at 88." (*not* ". . . are tying") [The
Lakers have 88 points, and so do the Pistons.]

Exercises

74.1 Cover page 148 and then write six things you can do with a ball.

1. .....*throw*..... it   3. .... it   5. .... it
2. .... it   4. .... it   6. .... it

74.2 Write at least:

1. three games where you can hit the ball (with various kinds of equipment).
   ..*baseball,*.......................................
2. three games where you can pass the ball. ....
3. three games where you can catch the ball. ....
4. two games where you can kick the ball. ....
5. one game where you can head the ball. ....

74.3 *True* or *false*? If *false*, correct the sentence to make it *true*.

1. The people who watch a football game are the audience.
   False. They are the crowd / the spectators.
2. The official who makes sure the rules are followed in tennis is the umpire.
3. Running can be an individual sport or a team sport.
4. Basketball has an umpire.
5. If the current score is Red Team 4, Blue Team 2, then the Blue Team is ahead.
6. Tennis is played on a field.
7. You play golf with clubs.
8. If both teams have the same score, the score is tied.

74.4 Fill in the blanks in this radio broadcast about baseball. Use the best word/phrase from the box.

beat	loss	victory	leading	tied	score

A baseball update from your 24-hour news station: At the end of a long game in San Diego, the Padres finally (1) ....*beat*.......... the Atlanta Braves by a (2) .... of 6 to 3. This was the first (3) .... for Atlanta this season. For the Padres, this was only the second (4) .... of the season. Meanwhile, in Montreal, the Expos are (5) .... the Chicago Cubs 4 to 0 in the sixth inning [part of a baseball game]. Chicago has been having a terrible game! And finally, the contest between the Toronto Blue Jays and the New York Yankees is still (6) .... at 3 runs each.

74.5 Answer these questions. If possible, ask a friend the same questions.

1. Are there any games or sports on page 148 that you watch but don't play? If so, what are they and where do you watch them?
2. Are there any games or sports on page 148 that you play/do yourself?
3. Are there any games or sports that are not played much in your country?
4. Which game or sport is the most popular in your country?
5. Which sport on page 148 is the most dangerous, in your opinion?
6. Which game or sport requires the most strength?
7. Which one has the biggest crowds?
8. Can you think of at least three more games/sports not included on page 148?

Movies and theater

box
seat
balcony
orchestra pit

curtain
stage
orchestra
aisle
rows

A Theater

At **the theater** you can see **plays**, e.g., *Hamlet* by Shakespeare, and **musicals**, e.g., *Phantom of the Opera* or *Rent*. They are **performed** on a **stage** by a **cast** of **actors**. The **lead** actors are the most important ones, and the **supporting** actors have smaller **parts**. You usually **reserve** theater **tickets** [arrange to buy them] **in advance** [some time before the performance]. The **audience** [the people watching the play/musical] **claps/applauds** [hits their hands together to make a sound]. This shows they **enjoyed** the **performance**.

B Movies

Movies/films are **shown** on a **screen** in a movie theater. Movies in a foreign language might have **subtitles** [translations across the bottom of the screen]. Some are **dubbed** in English [the original language is removed and replaced by English speech] or another language. The **director** of a movie (e.g., Steven Spielberg or Ang Lee) brings all parts of the project together. The **stars** (e.g., Jackie Chan or Julia Roberts) are the most important actors.

C Types of movies

There are many kinds of movies. Some movies fit into more than one category.

fantasy: about an imaginary world; may include magic and unreal types of animals, e.g., *Lord of the Rings*

action movie: has a lot of excitement, car chases, athletic action

horror movie: scares you with monsters, killers, etc., e.g., *Dracula*

science fiction movie: about imaginary scientific developments, often in the future, e.g., *E.T.*

thriller: an exciting story, often about trying to catch a criminal

drama: a story with interesting characters and exciting events

comedy: funny situations; makes you laugh

animation: cartoons, claymation, anime, e.g., *Tom and Jerry*

D Describing plays and movies

Words **critics/reviewers** might use in their **reviews** [opinion essays] on TV, in newspapers, or on online:

fast-paced: full of action

moving: producing strong emotions, often of sadness; a positive word

slow: boring, uninteresting

gripping: exciting and very interesting

powerful: has a big effect on our emotions

suspenseful: keeps you wondering what will happen next

hilarious: very funny

silly: very unrealistic; not serious, but not funny either

violent: includes lots of scenes with fighting and death

Exercises

75.1 The picture shows where someone sat at a theater.
Answer these questions.

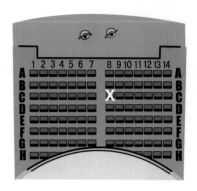

1. What section did the person sit in – the balcony,
   a box, or the orchestra? *the orchestra*
2. Which seat did he sit in – A1, A8, C1, or C8?
3. What is the space on his left – the aisle, the orchestra pit,
   or the stage?
4. Where are the actors – behind the curtain, in the orchestra,
   or on the stage?

75.2 What word or phrase is being defined?

1. A play or movie with singing. *a musical*
2. The group of actors in a play or movie.
3. The people who watch a play at the theater.
4. What they do with their hands at the end of a play.
5. The person who brings the parts of a movie together.
6. Journalists who talk on TV or write articles about movies and plays.
7. The name of the articles they write or the opinions they give on TV.
8. The translation of the story of a movie across the bottom of the screen.
9. To arrange to buy tickets before the performance.
10. The most important actors in a movie.

75.3 The movies below are considered classics [well-known and of a high standard]. For each
movie, add at least one word to columns B and C. Find information on the Internet or in
other sources as necessary. Complete rows 4–6 with information about movies you have
seen.

A Movie	B Category of movie	C Description of movie (adjectives)
1. *The Godfather* with Marlon Brando	drama *action*	violent *exciting*
2. The Harry Potter series with Daniel Radcliffe	fantasy	suspenseful
3. *The Lion King* by Walt Disney Productions	animation	funny
4.		
5.		
6.		

Music, art, and literature

A Kinds of music

People who **compose** [write] music are **composers**. There are many **genres** [kinds] of music.

classical: music by Beethoven, Tchaikovsky, Mozart, for example. It is often played by a **symphony orchestra**. [large musical group including violins, horns, etc.]

opera: a play in which all or most of the words are **sung**. Famous operas include *Carmen* by Bizet and *La Bohème* by Puccini.

jazz: music in which players often **improvise** [invent the music as they go along]. Jazz musicians important in history include Duke Ellington and Wynton Marsalis.

rock and **pop:** music in a style that is very popular, often for a short time. People who compose/write it are often called **songwriters**. Rock/pop **bands/groups** and **singers** important in history include the Beatles and Madonna.

B Musical instruments and musicians

cellist	violinist	pianist	guitarist	saxophonist	drummer
cello	violin	piano	guitar	saxophone	drums

C Art

Artists often **exhibit** [show] their **works** at an **art gallery** or a **museum**:

paintings; some **painters** produce **landscapes** [of places] or **portraits** [of people]
sculpture; some **sculptors** use stone, metal, or plastic

D Literature

Literature is writing that is important in a culture. **Fiction** is literature that is **imaginative** [not about real people/events]. Literature about real people/events is called **non-fiction**.

Kind of fiction	*Writer*
a **novel** [a story long enough to fill a book]	**novelist**
a **short story** [a story too short to fill a book]	**short story writer**
a **poem / poetry** [often in short lines; sometimes rhymes]	**poet**
a **play** [a piece of writing performed by actors in a theater]	**playwright**

Exercises

76.1 **What do you call the people who play the following instruments?**

1. piano ..*pianist*.............   3. guitar ....   5. saxophone ....
2. violin ....   4. drums ....   6. cello ....

76.2 **What type of art is each of these?**

1.    2.    3.

76.3 **Use the context and your own knowledge to fill in the blanks.**

1. Seiji Ozawa was the .....*conductor*..... of the Boston Symphony Orchestra.
2. A: Do you like .... music?
   B: Yes, very much. My favorite .... is Mozart.
3. I like .... music a lot. It's interesting to hear the musicians improvise.
4. He's a .... His first .... was performed in a very small theater.
5. The new art .... in New York will .... some of this artist's paintings.
6. She and her band played .... music. They were popular only for a short time. She was also a .... and composed most of their songs.
7. I haven't been to the .... since I saw *Carmen* last year.
8. *A Farewell to Arms* is a .... written by Ernest Hemingway. It's one of his best books. It is a piece of .... – not about real people.
9. Picasso was a great .... He painted .... of people, but they didn't look very much like real people.

76.4 **Name your favorites in each category. (The people you name can be living or dead.)**
Some of them may fit into more than one category.

Example: *Leonard Bernstein is my favorite composer. His most famous work is*
         West Side Story.

1. composer   6. pop or rock singer
2. song   7. play
3. genre of music   8. novel
4. band/group   9. poem
5. songwriter   10. novelist

A Background

In the U.S. and Canada, most **newspapers/papers** are **daily**. They **come out / are published** every day. They may have a special, larger **Sunday edition**. Some include a **weekly** [once a week] magazine with the Sunday edition. Most newspapers also have an **online edition** [on the Internet]. **Tabloid newspapers / Tabloids** are usually sold only in stores, not **delivered** [brought] to people's homes. They do not contain important news and are mostly for **entertainment** [fun; enjoyment]. Their short articles and pictures are usually about **celebrities** [famous people], diets, the supernatural, etc.

B Contents

national news: about the country where the newspaper is published
international news: about other countries
business news
sports news
features: longer articles about special subjects, e.g., a health issue

comics: a collection of cartoons
weather forecast: tells you what the weather will be like
reviews: opinions by **critics** about movies, plays, music, restaurants, etc.
editorials: opinions (often by the newspaper's managers) about important issues like politics

C People

editor: the person in control of the daily production
reporters/journalists: people who find information about news events and then **report** it [write about it in the newspaper] by writing articles.
photographers: people who take pictures published in the newspapers
freelancers: reporters and photographers who are not employees of any paper. They sell their work to papers one piece at a time.

D Headlines

Certain words (usually very short) are common in newspaper headlines. Here are some:

back: to support	Mayor **backs** school funding
bid (n., v.): an effort / a try / an attempt	UN fails in **bid** for peace talks
cut (v., n.): to reduce / make less / lower	City **cuts** road repairs
key: very important	Goalie **key** to L.A. soccer success
link (v., n.): to make a connection	Tomatoes **linked** to disease
probe (n., v.): an investigation	Senate begins **probe** of company
quit: to leave a job / resign	Top aide **quits** group
talks: discussions	Union holds **talks** with car makers

E *It said in the paper that . . . ; According to . . .*

To refer to something in the newspaper: It **says/said** in *The Times* that they've found the missing girl. **According to** *The Star*, the missing girl was found last night.

Exercises

77.1 Answer these questions about a country you know well.

1. What is the most important daily national newspaper?
2. What do most tabloid newspapers write about?
3. Is the Sunday edition of a newspaper usually different from other editions? How?
4. What parts of the newspaper do you usually read?
5. Do you read online editions of any newspapers? Which ones?
6. Are any newspaper journalists, editors, etc., famous? If so, name some.

77.2 Explain these headlines in your own words. Do not use the underlined words in your explanation.

1. **Mayor to quit**

   The mayor will leave his/her job.

2. **Legislature cuts taxes**

3. **New bid to cut teen smoking**

4. **U.S. backs European plan**

5. **Study links stress with heart disease**

6. **Police discover key witness**

77.3 Buy two different newspapers (in English or your own language) and complete these two tables. If possible, compare answers with a friend.

	Newspaper 1 (number of pages)	Newspaper 2 (number of pages)
national news	....	....
foreign/international news	....	....
features	....	....
business news	....	....
sports news	....	....

	Newspaper 1 (yes/no)	Newspaper 2 (yes/no)
weather forecast	....	....
comics	....	....
editorials	....	....
reviews	....	....
other (e.g., puzzles)	....	....

A Watching TV

plug it **in**

turn it **on** [≠ **turn** it **off**]

a remote control / a remote

You can also **turn** it **up** [increase the volume / make it louder; ≠ **turn** it **down**], or **change/switch channels** (e.g., from channel 2 to 4). Some people like to **channel surf** [change channels frequently to view different programs at the same time].

B Types of programs

soap opera: follows the lives of a group of **fictional** [not real] people. Many soap operas are on **daily** [once a day]. The stories are often romantic, exciting, dramatic, and hard to believe.

quiz show or **game show:** individuals, families, or teams answer questions or play games against each other. The winner gets a **prize**, e.g., a car, a vacation, money.

talk show: a host talks to famous people about their lives and careers. Sometimes there are comedy acts and music as well.

documentary: a film with factual information, often analyzing a problem in society.

news magazine: a program of brief informational films, interviews, and commentary.

a series: more than one program about the same situation or the same characters in different situations. This may be a **comedy** series (the programs are intended to be funny) or a **drama** series (the programs are intended to be serious or exciting).

current affairs / current events: a program about current social or political issues / problems. **Current** means "happening now / at the present time."

cartoons: animated programs or movies, often for children, sometimes for adults.

reality show: people who aren't professional actors are filmed as they take on a challenge, show their talent, etc.

rerun/repeat: a program that is being shown again (i.e., not for the first time).

C Networks, satellite TV, cable TV

A **network** is a group of TV **stations** that offers many of the same programs all over the country. Networks **broadcast** their shows [send out programs on TV or radio]. To get more TV channels, people might get **satellite TV** or **cable TV**. They **subscribe** to these services [pay a certain amount every month to a company]. For satellite TV you need a **satellite dish**. Cable TV is sent through wire cables underground.

D Talking about TV

What's **on** TV tonight? [What programs are showing on TV tonight?]
What time is the movie **on**? [What time does it start?]
How long are the **commercials**? [advertisements between and during programs]
Are they showing the game **live** [as it happens] or just **recorded highlights**? [parts of the game after it has been played, e.g., later in the day/evening]

Exercises

78.1 Imagine you are watching TV with a friend. What could you say in each situation below?

1. You want to watch a program on TV. Could you *turn the TV on / turn on the TV?*
2. You can't hear the program very well. Could you .... ?
3. You want to watch a different program. Could you .... ?
4. Now it's too loud for you. Could you .... ?
5. You don't want to watch anymore. Could you .... ?

78.2 In the description of TV shows, find at least one of the following (some shows fit into more than one category):

1. drama series ....
2. news magazine ....
3. game show ....
4. sports program ....
5. talk show ....
6. cartoon show ....
7. reality show ....
8. current affairs program ....
9. soap opera ....
10. comedy series ....

TIMES IN OUR LIVES
Ellen finds out she has an evil twin. Sandy can't hide her fatal attraction for David

CRIME CITY
The murder of an actress leads to an investigation of her ex-husband

60 MINUTES
The price of terrorism; lottery winners who go broke; charities that make a difference

WASHINGTON WEEK IN REVIEW
Discussion of political issues

GUESSING GAME
Contestants compete for cash prizes

JERRY'S SHOW
A librarian says that Jerry has a book that's 20 years overdue

FBI FILES The probe of two deaths unearths a frightening discovery

THE TONIGHT SHOW
Guests are top Olympic swimmers; music by the New Band

SPRINGFIELD
(animated) Brad visits the school psychologist and drives her crazy

NASCAR RACING
Live auto racing

REALITY HOUSE
Arguments occur as the housemates prepare to paint the house

78.3 Answer these questions about TV in a country you know well.

1. Who owns most TV channels – companies or the government?
2. How do most people get TV? By cable? By satellite? In some other way?
3. In total, how much TV do you watch every week? (i.e., how many hours?)
4. What are your favorite TV programs? What categories do they fit in (drama, sports, etc.)?
5. What day(s) or night(s) are they on?
6. Are you a channel surfer? Why or why not?
7. Do you enjoy watching commercials? Explain.
8. Do you often watch sports live on TV? If not, do you watch the highlights?
9. Do you ever watch reruns of TV shows? Which ones?

On the phone

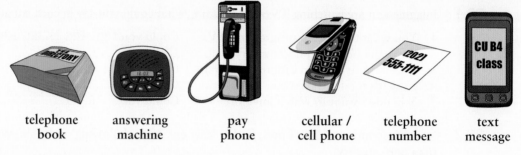

| telephone book | answering machine | pay phone | cellular / cell phone | telephone number | text message |

A Starting a phone conversation

At home:

A: Hello?
B: Hi. (**Is this**) Mary? / **Can I speak with** Mary? (*not* Are you Mary? / Is it Mary?)
A: This is Mary.
B: Hi. **This is** Ruth. (*not* I am Ruth. / Here is Ruth.)

At work:

C: Hayes Electronics.
D: Hello. **Can I / Could I / May I speak** to Ms. Gold, please?
C: I'm sorry, but her **line** is **busy**. [Her phone is in use; she is **on the phone**.] Would you like to **hold** [wait], or would you like her **voice mail**?
D: I'll hold. I really need to **get in touch** [communicate] with her right away.

> **note** People usually answer their **home phones** with "hello" (*not* with their name or phone number). People usually answer their **work phones** with their company's (or their own) names.

B Trying to get in touch

Yesterday, you and your friend Susan **played phone tag** [left phone messages for each other, back and forth].

4:30 p.m.	You try to **call** [phone] Susan, who lives far away. The call is **long-distance**. You **dial** her **area code** and then her **home number**. The phone **rings** [makes a sound], but a stranger answers. You've got a **wrong number**.
4:32 p.m.	You call **directory assistance** (or 411) to find the right number for her.
4:35 p.m.	You call Susan again. You **reach** her number, but she's **out** [not at home]. Her husband, Bill, answers and says that Susan **won't be back** [will not return] for two hours. You **leave a message**: "Could you ask her to call me when she gets back?" Bill **takes the message** [writes it down].
7:30 p.m.	Susan **calls** you **back**, but now you are out. She leaves a message on your answering machine. Her message is: "This is Susan. I'm just **returning** your call. I'll **give you a call** [call you] tomorrow."
9:45 p.m.	You get home and **listen to** her message. You decide not to call back on your **land line** [a telephone that is not a cell phone]. You use your cell phone to **text her cell** [send a text message to her cell phone]: "OK Sue, Talk 2 U soon." [talk to you soon]

Exercises

79.1 Give six words or expressions that include the word "phone" or "telephone".

1. *telephone call* ....   4. ....

2. ....   5. ....

3. ....   6. ....

79.2 Fill in the blanks in these phone conversations with logical words or phrases.

A   A: Classic Computers.
      B: Yes. (1) ..*This is*............ Kevin Lee at Offices Unlimited. I'm trying to reach
         Mr. Patterson. He left a (2) .... on my answering machine.
      A: I'm sorry, but Mr. Patterson is (3) .... Can I ask him to
         (4) .... later?
      B: Yes. My (5) .... is area code 999, 555-7267, and I'll be here until noon.

B   A: Hello?
      B: Hi. Debbie?
      A: No, (6) .... Diane. Debbie's not here.
      B: Oh. Do you know when she'll (7) .... ?
      A: I'm sorry, but I have no idea.
      B: Well, could I (8) .... a .... for her?
      A: Sure.
      B: Could you ask her to (9) .... this evening, please?
      A: OK. What's your name?
      B: Catherine. I'm a friend from work. She's got my number.

C   A: Hello?
      B: (10) .... Carlos?
      A: Yeah, speaking.
      B: Hi, Carlos. (11) .... Selena.
      A: Oh, hi. I was expecting you to call yesterday.
      B: I did – or at least I tried. I (12) .... your number
         about six times last night but it was always (13) ....
      A: Oh, sorry about that. I was (14) .... the phone with my brother for
         about an hour, and then someone from school called.
      B: Oh, OK. Anyway, I'm calling about . . .

79.3 Answer these questions about your own experience with telephones. If possible, ask another person these questions, too.

1. Do you mostly use a cell phone or a land line?
2. What do you say when you answer your phone at home?
3. Do you often text anyone? If so, who?
4. How much time do you spend on the phone each day?
5. What would you say if someone called your number by mistake (a wrong number)?
6. What is the emergency number for the police, fire department, or ambulance where you live?

Computers and the Internet

A Hardware and software

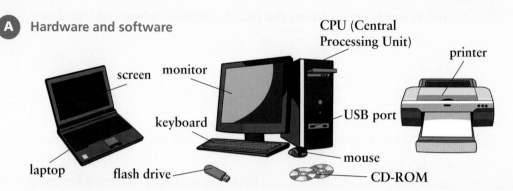

CPU (Central Processing Unit)
printer
screen
monitor
keyboard
USB port
laptop
flash drive
mouse
CD-ROM

Computer users need **hardware** [the machines] and **software** [computer programs]. The software is **stored** [kept] on a **hard drive / hard disk** inside the **CPU**. When users buy a computer, the **operating system** [the software that runs the computer] and other software may already be installed on the computer. If users need more software, they might buy it on **CD-ROMs** or **download** it from the **Internet**.

B Operating a computer

Using the **mouse**, you **click on** different **icons** [little pictures on the screen]. You write things using **word-processing** software. Here are some actions you can take while using it:

open a new document / file

save the document / file

cut

paste

open an existing document/file

print

copy

After you finish a document, you might **print out** a **hard copy** of it. When you are finished using a computer, you **turn it off**.

C The Internet

The Internet (sometimes called **the Net**) is a system connecting well over one billion computers around the world. The part of the Internet that most people use is called the **World Wide Web (the Web)**. When you connect to the Internet, you **go online**. Very often people go online using a **wireless** connection [no wires/cables connect the computer to the Internet]. Many hotels and restaurants offer free **Wi-Fi/wireless access**. Software called a browser finds **Web sites** for you. To find specific information, you can use a **search engine**, e.g., **Google**.

D E-mail

I **sent** you **an e-mail** yesterday. I know you did not receive it because it **bounced back** [was returned]. Maybe I have the wrong **e-mail address** for you. Can you **e-mail me**? Then I'll get my **message** to you by **replying** to [answering] your message.

I **check** my mail at least twice a day. Sometimes my **in-box** has 15 or 20 new messages in it. A lot of them are just **spam/junk** [unimportant messages], so I **delete** [erase] them. However, I always read messages from **senders** I know.

Exercises

80.1 Complete these common computer words and phrases.

1. ....*word*...... processing
2. soft ....
3. hard ....
4. flash ....
5. World Wide ....
6. .... address
7. operating ....
8. .... -ROM
9. bounce ....
10. lap ....

80.2 Write the computer command under each icon. Use the words in the box.

| cut | copy | print | paste | save |

1. .... 2. .... 3. .... 4. .... 5. ....

80.3 Fill each blank with a word or phrase from page 160.

I sat in a coffee shop and did some work on my (1) ....*laptop*........ computer. I was able
to go (2) .... in the coffee shop because it had free (3) .... access.
I (4) .... my e-mail and saw that I had 13 new (5) .... in my
in-box. Some of the messages were spam, so I (6) .... them. I received a
message from my boss. I (7) .... it and then (8) .... to it. Then I
(9) .... a message to one of my friends. The message bounced
(10) .... because I typed his e-mail (11) .... incorrectly. Before I
left the coffee shop, I (12) .... my computer off.

80.4 If you use computers, answer these questions. Also, ask someone else these questions.

1. Do you have a computer at home? If so, what kind is it?
2. Do you use a computer at school/work? If so, describe it.
3. What do you use the computer for?
4. Which software do you use the most?

80.5 If you use the Internet, answer these questions. Also, ask someone else these questions.

1. How often do you use the Internet?
2. Which Web sites do you often go to?
3. If you use a search engine, what kinds of information do you often search for?
4. If you use e-mail, how much time do you spend each day on it?

Unit 81

Education: Kindergarten to high school

A K–12

In the United States, **K–12** means "**kindergarten** through **twelfth grade**" [the last year of high school] for **public schools** [free education]. In most states, school is **compulsory** [you have to go] from ages 6 to 16. Different U.S. **school districts** [local areas with their own school systems] have different rules, but most children follow a system like this:

Approximate age	Kind of school
3 or 4	Some go to **nursery school** or **pre-school** (not compulsory).
5 or 6	Most children start kindergarten at this age. This is usually considered the first year of **elementary school / primary school**. Kindergarten is compulsory in some states. The next years of elementary school, grades 1–5 or 6 (**first grade** to **fifth** or **sixth grade**) are compulsory in every state.
10, 11, or 12	In many school districts, children go to **middle school** at this age. (In others, elementary school goes until eighth grade.) Middle school might be grades 5–8, grades 6–8, or 7–9. Some districts use the term **junior high school** for grades 7–9.
14–17	Students go to **high school / secondary school** (grades 9–12 or 10–12). Regular high schools offer academic and vocational programs. **Vocational high schools** offer training for a job, e.g., auto mechanic, beautician. **Specialized high schools** are for students with special interests, e.g., music, business.
18	Most students **graduate** [finish school successfully] and get a job or **go to college** for higher education. Students who leave school without graduating **drop out** of school and are called **dropouts**.

note
- Students go to school and go to college (**not** 'to the school/college').
- In the United States, college usually means study after high school (university, etc.).
- Public schools are run by local governments. They are free. Private schools and parochial [religious] schools are not free, and some can be expensive.
- Charter schools are special public schools available in some districts. Parents and teachers have more freedom to choose the course requirements [courses students must take] in these schools.

B A school schedule

Different states/districts have different course requirements. Certain **core subjects** [most important topics] are taught in most schools, e.g., **reading/English**, **writing**, **math** [mathematics], **science**, and **social studies** [history, politics, economics, etc.]. A **schedule** for one day in a typical high school might look like this:

8:00 Science	11:40 Lunch
8:55 Math	12:30 History
9:50 English	1:25 PE [physical education] / computers / etc.
10:45 Elective (music, art, etc.)	2:20 Foreign language

note Mathematics, politics, physics are singular; e.g., "Physics is my favorite subject."

Exercises

81.1 Here are some school subjects, but the letters are mixed up. What are the subjects?

1. TAHM *Math*
2. IRTHOSY
3. CNESCEI

4. NISGEHL
5. RAT
6. SIMCU

81.2 Answer these questions or complete the sentences without looking at page 162.

1. What does K–12 mean? *kindergarten through twelfth grade*
2. At what age do children go to nursery school?
3. At what age do they start elementary school?
4. Which year of elementary school is compulsory in some states but optional in others?
5. Three kinds of public high school are a regular school, a .... school, and a .... school.
6. Name four core subjects taught in high schools.
7. Which of these schools is free: parochial, private, or public?
8. What type of school comes between elementary school and high school?

81.3 Answer these questions about your own experience and your country.

1. Did you go to nursery school? Kindergarten?
2. At what age do most children start elementary/primary school?
3. In what ways is high school different from the U.S. system? How is it similar?
4. How many subjects did/do you study in high school?
5. Did you study any subjects that are not included on the opposite page? Which ones?
6. What was/is your favorite subject? Your worst subject?
7. How many classes did/do you have every day?
8. Did/do you attend public school or private school?
9. Until what age do students have to stay in school?
10. Are there a lot of high school dropouts?

81.4 Complete these sentences with the correct word or expression.

1. When she was a child, she lived in a small town and went .... with only fifty other students.
2. After I .... from high school, I went .... and studied history.
3. He wanted to finish school, but he needed to get a job and support his family. That's why he .... of school at 16.
4. They didn't send their children to kindergarten because it wasn't .... in their state.

81.5 The next unit is about college and higher education. Can you think of six subjects you can study at a university that you do not usually study at school (K–12)? Write down your answers, then turn to the next page.

Education: university / college

A Higher education in the United States

Higher education is education at a **university** or **college**. In the United States, "Where did you **go to school**?" often means "Which college/university did you go to?" The word college can mean a separate **institution** (e.g., Bowdoin College in Maine) or part of a university (e.g., the College of Engineering, part of the University of Washington). A student at a college or university is **in college**. A **community college/junior college** is a two-year, government-supported college. It often specializes in technical and vocational studies.

Students who want to **enter** a college or university go through an **application** [official request, usually in writing] process. If a student's application is **accepted,** he or she **is admitted / gets admission** [permission to enter] to the institution.

Tuition [the money you pay for courses] is lower at public colleges/universities than at **private institutions**. Some students receive a **scholarship** [money to pay all or part of the tuition].

B Undergraduates and graduate students

Undergraduates are studying for their first degree. [You get a degree when you complete university/college requirements successfully.] Four-year institutions usually give **B.A. (Bachelor of Arts)** and **B.S. (Bachelor of Science)** degrees. Community/junior colleges usually give two-year **associate's degrees**.

Graduate school is study for a degree beyond a bachelor's degree. A **graduate student works toward a master's degree** or a **doctorate** (often a **Ph.D.**)

C Classes and subjects

Most teachers at a college or university are **lecturers, instructors,** or **professors** [senior position which includes responsibility for research]. Graduate students who help teach courses are **teaching assistants** or **graduate assistants**.

You usually **take/study** these **subjects** at a university or college but not usually in high school. (*Note*: The underlined letters show the syllable with the main stress.)

agriculture	<u>art</u> history	engin<u>ee</u>ring	po<u>li</u>tical <u>sci</u>ence
anthro<u>po</u>logy	business	hotel adminis<u>tra</u>tion	psy<u>cho</u>logy
<u>ar</u>chitecture	education	phi<u>lo</u>sophy	soci<u>o</u>logy

The main subject that a student takes at college is his/her **major**, e.g., "Chris's major is psychology" or "Chris **is majoring in** psychology." Graduate students usually have to **do research** [careful and detailed study of one subject] to get a degree. For example, they may write a **thesis** [a report about their research] for a master's degree.

Exercises

82.1 Read these sentences spoken by college students. What subject is each person studying? Choose from the list on page 164.

1. "I'm concentrating on the modernist style and the work of Frank Lloyd Wright."
   architecture
2. "The way we use fertilizers on farms is better than it was 20 years ago."
3. "One of our biggest challenges is knowing where to locate new hotels."
4. "We're going to concentrate on Freud and Jung this term."
5. "I've been reading some books on time management."
6. "Expressionist painting was really a reaction to the work of the Impressionists."
7. "We've spent a lot of time discussing foreign policy."
8. "We're looking at new ways to utilize solar energy."

Now mark the stress in each of your answers above and practice saying the words. Check the index or a dictionary for help with pronunciation.

82.2 What do you call:

1. the money students pay for their courses?   *tuition*
2. the degree you get at the end of four years at a university?
3. students working toward this degree?
4. teachers at a university/college?
5. the process of trying to get accepted to a college/university?
6. students studying for a second degree?
7. the study of one subject in great depth and detail, often to get new information?
8. a two-year, government supported college?

82.3 Replace the underlined words with words that have the same meaning in the context.

1. Is he a student working toward a degree after his bachelor's degree? *graduate student*
2. Did she get money to pay for part of her tuition?
3. He's planning to get a two-year degree from a community college.
4. Where did you go to school?
5. Her main area of study is physics, I think.
6. She got a four-year degree from the university.

82.4 Answer these questions about higher education in a country you know well. If possible, compare your answers with someone else's.

1. Do some students receive scholarships to study at university or college?
2. Is the tuition free in some colleges or universities?
3. At what age do most students go to university or college?
4. How long do most undergraduate courses last?
5. What is the equivalent of a B.A. or B.S.?
6. Is the graduate school system similar to that in the U.S.? Explain.

Law and order

A The police

The **law** might say a certain action is wrong – it is **illegal / against the law**. Someone who **commits a crime / breaks the law** is a **criminal**. The police **investigate** crimes [try to find out what happened and who is responsible]. If they find a **suspect** [a person who may have committed the crime], they **question** the person [ask questions]. They may then arrest that person [take him/her to the police station] and **charge him/her with** the crime [officially say the suspect committed the crime]. The suspect could spend some time in **jail/prison** [a place where people are locked in] after the arrest. The suspect may then **go to court** for **trial**.

B The court

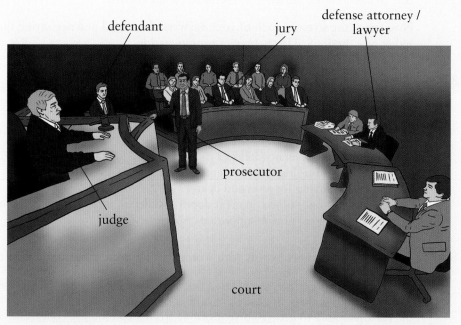

defendant   jury   defense attorney / lawyer

prosecutor

judge

court

Someone **on trial** for a crime is the **defendant**. In **court**, the prosecutor [the **lawyer** for the government] must **prove** [show something is true] that the defendant committed the crime – is **guilty**. The **defense attorney** [the lawyer for the defendant] tries to show that the defendant is **not guilty / is innocent**. The **jury** listens to all the **evidence** [information about the crime, for and against the defendant] and then **renders a verdict** [makes a decision].

C Punishment [what a person must suffer if they do something wrong]

If the jury **finds** the defendant **guilty**, he/she **is convicted of** the crime [the jury's verdict is "guilty"]. The judge will give a **sentence** [a punishment]. If a person is convicted of a **felony** [very serious crime] like **murder**, the sentence may be many years in prison. The defendant then becomes a **prisoner** and lives in a **cell** [a small room in a prison].

For a crime that is not very serious (often called a **minor offense**, e.g., illegal parking), the police do not **make** any arrest and the court does not **hold** a trial. The police might give the person a **ticket** [piece of paper describing the offense]. The punishment is usually a **fine** [money the **offender** has to pay].

Exercises

83.1 Here is the beginning of a story. Complete it by putting the sentences in the correct order.

....*1*.... Last week $100,000 was stolen from a bank on Main Street.

.... they found both men guilty.

.... and charged them with the robbery.

.... After the jury listened to all the evidence,

.... They were sent to prison for seven years.

.... The trial took place six months later.

.... They finally arrested two men

.... The police questioned a number of people about the crime.

83.2 Answer the questions.

1. Who investigates crimes?   *the police*
2. Who sentences people?
3. Who lives in prisons?
4. Who decides if someone is innocent or guilty?
5. Who presents evidence in court?
6. Who commits crimes?

83.3 Fill in the blanks.

1. I have never ....*broken*........ the law – never .... a crime.
2. In the United States, it is .... the law to drive a car without a driver's license.
3. If you park illegally, you will have to pay a ....
4. The police were fairly sure the woman had committed the crime. Still, they knew they might not be able to .... it in court.
5. The jury must decide if the defendant is innocent or ....
6. In order to reach their decision, the jury must listen carefully to the ....
7. If a defendant is .... of murder, the .... may be life in prison.
8. He has been in trouble with the police once before, but it was only a minor ....

83.4 Read the article. Assume the crime took place in a country you know well. If possible, discuss your answers with someone else.

> **T**wo 15-year-old girls broke into a house in the middle of the day when the homeowner was out and took money and jewelry worth about $900. The homeowner reported the crime to the police when she returned home at 6 p.m.

1. Will the police investigate this crime?
2. How will they investigate? What will they do?
3. If the two girls are caught, what will happen next?
4. Can the girls be sent to prison? What do you think their sentence would be?

A Against the law

If you do something **illegal** [wrong / against the law], then you have committed a crime. Most people commit a minor crime at some time in their lives, e.g., driving above the speed limit, parking illegally, or stealing candy when they were children.

B Crimes

Crime	Criminal [person]	Verb
theft [general word for stealing]	**thief**	**steal** (also **take**)
robbery [stealing from people or places]	**robber**	**rob**
breaking and entering [forcing one's way into someone's house]	**intruder**	**break into**
burglary [stealing from a store/house after breaking in]	**burglar**	**burglarize / burgle**
shoplifting [stealing from a store while pretending to shop]	**shoplifter**	**shoplift**
murder [killing someone by intention]	**murderer**	**murder**
manslaughter [killing someone without intention]	—	—

C Crime prevention

How do the police, courts, and **lawmakers** [senators, congress members, etc.] try to **fight crime** [take action to stop crime]? Here are some steps they might take. Not everyone thinks these are good ideas:

Police **carry** guns. [have guns with them as they walk or ride around]
Police **set up checkpoints** [blocked places on the roads] and question people who pass.
The courts give **tougher/harsher** punishments for crimes than in the past (e.g., bigger fines or longer **prison terms**).
Lawmakers make **capital punishment** [death for criminals] legal for crimes such as murder.

Individuals can help **prevent** crime [stop crime from happening]. Here are some things you can do to **protect yourself** [keep yourself safe] and your **property** [home, land, things you own]:

Don't walk along dark streets **late at night** (e.g., midnight)
    by yourself. [alone]
Lock all doors and windows when you leave the house.
Don't wear a lot of expensive **jewelry** (e.g., rings, necklaces)
    when you go out.
Don't keep your **wallet** in a back pocket or in a pocketbook /
    handbag / purse that does not close tightly.
Leave lights **on** at home when you go out.
Install [put in] a **burglar alarm** (which makes a loud noise
    if someone breaks into your home).
Put money and **valuables** [jewelry, passports, etc.]
    in a **safe**. [a strong metal box that is very hard to open]

wallet

safe

Exercises

These exercises also review some vocabulary from Unit 83.

84.1 Organize the words in the box into three groups: crimes, people, and places.

Example: *Crimes: murder, . . .*

murder	thief	prison	attorney	robbery
burglar	cell	criminal	court	police station
manslaughter	judge	prisoner	jury	shoplifting

84.2 Respond to the statements/questions, confirming the crime in each.

1. A: He broke into the house, didn't he?
   B: Yes, he's been charged with ..*burglary*..................

2. A: He killed his boss?
   B: Yes, he's been charged with ....

3. A: She stole jewelry from that department store while she was shopping, didn't she?
   B: Yes, and she's been charged with ....

4. A: The woman on the motorbike didn't mean to kill the bicyclist.
   B: No, she didn't. That's why she's been charged with ....

5. A: He took the money from her bag?
   B: Yes, but they caught him, and he's been charged with ....

84.3 How safe are you? Circle *yes* or *no*. Notice the number for each answer.

1. Do you often walk in high-crime areas?	yes = 1	no = 0
2. Do you often walk by yourself late at night?	yes = 2	no = 0
3. Do you keep your wallet in a safe place?	yes = 0	no = 1
4. Do you wear an expensive watch or expensive jewelry?	yes = 1	no = 0
5. Do you check doors and windows before you go out?	yes = 0	no = 2
6. Have you installed a burglar alarm?	yes = 0	no = 1
7. Do you leave lights on when you go out?	yes = 0	no = 1
8. Does someone watch your house/apartment while you are out?	yes = 0	no = 2
9. Do you have a safe in your home?	yes = 0	no = 1

Now add up your score: less than 3 = very, very safe; 3–5 = fairly safe; 6–8 = you should be a lot more careful; more than 8 = you are in danger!

84.4 Consider each statement. Do you agree, disagree, or have no opinion? Explain. Discuss your answers with another person if possible.

1. It is good for the police to carry guns.
2. Capital punishment should be the sentence for serious crimes, such as murder.
3. Harsher punishments for criminals will reduce crime.
4. No matter how hard we fight crime, it will always be a problem.

Politics

A Types of government

democracy: Leaders are chosen by the people.
monarchy: A country with a king or queen. In many monarchies (e.g., the United Kingdom, Thailand), the **monarch** [king or queen] does not actually **rule**. [manage the details of government]
dictatorship: One person rules with total power. This person is called a **dictator**.

B Political beliefs

Abstract noun	Personal noun / adjective
conservatism	conservative
socialism	socialist
liberalism	liberal
communism	communist

C Political positions

To describe liberal or conservative people/beliefs, people in the United States use phrases with left, right, and center.

on the left /   **middle of the road /**   **on the right /**
left of center [liberal]   **in the center** [moderate]   **right of center** [conservative]

> *note*   **Liberal** and **conservative** mean different things to different people in different places.

D Elections

In a democracy, people **vote for** [choose in a formal way] the **candidate** they prefer for an **elective office**, e.g., president, senator, governor, mayor. They do this in an **election** [the time when people choose someone by voting for them].
More than 40 percent **voted** for the Democrats.

Usually at least two candidates **run for** an **office** [try to be elected to do a job]. In the United States, national elections **take place / are held** [happen] every four years. Candidates usually belong to a **political party**, e.g., Republican, Democrat, Green Party. After someone is **elected**, he/she **takes office** [begins working in the job].

E Political systems and government

In the United States, **Congress** is the **legislative (law-making)** branch of government. Congress has two houses: the Senate and the House of Representatives. Its **senators** [from the Senate] and **representatives** [from the House of Representatives] are called **congresspersons** and are elected. The President and the leaders of Congress may belong to different political parties. This type of system is called **presidential** government. Other countries, such as the United Kingdom, use **parliamentary** government. In this system, when a political party (or group of parties – a **coalition**) wins a **majority** [51% or more] of seats [official positions in Parliament] in a national election their leader becomes **Prime Minister** [head of government]. This majority party (or coalition) is **in power**. Other parties are **in opposition**.

Exercises

85.1 Complete this word-building table. Use a dictionary to help you, if necessary.

Abstract noun	Person	Adjective
politics	politician	political
dictatorship	....	....
socialism	....	....
conservatism	....	....
liberalism	....	....

85.2 Fill in the blanks to complete this description of the political systems in the U.S. and the U.K. Write one word in each blank.

In the United States, the President and the (1) ....*Congress*...... are elected separately. The political (2) .... with more than 51% of the seats has a (3) .... in Congress. The President may or may not belong to the same party. Presidential (4) .... take place every four years.

In the United Kingdom, national elections are (5) .... at least every five years. (An election could take place sooner.) The political (6) .... in the United Kingdom is different from that in the United States; in the United Kingdom, the political (7) .... that wins a (8) .... of the seats in Parliament will be in power, and their leader becomes (9) .... Minister.

85.3 Answer these questions about a country you know well. If possible, ask someone else the same questions.

1. Which party is in power at the moment?
2. When was this party elected?
3. Who is the leader of this party?
4. Is this person the President or Prime Minister of the country?
5. How many major (important) political parties are there?
6. Do you think the party that is currently in power will win the next election?
7. Would you describe yourself as left of center, right of center, or moderate?
8. Have your political views changed much during your lifetime? Explain.

85.4 **How to increase your English vocabulary in politics:**

Buy three newspapers (in English if possible, or in your own language), and find the same story about politics in each one. Read the articles and underline any words that appear in all of them and any other words you think are important. If you are reading a newspaper in English, try to guess the meaning of these words from the context and then use a dictionary to check. This exercise is equally useful if you read articles in your own language. Use a bilingual dictionary to find the English translation/explanation for your words. Then look them up in an English-English dictionary too.

Bureaucracy

A What is it?

A bureaucracy is an official system with rules and procedures used by **officials** (**bureaucrats**) in an organization or a government. Many people use **bureaucracy** as a negative word, referring to unnecessary rules, waiting in **long lines**, and lots of **documents** and **forms**.

B Documents

Here are documents you might need to **obtain** [get] or show.

certificates: official pieces of paper stating certain facts, e.g., a **birth certificate** gives facts about your birth; a **marriage certificate** states that two people are married
passport: identification that allows you to leave your country and enter others
visa: gives you permission to enter, pass through, or leave a foreign country
driver's license: permits you to drive on public roads
fishing license: allows you to catch fish in a certain state, country, etc.

Officials often **check** [look at / examine] your documents, e.g., the police may check your driver's license; customs officials may check your passport. Sometimes you will be asked for **identification/ID** [any document (e.g., a driver's license) that shows who you are].

Some documents are **valid** [acceptable] for a fixed period of time, e.g., a visa may be for six months. At the end of that time, your visa **runs out / expires** [it finishes / comes to an end]. If you want to stay in the country, you must **renew** it [get a new one for a further period of time]. You can renew a visa, a passport, a **membership card** for a club, etc.

C Forms

Sometimes you need to **fill in / fill out forms** [write information in the spaces].

customs form: a form to fill out when you enter another country by airplane
registration form: a form to fill in when you take a course or go to school
application form: a form for details about yourself as you try to get a job, a credit card, etc.
income tax forms: forms to fill out when you pay your income taxes

Most forms require you to **sign** them [write your signature]. Some also require you to print your name, e.g.:

Signature *Luis Santos*

Print name **Luis Santos**

D Formal language

Forms often ask for such information as:

date of birth (When were you born?)
country of origin (Where do you come from?)
sex/gender (Are you male or female?)
marital status (Are you single or married?)
date of arrival/departure (When did you arrive/leave?)

Exercises

86.1 Write at least two words that can be used before these nouns.

1. ....._identification_..... card   3. .... license
   ....
2. ....   4. .... form
   .... certificate

86.2 Complete these sentences.

1. Will you need to ...._obtain_....... a visa if you go to Canada?
2. Nobody .... my passport when we went from Belgium to France.
3. Could you .... this form, please?
4. They sent the form back to me because I had forgotten to .... it at the bottom.
5. Unfortunately my visa .... next week, so if I want to stay here, I'll have to .... it.
6. You should get there early because there are always long ...., and you may have to wait a long time.
7. I want to take an English course in California, so I wrote to a few schools and asked them to send me an .... form.

86.3 Put a check mark (✓) next to any of these documents that you have.

.... a passport   .... an insurance card
.... a driver's license .... a marriage certificate
.... a birth certificate .... a fishing license

86.4 Complete the paraphrase of each question.

1. What's your date of birth? When ...._were you born?_...............
2. What's your country of origin? Where .... ?
3. What's your sex? Are you .... ?
4. What's your marital status? Are you .... ?
5. What was your date of arrival? When .... ?
6. When's your date of departure? When .... ?

86.5 Here are some common complaints about bureaucracy. Have you ever had these problems? Which ones? Describe your experiences.

1. waiting in one line, then discovering you should be in another line
2. not being able to get through on the telephone
3. delays, e.g., waiting a long time for a new passport
4. being asked to repeat information over and over again, especially over the telephone
5. officials losing information you have given them
6. officials who act like police officers but who are ordinary office workers

Have you had any other problems with bureaucracy? Describe them.

War and peace

A How wars break out [start]

Wars often start because of a **conflict** [strong disagreement] between countries or groups of people about **territory** [land that belongs to one group or country]. Look at the diagram on the right and read the description on the left.

Country A **invades** country B [A enters B by force and in large numbers], and **captures** (also **takes / takes control of**) the city of X. **Soldiers** from country B have to **retreat** [go backward] (≠ **advance**) to the city of Y. A's **military forces** – their **army** and **air force** – then attack the city of Y [take violent action to damage it], but B's soldiers **defend** it [take action to protect it] successfully.

Country A

Country B

B During a war

Country B has asked for help from its **allies** [countries that are friends with country B]. The allies send **aid** [help] in the form of extra **troops** [groups of soldiers] and **supplies** [food and other things that are needed, e.g., blankets and medicine]. Soldiers **shoot/fire** at each other and at **civilians** [ordinary people who are not soldiers], and **bombs fall on** the country's main cities every day. Hundreds of soldiers are either killed or **wounded** [injured].

C Peace talks

For the civilians who are still **alive** [not killed], the situation gets worse. Food supplies **run out** [they are almost gone/finished]. The soldiers get tired, and both sides begin to see that neither side can win the war; they agree to meet for **peace talks** (*pl*). They try to **agree on** a **peace treaty** [an agreement to end the war]. They may agree to a **ceasefire** [an agreement to stop fighting for a period] while they talk. Finally, if the war ends, there is a permanent end to **hostilities** [fighting].

D Terrorism

Terrorism is violent action for political or other reasons. Some **terrorists hijack** [take control of] airplanes, ships, etc. A terrorist may **plant a bomb** [secretly put a bomb] in a public place (e.g., a market, a train station) to kill many civilians. A **suicide bomber** may carry the bomb himself/herself; when it **explodes / blows up**, he/she dies.

Terrorists might take the people inside an airplane or a building as prisoners. These prisoners are called **hostages**. The terrorists say they will **release** the hostages [free them] if the government **meets** their **demands** [gives them things they ask for]. Some governments **negotiate** [discuss things] with terrorists and may meet some of their demands. Other governments may **refuse** [not agree] to negotiate with terrorists.

Exercises

87.1 Match the words on the left with the correct definition on the right.

1. ally
2. release
3. conflict
4. troops
5. invade
6. wound
7. territory
8. cease-fire

a. land controlled by a country
b. an end to fighting
c. permit to go free
d. injure
e. groups of soldiers
f. friendly country
g. strong disagreement
h. enter another country by force, in large numbers

87.2 Complete the sentences.

1. A: Is the soldier dead?
   B: No, he's ...*(still) alive*......

2. A: Will they agree to a ceasefire?
   B: No, they'll continue ....

3. A: Did the army try to advance?
   B: Yes, but they couldn't. They had to .... to the territory they came from.

4. A: Do the people still have lots of food and other supplies?
   B: No, they're beginning to .... of the things they need.

5. A: I heard that a bomb .... in Country A's largest city.
   B: Do you think a war with Country B will .... ?
   A: No. I think terrorists .... the bomb. It wasn't an .... by Country B.

6. A: The terrorists .... the plane.
   B: Are they keeping the passengers as .... ?
   A: Yes. They will .... them only if the government meets their ....

87.3 Writers try not to use the same word over and over again. Underline each word or phrase in this article that restates an earlier idea in bold. e.g., <u>conflict</u> restates "war."

> Caught up in **war**, the people of City Y badly need **food and medicine**. The <u>conflict</u> makes it impossible for trucks to bring in essential supplies. **Ordinary people** are giving some of their food to **the soldiers** who are defending them, but soon the troops and the civilians will all be very hungry. The center of the town is being slowly destroyed. A bomb **blew up** in a busy market and destroyed dozens of shops when it exploded. Soldiers **fire** at anyone who moves. This morning we saw troops shoot at a group of children on their way to school. It was terrible. **Aid** agencies have tried to help the **wounded**, but doctors are not able to reach some badly injured people in the center of the city.

87.4 Answer these questions. If possible, discuss your answers with someone else.

1. Why do terrorists take hostages?
2. Why do some governments always refuse to negotiate with terrorists?

Pollution and the environment

A Important definitions

Many people are worried about the **environment** [the air, water, and land around us] because human activity **harms/damages** it. Some of these activities cause **pollution** [dirt, harmful chemicals, etc.] in air, water, and **soil** [the top layer of the land].
Some problems are:

Weakening of the **ozone/O_3 layer**: a layer of **gas** that protects people from some of the sun's harmful radiation.

The **greenhouse effect**: caused by an increase in some gases (e.g., carbon dioxide / CO_2) in the earth's **atmosphere** [air]. It **traps** the sun's heat [prevents it from leaving the earth]. This effect **contributes to** [partly causes] global warming. (See below.)

global warming: a **long-term** [lasting many years] increase in the **average temperature** of the planet [earth].

acid rain: rain that contains dangerous chemicals; this is caused by smoke from factories.

B Common causes of damage

smoke from **factories**

emissions / exhaust fumes from cars and trucks

industrial **waste** [unwanted material] in rivers, lakes, seas, etc.

gases from refrigerators or from some plastics; they can damage the ozone layer

C How to protect [stop damage to] the environment

- Don't **throw away** bottles, newspapers, etc. Instead, **recycle** them [use again].
- Walk, bicycle, or use **public transportation** (e.g., buses, subways), if possible.
- Don't drive **gas-guzzling** cars [cars that use a lot of gas]. Use **fuel-efficient vehicles** instead.
- **Carpool** [a group of car owners who agree to share their cars; a different car is used for the group each day] to go to work or school.
- Don't **waste resources** [make bad use of resources, e.g., water, gas, wood]. Instead, try to **conserve/save** them [use a small amount, and not waste them].

> *note*   A **resource** is a valuable possession. **Natural resources** include water, air, and forests. **Human resources** include knowledge, skills, and the work people do. These phrases are often plural.

Exercises

88.1 Fill in the blanks to form a compound noun or phrase from page 176.

1. the ....*ozone*........ layer
2. .... rain
3. industrial ....
4. .... transportation
5. .... warming
6. .... fumes
7. the greenhouse ....
8. natural or human ....

88.2 Complete these tables. If necessary, use a dictionary to help you.

Noun	Verb
waste	....*waste*..........
....	conserve
....	destroy
pollution	....
damage	....

Noun	Adjective
damage	....
....	environmental
harm	....
danger	....
....	natural

88.3 Complete the definitions.

1. Conservation is the protection of natural things, e.g., ..*plants*.......... and ....
2. Acid rain is rain that contains dangerous chemicals. It is caused by ....
   ....
3. The ozone layer is a layer of gases that stops dangerous radiation from the sun from
   reaching ....
4. The greenhouse effect takes place when certain gases in the atmosphere trap ....
   ....
5. Global warming is an increase in ....
6. CFCs (chlorofluorocarbons) are a type of chemical that ....
   ....

88.4 If we want to protect the environment, there are certain things we should and shouldn't do.
Complete these two lists.

We should:
......*recycle*...... paper, bottles, and clothes.
.... public transportation instead of cars, if possible.
.... water and energy.

We shouldn't:
.... paper, bottles, and clothes.
.... the ozone layer.
.... water and energy.

88.5 Test your knowledge of conservation issues. *True* or *false*?

1. CFCs protect the ozone layer.
2. Aluminum cans cannot be recycled.
3. A hole in the ozone layer could increase skin cancer.
4. Cutting down trees increases carbon dioxide in the atmosphere.

A Departure

If you have an **e-ticket** [issued via the Internet], you can print your **boarding pass** at a **check-in counter** in the airport. If you have a paper ticket, a **ticket agent** [airline representative] **checks** [examines] your ticket and your **photo ID** [a document that shows who you are]. The agent gives you a boarding pass that shows your **flight gate** number (e.g., Gate 14) and your seat number (e.g., 15C). If you have luggage to **check** [to go in a separate area of the plane], you get a **claim slip** [a piece of paper showing the luggage is yours].

You **go through security**, where your **carry-ons** [small bags you take with you onto the plane] are **screened**. You step through a **metal detector**. Then you go to the gate area for your **flight**. Once you've **boarded** the plane, you can **store** [put] your carry-ons under the seat in front of you or in the **overhead compartment** above you. The plane then **taxis** [moves slowly] toward the **runway**, and when it has permission to **take off** [leave the ground], it **accelerates** [goes faster] along the runway and takes off [begins to fly].

B The flight

The **captain** [the pilot] or the **flight attendants / cabin crew** [people responsible for passengers' safety and comfort] may **announce** [say so everyone can hear]:

- Please **fasten your seat belts** and put your seat in the **upright** position.
- At this time, please turn off and **stow** [put away] any **portable electronic devices**. [electronic articles that you can carry, e.g., a cell phone]
- We are now **cruising** [flying at a steady speed] at an **altitude** [height] of 30,000 feet (9,144 meters).
- We would like to **remind** you [ask you to remember] that this is a nonsmoking flight.

C Arrival

After the plane **lands** [arrives on the ground], it taxis to a gate. After the doors open, you **get off** the plane and walk through the **terminal building** [where passengers arrive and depart] and go to the **baggage claim**, where you get your luggage. After international flights, you then **pass through customs** [where your bags are checked for illegal goods or large purchases]. You get **ground transportation** [a bus, taxi, train, or shuttle] to your **destination**. You can also **rent** a car at most airports.

Exercises

89.1 Complete the words or phrases using words in the box.

off	security	claim
counter	pass	detector
ID	transportation	

1. check-in ..*counter*................
2. baggage ....
3. ground ....
4. boarding ....
5. metal ....
6. photo ....
7. take ....
8. go through ....

89.2 What do you call . . .

1. a place where you can store your carry-ons?   *overhead compartment*
2. the place you pass through after an international flight?
3. a ticket issued to you electronically over the Internet?
4. the bags you bring on the plane with you?
5. the part of the airport where the plane accelerates and takes off?
6. the people who take care of your safety and comfort on the plane?
7. the building at the airport where passengers leave and arrive?
8. the height at which a plane flies?

89.3 Complete part of a letter about an unpleasant flight.

> Dear Tom,
>
> I've just arrived in L.A., but I'm still recovering from a really terrible flight. We
> (1) ..*took off/departed*.. two hours late because of bad weather. Then, over the Rockies,
> we hit more bad weather. The (2) .... announced that we had to
> (3) .... our seat belts and remain seated, which got me worried, and for half
> an hour we (4) .... through a terrible storm. It was still raining and very windy
> when we (5) .... in South Korea, and I was really glad to (6) ....
> the plane and get into the terminal. Fortunately, things have improved since then. I really
> hope the return (7) .... is a lot better.

89.4 Think about the whole experience of flying (from check-in to the time you leave the airport
at your destination). Answer these questions. If possible, discuss your answers with someone else.

1. What is the most interesting part, and what is the most boring part of a flight?
2. Where do you often have delays, and why?
3. Is there any part that frightens or worries you?
4. What do you usually do during flights?
5. Do you always eat the food they serve you?
6. Is there one thing that would improve flying and make the experience better?

Hotels

A Places to stay

a hotel: You pay for your room. Meals are usually extra, except that breakfast may be included. Most hotels have a restaurant and/or a coffee shop. Many hotels offer **suites** [a group of two or three rooms]. Some hotels have "**inn**" [an older word for a small hotel] in their names, e.g., Lake House Inn.

a motel: Less expensive than a hotel. Parking is free; often you can park your car right outside your room. There's usually no restaurant.

a bed and breakfast (B&B): a small, simple hotel or private house that rents rooms. Breakfast is included in the price.

a youth hostel: Very inexpensive; you share a room with other people.

B Staying at a hotel

We stayed at Caesars Palace in Las Vegas for three nights in July, but I **made a reservation / reserved** a **room** [arranged for a room to be held] three months **in advance** [earlier; in other words, in April] because it was the middle of the tourist season [period of time]. When we arrived, we **checked in** at the **registration desk** / at the **front desk**; then the **bellman/porter** took our suitcases up to the room. I gave him a **tip** (n., v.) – $1 for each suitcase. The staff was very friendly, and

housekeeping did a great job of keeping our room clean. We were very **comfortable**. The only problem was with the TV, which didn't **work** [function] very well. (You could also say "There was **something wrong with** the TV.")

C Useful words and expressions

a single room: For one person.

a double room: a room for two people with one large bed or two single beds. One person can stay in a double room, but if there are two, we call it **double occupancy**, e.g., "$50 dollars per person, double occupancy." [The price for the room is $100.]

a non-smoking room/floor: Smoking isn't allowed.

a king-size bed

Could I **make a reservation / reserve a room / book a room** for next Thursday?

Could I have a **wake-up call** at 7 a.m., please? [Could you call to wake me at 7 a.m.?]

Could you **put it on my bill**, please? [add the cost to the bill, e.g., for a meal you order in your room]

I'm **checking out** [leaving the hotel at the end of your stay]. Could **I pay my bill**, please? [pay for everything]

Could you **call** [telephone for] a taxi for me to go to the airport?

Are you **full / fully booked** [completely full, no rooms available] all next week?

Is breakfast **included**? [Does the price include breakfast?]

Exercises

90.1 Here is the first sentence in a person's story about a hotel stay. Put the other sentences in order to complete the story.

....*1*.... I reserved a single room at the hotel.
.... I watched TV until I fell asleep.
.... I paid my bill at the front desk and checked out.
.... I checked in at the registration desk.
.... I went up to my room.
.... I had a wake-up call at seven o'clock.
.... I arrived at the hotel.
.... I got up and took a shower.
.... I had breakfast.
.... A bellman took my luggage upstairs.
.... I gave the bellman a $2 tip.

90.2 **What would you say in these situations?**

1. You want to stay in a hotel for two nights next week. You will share it with one of your friends. Neither of you smokes. You call the hotel. What do you say?
   I'd like to make a reservation for a double room, nonsmoking, for two nights. I'd like two beds, please. We'll be arriving next Thursday and checking out Saturday.

2. You are at the hotel registration desk, and you are planning to leave in about 15 minutes. What could you ask the clerk?
   ....

3. You want to wake up at 7 a.m., but you don't have an alarm clock. You call the front desk. What do you ask?
   ....

4. You have a snack in the hotel lobby restaurant. The waiter asks how you want to pay. What's your reply?
   ....

5. When you turn on the shower in your room, the water comes out very, very slowly. What could you say at the front desk or when you call downstairs?
   ....

6. You want to go to the nearest bank but don't know where it is. What do you ask at the front desk?
   ....

90.3 **You are staying at a good, big-city hotel in a country you know well. What would or wouldn't you expect? If possible, compare your answers with someone else's.**

1. a room without a private bathroom
2. a hair dryer in the bathroom
3. a color television in the room
4. a fax machine in the room
5. a coffeemaker in the room
6. air conditioning in the room

A sightseeing vacation

A Sightseeing

You may **do a little sightseeing** on vacation, or you may do a lot of sightseeing. You might go to a museum or an art gallery, or see/visit:

a palace

a cathedral

a market

a temple

a statue

a famous building

Many people go on a tour of a town (usually on a bus); they can also take a tour of the palace / the cathedral / the art gallery, etc. When you go sightseeing, it helps to buy a guidebook [a book of information for tourists] and a map.

B Tourist activities

go shopping
take photographs/pictures
spend a lot of / lots of **money**
buy **souvenirs** [typical products from the country]
get lost [lose their way]
go out most evenings (e.g., go to a restaurant or dance club)
have a good/great time [enjoy themselves]

C Describing places

The word **place** can describe a building, an area, a town, or a country: Quebec City is a lovely **place** [city], and we found a really nice **place** [hotel, etc.] to stay. The city is full of interesting places [areas/buildings].

Venice is beautiful, but it's always **packed** [very crowded / full] with tourists in summer.
New York is very **cosmopolitan**. [full of people from different countries and cultures]
Puerto Rico has lots of **historical monuments**. [places built long ago, e.g., forts]
Many beautiful cities have become very touristy. [negative: "too much tourism"]
São Paulo is a really **lively** place [full of life and activity], and the nightlife is great.

> *note*   If you want to ask if it is "a good idea" to visit a place, you can use **worth + -ing**:
> A: If I go to Mexico, is it **worth** spending a few days in Guadalajara?
> B: Yes, definitely. And if you want to travel around, it's **worth** renting a car.

Exercises

91.1 Read this letter that John wrote to his family while he was on vacation. Write a word or a phrase in each space.

> July 19th
>
> Hi everyone, I've been in Paris for almost a week now and I'm having a
> (1) ..*great time*.............. . I spent the first few days (2) .... — the Eiffel
> Tower, Notre Dame, and all the usual tourist attractions. Most places are absolutely
> (3) .... with tourists (it's the time of the year, I suppose), so yesterday
> I decided to go (4) .... and bought a few (5) ....
> Today I've been to a couple of very interesting art (6) .... I got
> (7) .... on my way back to the hotel, but it didn't matter because
> I discovered a really fascinating (8) .... with lots of little stalls selling
> just about everything from apples to antiques. I ate in the hotel the first night, but usually I
> (9) .... and have dinner in a restaurant — the food is fantastic. I guess
> I've (10) .... a lot of money, but it's a great place. I've
> (11) .... lots of photos, so you'll be able to see for yourselves when I get
> back home on the 24th.
>
> See you then,
>
> John

91.2 Which of these places do you like to visit when you're on vacation? Explain why.

museums	movie theaters	markets
dance clubs	theme parks	restaurants
ancient ruins	tourist shops	churches/cathedrals/temples
art galleries	castles/palaces	the theater / the opera / the ballet / concerts

91.3 Answer the questions. Use words and phrases from page 182.

1. A: You have quite a few photos of your trip, don't you?
   B: ..*Yes, we took lots of pictures.*.............................

2. A: There's a big mix of people in Toronto, isn't there?
   B: Yes, it's very ....

3. A: Was it very crowded?
   B: Yes, it was ....

4. A: There's a lot to do in the evenings, isn't there?
   B: Yes, the ....

5. A: Did you enjoy yourselves?
   B: Yes, we ....

91.4 Without using one place more than twice, name a town or city you know well that is:

lively	packed with tourists in summer	very touristy
cosmopolitan	famous for its historical monuments	not worth visiting

At the beach and in the country

A Places to stay

When people **go on vacation,** they stay in **various** [different] places. Some go to hotels, and others rent a "vacation home" – a house or **cabin** [a small wooden house, often in the woods or mountains]. Some prefer sleeping in a **tent** at a **campsite** [an outdoor area for staying a short time].

a cabin

a tent

B At the beach

Many people spend their vacation at **beach resorts** [places by the sea for vacationers, e.g., Acapulco, St. Tropez, Boracay], where they can spend most of their time on the beach. Some people enjoy swimming; others love **sunbathing** [lying on the beach in order to get **a suntan**]. If you like sunbathing, you should use **suntan lotion** or **sunscreen/sunblock** to **protect** your **skin.** If you don't have any protection, you may get **sunburned,** which is painful and can be dangerous.

Swimming can also be dangerous if there are **rocks** under the water or if the sea is **rough,** e.g., with big **waves.**

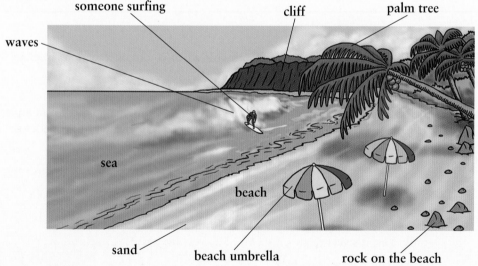

someone surfing   cliff   palm tree

waves

sea

beach

sand   beach umbrella   rock on the beach

C In the country

People who live in cities often like to **get away** [leave the place where they live] on weekends or in the summer and enjoy the **peace and quiet** [calm and tranquility] of **the country** (also called the **countryside**). Some people just like to **put their feet up** [relax and do nothing] and occasionally go for **a stroll** [a slow casual walk], while others enjoy **hiking** [long walks in the country, often across hills and valleys]. And the countryside is a great place to have **a picnic** [eat a prepared meal of cold food outside].

| *note* | Learners sometimes say "I love to be in the nature." This is not correct in English. Instead we say: "I love being close to nature." **or** "I love being in the country." |

Exercises

92.1 Write at least five words beginning with "sun." Use a dictionary for extra ideas. You can check your answers on page 184 and in the index.

sun *tan* ....   sun ....   sun ....

sun ....   sun ....

92.2 Match a word from the left with a word from the right to form six words or phrases.

1. sandy   a. waves
2. suntan   b. bathe
3. beach   c. beach
4. high   d. lotion
5. sun   e. umbrella
6. big   f. cliff

92.3 Now answer these questions.

1. Why do most people go to beach resorts?
   to spend time lying on the beach, sunbathing, and swimming
2. Why do people sunbathe?
3. Why do people use sunblock or sunscreen?
4. How does it feel if you get sunburned?
5. What sport requires big waves?

92.4 Write a logical word or phrase in each blank in this paragraph.

I live and work in the city, but I like to (1) ...*get away*............... on weekends, if possible. My parents have a small house in the (2) ...., about 60 miles to the north, and it's a great place to go if you want some peace and (3) .... In the summer, you can just (4) .... by the pool during the hottest part of the day, then in the evening go for a (5) .... through the town or over the fields. Sometimes we go out for the whole day and have a (6) .... somewhere, by the lake or near the forest.

92.5 Complete each sentence by adding one word.

1. Would you prefer a vacation at a beach ...*resort*............. or in the country?
2. Would you prefer to stay in one place, or would you rather [prefer to] go to .... places?
3. Would you prefer to stay in a hotel or outside in a .... ?
4. Would you prefer to stroll through town or go .... in the country?
5. Would you prefer somewhere that is lively, or would you rather go to a place where there is .... and quiet?

Look at the questions again. Which would you prefer? If possible, discuss your answers with someone else.

Time

A Prepositions: *at, on, in*

at a specific time: at 8 o'clock, at 3:30, at midnight
on a day: on Monday, on July 14, on the third day, on weekdays/weekends
in a period: in May, in 2001, in the morning/afternoon/evening [but: at night]

B Words that are often confused

I will stay here **until/till** she calls. [I will go after she calls.]
I will be in the office **until/till** 4 o'clock. [I will leave the office at 4:00.]
I will be in the office **by** 4 o'clock. [I will arrive at the office not later than 4:00.]

I've worked in this office **for** six months. (**for** + a period of time. This tells you "how long.")
I've worked in this office **since** May. (**since** + a point in time, i.e., a day, year, etc. This tells you the starting point)

I worked for a newspaper **during** my senior year in college. (This tells you "when.")

I worked for a newspaper **for** one year. (*not* I worked for a newspaper during one year.)
I'm going back to Brazil **in** 10 days. [10 days from now]
We arranged our next meeting **for** April 7. [to be on April 7]

> *note* "**During** a period" may mean a part of that period or the whole period, e.g., "during my senior year in college" can mean part of that year or the whole year. The context usually makes it clear, but if we want to stress or emphasize that an action occupied the whole period, we often use **throughout**, e.g., "It rained **throughout** the night." [It didn't stop raining.]

C Approximate times: past and future

I've known my dentist **for ages** [for a long time], but I haven't had a checkup **recently/lately**. (e.g., in the last few months)
I haven't seen Tom **recently/lately**. (e.g., in the last few days or weeks)
I used to go to a Korean dentist, but that was **a long time ago**. (e.g., 5–10 years ago)
My sister went to the dentist **the other day**. [a few days ago]
This temporary tooth will be OK **for the time being**. [for now / until I get a permanent one]

D Periods of time

There are 60 **seconds** in a minute, 60 minutes in an hour, 24 hours in a day, 7 days in a week, about 4 weeks in a **month**, about 52 weeks in a year, 10 years in a **decade**, 100 years in a **century**, 1,000 years in a **millennium**.

E Time passing: *take* and *last*

My English course **lasts** 10 weeks. [It continues for 10 weeks.]
How long does the movie **last**? [How long is it from the beginning to the end?]
It **takes** me [I need] half an hour to get to school.
We can walk, but it'll **take** [we'll need] a long time.

Exercises

93.1 Complete the paragraph with *at*, *on*, or *in*.

> There's one bus from the city that gets here (1) ...*at*... 10:00 (2) .... the morning, and then another that arrives (3) .... 4:00 (4) .... the afternoon. That's (5) .... weekdays, but (6) .... weekends the schedule is a little different. (7) .... Saturday there are still two buses, but the second one arrives (8) .... 5:30. (9) .... Sunday there is just the one bus (10) .... 2:00. And (11) .... the winter, the buses don't run at all (12) .... Sundays.

93.2 Circle the correct answers.

1. The teacher told us to finish our homework (by)/ until Monday.
2. We can't leave by / until the others get back.
3. I've been in the army for / since I was 18.
4. They've worked here for / during six months.
5. She's going back to Thailand in / until three months.
6. He left the office during / throughout the lunch break.
7. I made a reservation at the restaurant by / for next Saturday. I hope that's OK.
8. It was hot by / throughout August; we didn't have one day under 90 degrees.

93.3 Complete these sentences with a number that makes sense to you. Don't worry if you don't know the exact answer.

1. The best athletes can run 100 meters in less than ....*10*........ seconds.
2. The Olympic Games usually last about .... weeks.
3. Picasso was born in the .... th century.
4. President John F. Kennedy died in 1963. That's .... years ago.
5. It takes approximately .... hours to fly from Tokyo to New York.

93.4 Replace the underlined time expressions with approximate time expressions.

1. I went to the library <u>a few days ago</u>.   *the other day*
2. This dictionary isn't great, but it'll be OK <u>until I'm more advanced</u>.
3. I haven't been to the movies <u>for the last three weeks</u>.
4. And I haven't been to a concert <u>for three or four years</u>.
5. I went to Hawaii with my parents, but that was <u>10 years ago</u>.

93.5 Complete these sentences about yourself.

1. On weekdays I usually get up at .... and leave home at ....
2. I always brush my teeth in .... and at ....
3. I usually take a vacation in ....
4. I have been in my current school/job for ....
5. I have been studying English since ....
6. It takes me .... to get to school/work.

A Cardinal numbers

379 = three **hundred** (and) seventy-nine
5,084 = five **thousand** (and) eighty-four
2,860 = two thousand eight hundred (and) sixty
470,000 = four hundred (and) seventy thousand
2,550,000 = two **million**, five hundred (and) fifty thousand
3,000,000,000 = three **billion**

> **note** There is no plural **-s** after hundred, thousand, million, and billion when these words are part of a number. By themselves, they can be plural, e.g., **thousands** of people; **millions** of insects.

B Ordinal numbers and dates

We write **March 4** (or March 4th), but say **March (the) fourth** *or* **the fourth of March**.
1905 = **nineteen oh five**
2010 = **two thousand (and) ten** *or* **twenty ten**

C Fractions and decimals

1 1/4 = one and **a quarter / a fourth**   1.75 = one **point** seven five
1 1/2 = one and **a half**   1.25 = one point two five
1 3/4 = one and **three quarters/fourths**   1.5 = one point five
1 1/3 = one and **a third**   1.33 = one point three three

D Percentages

26% = twenty-six **percent**
More than 50% is the **majority**; less than 50% is the **minority**.

E Arithmetic

There are four basic processes for doing [calculating] **mathematics** / math problems:

+ addition   6 + 4 = 10 (six **plus/and** four **equals/is** ten)
– subtraction   6 – 4 = 2 (six **minus** four equals/is two)
x multiplication   6 x 4 = 24 (six **times / multiplied by** four equals/is twenty-four)
÷ division   4 ÷ 2 = 2 (four **divided by** two equals/is two)

F Saying *0* or saying *zero*

telephone numbers: 555-0724 = five five five, **oh** seven two four
mathematics: 0.7 = **zero** point seven / point seven; 6.02 = six point **oh** two
temperature: –10 degrees = ten (degrees) below **zero** / minus ten (degrees)
most sports games: 2–0 = two (to) **nothing** / two oh / two (to) zero

G Numbers in street addresses

Buildings on one side of a street usually have odd numbers (e.g., 1, 3, 55, 179). The buildings on the other side usually have even numbers (e.g., 2, 4, 68, 282).

Exercises

94.1 How do you say these numbers in English? Write your answers after each one.

1. 462 .*four hundred (and) sixty-two*.....................................
2. 2 ½ ....
3. 2,345 ....
4. 6.75 ....
5. 0.25 ....
6. 1,250,000 ....
7. 10.04 ....
8. 47% ....
9. September 10 ....
10. July 4 ....
11. 555-8077 (phone number) ....
12. –5° Fahrenheit ....
13. In 1903 ....
14. In 2036 ....

Now practice saying them. If possible, record yourself saying them and then record someone who speaks English very well. Listen to both. How do you sound?

94.2 Correct the mistakes in these sentences.

1. After the game, I heard the crowd was over twenty ~~thousands.~~ *thousand*
2. We arrived on the ten September.
3. I graduated in two oh oh nine.
4. My birthday is thirty-one August.
5. The class is two and half hours long.

94.3 Write answers to these math problems.

1. 23 and 36 is ..*59*...... .
2. 24 times 8 equals ....
3. 80 minus 20 is ....
4. 65 divided by 13 equals ....
5. Add 10 and 6, multiply by 8, then subtract 40, and divide by 11. What number do you get? ....
6. Divide 33 by 11, multiply by 7, add 10, and subtract 16. What number is left? ....

94.4 Answer these questions. Write your answers in words.

1. When were you born?
2. How much do you weigh?
3. What is your apartment or house number? Is that an odd or even number?
4. What is the approximate population of your city or town?
5. What is the approximate population of your country?

Distance, size, and dimension

A · Distance

These are common ways of asking about distance, with typical replies.

How far is it?	Not very **far**. The closest one is about **a mile away**.
Is it **a long way**?	No, **just around the corner**. / No, **a short walk**. [very near]
Is it very far?	No, not far. / No, just **a five- or ten-minute walk**. [fairly near]
Is it a long way?	Yeah, **a fairly long way**. / Yeah, over a mile.
Is it very far?	Yes, it's a long way. / Yes, it's miles. / Yes, it's **too far to walk**.

B · Size and dimension

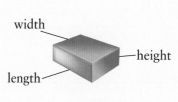

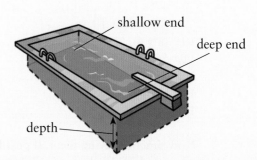

shallow end

deep end

width

height

length

depth

We can describe size using the nouns above or the adjectives formed from them, like this:

What's the **length / width / height / depth / size** of . . . ? *or* How **long / wide / high / tall / deep / big** is . . . ?

> **note**
> • Notice that in the answer to these questions, an adjective follows the measurement: The yard is about 30 feet **wide**. [**The width** is about 30 feet (9 meters).]
> • We generally use **tall** to describe people, trees, and buildings; and **high** to describe mountains. We also say **high-rise** buildings.

C · Size in people and things

a **tall** girl [≠ a **short** girl]
a **fat** person [≠ a **thin/slim** person] (See Unit 47 for more details.)
a **long** book [many pages; ≠ a **short** book]
a **deep** lake [many feet deep; ≠ a **shallow** lake]

a **wide** road [≠ a **narrow** road]

a **thick** book [≠ a **thin** book]

> **note**
> We can use **big** or **large** to describe size in North American English, but not **great**. For English-speaking people, **great** (informal) often means "wonderful," e.g., a **great** movie. But we can use **great** before **big** to say that something is very big, e.g., a **great big** dog. If you want to ask about size in clothes, you can say: **What size are you?** *or* **What size (shoes) do you take/wear?** If you don't know, you need someone to **measure** you.

Exercises

95.1 Think about the place you are in now and answer these questions, using some of the expressions from page 190.

1. How far is it to the nearest store?
2. How far is it to a bank?
3. Is it very far to the nearest bus stop?
4. Is it very far to a post office?
5. Is it a long way to the nearest swimming pool?
6. Is the next big town or city very far away?
7. How far are the train tracks?
8. Is it far to the downtown area?

If possible, ask someone else the same questions and compare your answers.

95.2 Write down eight different questions you could ask about the distance, size, or dimensions of the person and things in the pictures.

 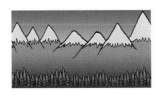  

95.3 Answer each question in the negative. Use "no" plus the opposite of the statement in the question.

1. A: Is it a long movie?
   B: No, *it's pretty short.*..

2. A: Is he fat?
   B: No, ...

3. A: The water's fairly deep, isn't it?
   B: No, ...

4. A: Their office is in a low building, isn't it?
   B: No, ...

5. A: Is the road very wide at that point?
   B: No, ...

6. A: It's a pretty thick book, isn't it?
   B: No, ...

7. A: She's fairly tall, isn't she?
   B: No, ...

8. A: They live in a small place, don't they?
   B: No, ...

Shapes, colors, and patterns

A   Shapes

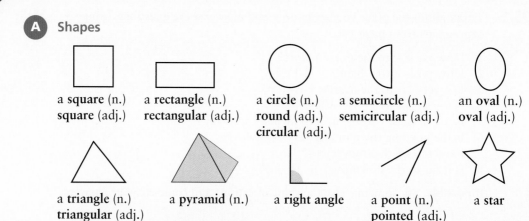

a **square** (n.)   a **rectangle** (n.)   a **circle** (n.)   a **semicircle** (n.)   an **oval** (n.)
square (adj.)   **rectangular** (adj.)   **round** (adj.)   **semicircular** (adj.)   **oval** (adj.)
                                         circular (adj.)

a **triangle** (n.)   a **pyramid** (n.)   a **right angle**   a **point** (n.)   a **star**
triangular (adj.)   **pointed** (adj.)

a **square** box, a **round** table, a **pointed** end, a **rectangular** field, an **oval** shape

> **note**   We can also form adjectives to describe shapes in this way: The ball was
> **egg-shaped**; a **heart-shaped** wedding cake; a **diamond-shaped** pin.

B   Colors

You will already know most of the common colors. Here are some that are less common:

Mix **black** and **white** to make **gray**. Mix **red** and **blue** to make **purple**.
Mix **green** and blue to make **turquoise**. **Pink** is a color between red and white.
Beige is a very light **brown** with some **yellow** in it.

C   Shades of color [degrees and variation of color]

turquoise   beige
pink
purple
gray

She bought a   He was wearing   My new shirt
dark green skirt. **light** blue jeans. is **pale** yellow.

> **note**   With some colors, we use **pale** rather than **light** (e.g., pale yellow, pale pink)
> because they are already light colors.

D   Patterns (also called designs)

striped shirt   **plaid** skirt   **floral** tie   **checked** dress

E   Use of the suffix -ish

When we want to say that a shape is almost round or a color is nearly green, we can express
this idea by adding the suffix *-ish*: a **roundish** face; a **greenish** tie; a **yellowish** color.

Exercises

96.1 Describe these pictures using the correct noun and adjective.

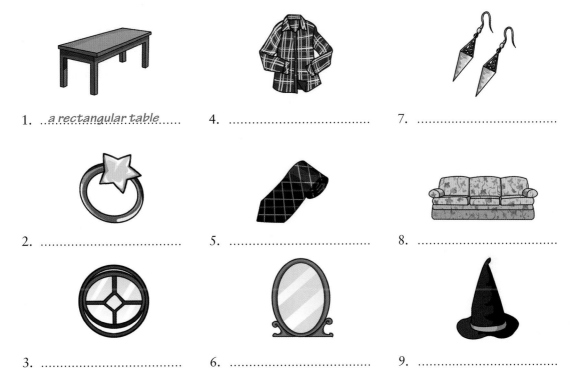

1. *..a rectangular table......*   4. ....   7. ....

2. ....   5. ....   8. ....

3. ....   6. ....   9. ....

96.2 What object is described in each sentence?

1. It has a point at one end, and that's the end you use to write with.   *a pencil or pen*
2. It is rectangular and usually green. There are lines on it, and people play a game on it.
3. At certain times of the month it's completely round. At other times, it's closer to a semicircle.
4. It's orange, fairly long, and usually pointed at one end. You eat it.
5. It can look dark blue, light blue, turquoise, or even dark green. It contains water.
6. It's oval-shaped, white or beige or light brown in color. It has a hard outside. The inside, often fried, is a common breakfast food.
7. It's usually made of wire or plastic. The bottom part is triangular. At the top there is another piece in the shape of a semicircle. You put shirts or jackets on the triangular part and hang them up.
8. It has four equal sides and four right angles.
9. It has three sides and three angles. No more than one angle can be a right angle.
10. It's grayish on the outside, pink on the inside, it swims, and you eat it.

96.3 Describe what you are wearing, including the exact color of everything. Use a bilingual dictionary as necessary to find the names of colors or designs.

Abbreviations and shortened words

A Letters or words?

UN	United Nations	PC	personal computer
U.S.A.	United States of America	ATM	automated teller machine
EU	European Union	ID	identification
HD	high definition	DVD	digital video disk

Other abbreviations are read as words:

OPEC /'oʊˌpek/ Organization of Petroleum Exporting Countries
PIN /pɪn/ personal identification number

B Written forms only

Some abbreviations are written forms only; they are still pronounced as full words.

Mr. /'mɪs·tər/ [any man]   St. /seɪnt/ (as in Saint Mark's Square)
Mrs. /'mɪs·əz/ [a married woman]   St. /striːt/ (as in Main Street)
Ms. /mɪz/ [a woman who may be   Dr. /'dɑk·tər/ (Doctor)
          single or married]

C Abbreviations as part of the language

Some abbreviations from Latin are used commonly in English.

Abbreviation	Pronunciation	Meaning*	Latin
etc.	/etˈset·ə·rə or etˈse·trə/	and so on	et cetera
e.g.	E-G	for example	exempli gratia
i.e.	I-E	that is to say / in other words	id est

*Note: We say them as:

"et cetera" *or* "and so on"
"e.g." (as letters) *or* "for example"
"i.e." (as letters) *or* "in other words"

D Shortened words

Some English words can be shortened, especially in spoken English. Here are some common ones:

phone (telephone)	bye (goodbye)	math (mathematics)	bike (bicycle)
cell (cell phone)	board (blackboard)	plane (airplane)	TV (television)
photo (photograph)	mom (mother)	dad (father)	gym (gymnasium)
paper (newspaper)	rep (representative)	ad (advertisement)	exam (examination)
the flu (influenza)	lab (laboratory)	vet (veterinarian)	

[an illness like a cold   [a special room
 but more serious]   where scientists work]

Exercises

97.1 Complete each item to show what the letters stand for. Cover page 194.

1. EU = European ..*Union*..........
2. PC = personal ....
3. U.S.A. = United ....
4. ATM = automated ....
5. UN = United ....

6. OPEC = Organization of
   Petroleum ....
7. PIN = personal ....
8. HD = high ....

97.2 Rewrite this note to a family friend. Make it less formal by using shortened words and abbreviations where possible.

> Michael,
>
> Peter had a mathematics examination this afternoon, and then he had to take his bicycle to the repair shop, so he'll probably get home a little late. You can watch television or read the newspaper while you're waiting for him. If there's a problem (for example, if Doctor Brown calls about the influenza vaccination), my office telephone number is next to the photographs in the dining room. I've got my cell phone with me too. Peter's father and I should be home by about five o'clock.
>
> Margaret (Peter's mother)

97.3 What abbreviations in written English are often used for these words or phrases?

1. and so on   *etc.*
2. for example
3. Street

4. in other words
5. Mister
6. Doctor

97.4 Complete these sentences with abbreviations or shortened words.

1. If you go to any of the Mediterranean islands, ...*e.g.*......., Sardinia, or Corsica, it's a good idea to rent a car.
2. When you pay by check in a store, they usually ask you for some ....
3. A: Do you need to order more supplies?
   B: Yes, I'll call our sales .... today.
4. I asked my teacher to write the word on the ....
5. If you go to the bookstore, you can buy books, pens, writing paper, ...
6. I could not reach our director last week. She had the .... , so she was out of the office.
7. To sell my car, I put an .... in the paper. I got three replies in one day.
8. There's a great nightclub on Main .... , but you can't get in unless you're of legal age, ... , over 21.
9. I have to say .... now. I have to go home and make dinner.
10. I took a .... to Italy and went to Venice. I saw .... Mark's Square.

Unit 98

Signs, warnings, and notices

A   Informative signs

Some signs give you information:

OUT OF ORDER

for a machine that is not working, usually in a public place, e.g., an ATM or a public toilet.

NO VACANCY

outside a motel. It means the motel is full – there are no rooms left.

SOLD OUT

outside a theater or concert hall. There are no tickets left – all the tickets are sold.

B   Don't do this!

Some signs or notices tell you not to do certain things:

C   Watch out!

Some signs or notices are warnings – they tell you to be careful because something bad may happen:

FRAGILE HANDLE WITH CARE

[Be careful; this will break easily.]

CAUTION! WET FLOOR

[Be careful not to slip on the floor; it was just washed.]

WATCH YOUR STEP

[Be careful not to fall, e.g., when getting off a bus.]

BEWARE OF PICKPOCKETS

[Be careful; there are people here who will steal things from your bag or pocket without you knowing.]

D   Notices and warnings on food and medicine

Keep this and all other medications out of the reach of children.
[Don't leave medicines in a place where children can get to them.]

Do not exceed recommended dosage.
[Don't use more of this medicine or take it more often than your doctor or the label on the package says.]

Not to be taken by mouth.
[Do not eat or drink this.]

Best if used before May 5.
[Don't eat or drink this after the date.]

Exercises

98.1 Complete these signs, warnings, and notices without looking at page 196. (Sometimes there is more than one possibility.)

1. BEWARE OF ..*pickpockets*..........

2. WATCH YOUR ....

3. DO NOT ....

4. NO ....

5. THANK YOU for ....

6. HANDLE WITH ....

7. OUT OF ....

8. KEEP ....

98.2 Where would you expect to see these signs, warnings, and notices?

1. **No vacancy** *outside a motel*

2. Best if used by July 31

3. **No Parking**

4. **NOT TO BE TAKEN BY MOUTH**

5. **OUT OF ORDER**

6. **Sold out**

7. FRAGILE

8. Keep off the grass

98.3 What signs, warnings, or notices are possible in each of these places?

1. a zoo *Do not feed the animals.*
2. a waiting area in a busy airport
3. the door of a hotel or motel room at 8 o'clock in the morning
4. in front of a driveway
5. inside a theater
6. on a bus

98.4 Now write some different signs of your own. Think of six possible signs, warnings, and notices you could put in one of these places:

1. a school
2. a hospital
3. a language school
4. a place where people work, e.g., bank, factory, office

Where would you put these signs? If possible, do this activity with another person or show it to another person.

98.5 Find six more signs, warnings, and notices in the next week. In a notebook, write down what they say. If a sign is not in English, write an English translation.

Vague language

In spoken English, we often use words that are **vague** [not clear/precise/exact].

I have a **vague idea** where it is. [I know the general area, but I don't know exactly where.]
I have a **vague memory** of the game. [I can remember some of it, but not very clearly.]

A Thing(s)

- To refer to actions, ideas, and facts:
  The main **thing** [fact] about John is that he likes everything to be well organized.
  Hitting that child was a terrible **thing** [action] to do.
- To refer to *countable* objects (often the speaker and listener know what the object is, or the speaker has forgotten the name of it at the moment of speaking):
  What's that **thing** (bicycle) doing in the house?
  Put those **things** (cups and saucers) in the cabinet.
- To refer to a general situation:
  How are **things** at school? [school in general]
  Lately, **things** have been going really well. [life in general]

B Stuff

We sometimes use **stuff** *(informal)* to refer to *uncountable* nouns (or a group of countable nouns) when it is not necessary to be precise and give the exact name. Often the listener knows what the speaker is talking about.

Just leave that **stuff** [different items of clothes] on the floor. I'll clear it up.

I play guitar but not much classical **stuff**. [music]

C Kind of / Sort of . . .

The walls are **kind of** yellow. [not exactly yellow, but similar to yellow]
I'm **kind of** hungry. [a little bit hungry]
He gets . . . uh . . . **sort of** . . . nervous when you mention the word *exams*. [a little bit nervous]
A: Did you like the concert?
B: Yeah, **sort of / kind of**.

| note | Kind of and sort of are often used interchangeably. |

D Approximately

These words have the same meaning, but **approximately** is more formal than the others:

The train should arrive in **approximately** 20 minutes.
It's **about** three miles to the house.
I'll see you **around** noon.
We are expecting 100 guests, **more or less**.

Exercises

99.1 What could *thing(s)* and *stuff* mean in these sentences? Use a dictionary or speak with another person to get ideas if necessary.

1. I never wear that stuff; it has such a strong smell.   *perfume or after-shave lotion*
2. This thing is stuck in the lock.
3. We don't need these things. We can eat the fried chicken with our fingers.
4. What's that white stuff called that you mix with water to make bread?
5. Can you turn that thing off? That music is giving me a headache.
6. I couldn't get any more stuff in my suitcase.
7. It's a wonderful thing and keeps my young children occupied for hours.
8. It's good stuff. My hair feels really soft, and it didn't cost a lot.

99.2 Add a word or a phrase in each blank to make this conversation less precise and more natural.

A: How many people were at the conference?
B: .... 400.
A: Did you enjoy it?
B: Yes, ...
A: You don't seem very sure.
B: Well, there were some good .... , but it was
.... long.
A: And how did John's talk go?
B: Well, he was .... nervous at the beginning, but then he got more confident, and I think it went really well.
A: Did he have a big audience?
B: .... seventy-five.
A: That's pretty good.
B: I think John was .... disappointed – he wanted
.... a hundred.

99.3 Reply to each of these questions with a vague response.

1. A: Was the party fun?
   B: Yeah, *kind of* ....

2. A: Did you get everything you wanted?
   B: Yeah, ...

3. A: Did you say the walls were blue?
   B: Yeah, ...

4. A: Will there be twenty chairs in the room?
   B: Yeah, ...

5. A: Is it a serious movie?
   B: Yeah, ...

6. A: Do you remember your fifth birthday party?
   B: Yeah, I have ....

Formal and informal English

Your dictionary probably marks some words or phrases as *formal* and others as *informal*. You need to be careful with informal language because it may not be appropriate in certain situations.

A Formal English

Formal English is more common in writing than in speaking. It is found in signs, notices, business letters, and legal English. You will also hear examples in spoken English (announcements in airports, some speeches, etc.)

Café notice: Only food **purchased** [bought] here may be eaten on **the premises** [here].
Police statement in court: I **apprehended** [stopped] him outside the supermarket.
Theater announcement: The play will **commence** [start] in two minutes.
Formal business situation: The meeting will **resume** [start again] this afternoon at 2 p.m.
Lawyer: My client had a broken ankle. **Thus** [so] he could not have driven the car.
Formal letter: I **regret to inform you** [I am sorry to say] that we **are unable to** [can't] **grant** [give] you . . .
Announcements: If you **require** [need] **further assistance** [more help], please contact . . .
Outside a restaurant: Parking for **patrons** [customers] only.

B Informal English

In general, informal language is more common in spoken English than in written English. Certain types of language are often informal:

- Most uses of *get* are informal. (See Unit 28 for more details.)
- Many phrasal verbs are informal. (See Units 22 and 23 for more details.)
- Many idioms are informal. (See Unit 13 for more details.)

Here are some examples using words from above and other common informal words:

Those **kids** [children or young people] like to **hang out** at the park. [spend a lot of time at a place]
We always keep a first-aid kit **handy**. [nearby, easy to reach]
I offered the **guy** [man] 30 **bucks** [dollars] for the **bike** [bicycle], but he wasn't interested.
I **bet** [am almost sure] we'll **get** [obtain] the money **pretty** [fairly] soon.
What's up? [What's the matter? / What's new?]
Wanna (Want to) go out? [Would you like to go out?]
Do you **feel like** going home? [Do you want to go home?]
Take care. [Good-bye.]

Slang is a form of *very* informal language (e.g., **dude** = "man, guy"). Many people think slang words are impolite and unacceptable in most situations.

Exercises

100.1 Put the words on the left into the correct columns in the table.

purchase handy
kids resume
thus guy
five bucks commence
apprehend patron

Formal	Informal
purchase	

For each of the words below, find a synonym from the table above.

buy ...*purchase*.... catch/stop .... dollar ....
man .... easy to reach .... start again ....
therefore .... customer .... children ....

100.2 Rewrite these sentences in less formal English.

1. Is that your bicycle? *Is that your bike?*
2. I think the show will commence fairly soon.
3. Would you like to go out for dinner?
4. What's the matter?
5. The man in the market sold me this ring for 20 dollars.
6. Where did you purchase that book?
7. They will never apprehend him.
8. On our vacation, we're going to spend time at the pool every day.
9. Where did the children obtain that video game?

100.3 Rewrite this letter in more formal English.

> Hi Mr. Kim:
>
> We're really sorry to say that we can't lend you the sum of 500 bucks that you asked for, but maybe we could give you a loan for some of the money. Sorry, dude. If you still want this, maybe you could call up our assistant manager. She could talk to you about it.
>
> Take care,

100.4 Use your dictionary to find out if the underlined words are formal or informal. Write the meaning.

1. I thought the movie was a drag. *(informal) "boring / a bore"*
2. There is no public restroom on the premises.
3. He talks too much; I wish he would shut up.
4. Someone ripped off my bag.
5. Smoking is prohibited.

Phonetic symbols

Vowel sounds

Symbol	Examples		Symbol	Examples
/ɑ/	hot, father, sock, star		/ɔ:/	saw, thought, ball
/æ/	hat, last, bag		/ɔɪ/	boy, join
/ɑɪ/	bite, ride, sky, height		/oʊ/	go, boat, below
/ɑʊ/	house, now		/ʊ/	put, good
/e/	let, head, said		/u:/	food, blue, shoe, lose
/eɪ/	late, name, say		/ʌ/	*stressed*: sun, love, under
/i:/	sleep, me, happy		/ə/	*unstressed*: alone, label, collect, under
/ɪ/	fit, pin, if		/ɜ/	*before* /r/: bird, turn, earn

Consonant sounds

Symbol	Examples		Symbol	Examples
/b/	bid, rob		/r/	read, carry, far, card – *In some parts of North America is not always pronounced at the ends of words or before consonants.*
/d/	did, under			
/ð/	this, mother, breathe			
/dʒ/	judge, gentle			
/f/	foot, safe, laugh		/s/	see, mouse, recent
/g/	go, rug, bigger		/ʃ/	shoe, cash, nation
/h/	house, behind, whole		/t/	team, meet, matter, sent
/j/	yes, useful, music		/tʃ/	church, rich, catch
/k/	kick, cook, quick		/θ/	think, both
/l/	look, ball, feel, pool		/v/	visit, save
/ᵊl/	settle, middle – a *syllabic consonant*		/w/	watch, away, wear; which, where – *Many North American speakers pronounce* /w/ *in such words and many pronounced* /hw/.
/m/	many, some, damp			
/n/	none, sunny, sent			
/ᵊn/	kitten, button, mountain – *a syllabic consonant*		/z/	zoo, has, these
/ŋ/	ring, think, longer		/ʒ/	measure, beige, Asia
/p/	peel, soap, pepper			

Pronunciation problems

when "a" is /eɪ/	*when "i" is /ɑɪ/*	*when "o" or "oo" is /ʌ/*	*when "u" is /ʌ/*
patient	pilot	glove	punctual
Asia	virus	oven	luggage
dangerous	dial	month	hungry
pavement	hepatitis	front	discuss
bacon	minus	color	function
phrase	license	government	publish
engaged	diet	dozen	customs
came	striped	flood	luck
lately	tiny	blood	corrupt

When ow is /oʊ/, e.g., throw, blow, show, know, elbow

When ou or ow is /ɑʊ/, e.g., round, drought, blouse, now, towel, shower

When ou is /uː/, e.g., soup, group, through, wound *(n.)*, souvenir, routine

When ou is /ʌ/, e.g., cousin, couple, trouble, tough, rough, enough

When ir, or, or ur is /ɜr/, e.g., bird, shirt, worth, work, purple, burn, burglary, curtain

When er or or is /ər/, e.g., under, cover, mother, advisor, color, doctor

When a, au, or aw is /ɔː/, e.g., tall, fall, cause, audience, exhausted, draw, raw, law

When a or o is /ɑ/, e.g., calm, father, wallet, star, hot, stopped, possible

When a or u is /ɪ/, e.g., busy, business, damage, orange*, minutes*, lettuce*

When o is /uː/, e.g., move, prove, improve, lose, choose, loose

When ea is /e/, e.g., dreadful, jealous, health, dead, bread, instead, pleasant, weather, weapon

* These sounds may be pronounced /ɪ/ or /ə/

Silent letters (the underlined letters are silent):

island, knee, knife, know, knock, knowledge, wrong, wrist, muscle, castle, whistle, fasten, listen, bomb, lamb, thumb, comb, scissors, science, psychology, honest, hour, cupboard, answer, guess, aisle, half, should, would, Christmas, mortgage

Disappearing syllables (the underlined letters often disappear or are reduced to a /ə/):

fattening, miserable, temperature, vegetable, every, several, comfortable, favorite, laboratory, chocolate, restaurant

Problem pairs:

quite /kwɑɪt/ *and* quiet /ˈkwɑɪ·ət/   desert /ˈdez·ərt/ *and* dessert /dəˈzɜrt/

soup /suːp/ *and* soap /soʊp/   lose /luːz/ *and* loose /luːs/

Note: The pronunciation of these letters at the end of words is often like this:

-ous /əs/, e.g., famous, dangerous, unconscious, ambitious, cautious, jealous

-age /ɪdʒ/, e.g., luggage, baggage, village, damage, cabbage, bandage, message, manage

-able /ə·bəl/, e.g., comfortable, reliable, suitable, unbreakable, vegetable, fashionable, miserable

-tory, -tary /tə·ri/, e.g., directory, history, documentary

-ture /tʃər/, e.g., picture, signature, departure, capture, temperature, literature, feature

-ate /eɪt/ at the end of verbs, e.g., educate, operate, communicate

-ate /ət/ or /ɪt/ at the end of nouns and adjectives, e.g., graduate, approximate, certificate

Index

dislike (v.)
illegal
illogical
impatient
impolite
impossible
incorrect
informal
invisible
irregular
irrelevant
irresponsible
misspell
misunderstand
overcharge
oversleep
prefix
redo
reopen
unable
undressed
unemployed
unfriendly
unhappy
unlike
unlock
unpack

Unit 7

actor
administration
artist
darkness
director
discussion
driver
economist
education
educator
explanation
guitarist
happiness
improvement
information
journalist
management
manager
posting
programmer
punctuality
selection
similarity
spelling
stupidity
suffix

translator
weakness
writer

Unit 8

attractive
careful
careless
cloudy
comfortable
comprehensible
creative
dangerous
dirty
drinkable
famous
flexible
foggy
helpful
homeless
incomprehensible
industrial
inedible
inflexible
knowledgeable
musical
painful
painless
political
practical
reliable
sunny
thoughtful
thoughtless
unbreakable
uncomfortable
undrinkable
unreliable
useful
useless
washable

Unit 9

answer (n., v.)
bank (n.)
bank on (v.)
break (n., v.)
call (n., v.)
chat (n., v.)
cost (n., v.)
diet (n., v.)
dream (n., v.)
drink (n., v.)

file (n., v.)
groceries
guess (n., v.)
laugh (n., v.)
look (n., v.)
package (n., v.)
pull (n., v.)
push (n., v.)
rain (n., v.)
reply (n., v.)
rest (n., v.)
smell (n., v.)
smile (n., v.)
tag (n., v.)
taste (n., v.)
turn (n., v.)
wait (n., v.)
walk (n., v.)

Unit 10

admissions office
alarm clock
babysitter
bathroom
bedroom
brother-in-law
cell phone
coffee break
coffee cup
coffee shop
compound noun
credit card
dining room
dress shoes
DVD player
father-in-law
front office
haircut
income tax
laptop
light bulb
math teacher
mother-in-law
paper clip
post office
running shoes
stop sign
sunglasses
tennis shoes
textbook
toothbrush
traffic light
washing machine
wedding ring

Oh, that's awful / bad news /
 terrible / too bad
Oh, what a nuisance/pain
Sure, if you like
That sounds cool / like fun /
 wonderful / interesting /
 unusual
That's great news!
That's great / fantastic /
 wonderful
That's OK with me
visa
Whatever (you like)
Whenever (you like)
Wherever (you like)

Unit 22

bring up
call (someone) back
carry on
cut (something) off
drink up
eat up
fall down
find out
finish up
get along (with)
give (something) back
go back
go off
go on
go up
hurry up
keep on (doing something)
lie down
look (something) up
phrasal verb
pick up
put (someone) off
put (something) out
put back
save up (for)
see (someone) off
sit down
stand up
take (something) back
take off
use up
wake up

Unit 23

break down
carry on

come in
get by
get over (something)
go up
grow up
intransitive verb
look after (something)
make up
phrasal verb
pick (something) out
put (something) on
set up
stand up
stay up
transitive verb
turn (something) off
turn (something) up
turn down
turn on
work out
write (something) down

Unit 24

Do you have . . . ?
breakfast
dinner
examine
have a baby
have a great/nice/terrible
 time
have a heart attack
have a party
have a(n) argument/debate/
 discussion/meeting
have steak / a sandwich / a
 drink
Have you got . . . ?
have/take a look
have/take a shower
have/take the bill
haven't got
I have / 've got a problem.
I have / 've got an idea.
lunch
pregnant

Unit 25

do a job
do anything / nothing /
 something
do homework
do research
do someone a favor

do the shopping
don't do anything
make (a) noise
make a decision
make a difference
make a meal
make a mistake
make friends
make money
make progress
take (45 minutes)
take a break/nap/rest
take a bus/taxi/train
take a course
take a picture
take an amount of time
take an exam / a test
take the time
take your/my/his, etc., time

Unit 26

break a promise
break the law
break the news
break the world speed
 record
give my regards
give someone a call
give someone a hand
give someone a ride
give the situation some
 thought
I see
I see what you mean
I'll see
keep + -ing
keep a record
keep in touch
keep quiet
keep someone/something
 safe
keep someone/something
 warm
keep your promise
see the point
See you (later)

Unit 27

catch (a ball / falling leaf /
 stick etc.)
catch (someone) doing
 something
catch a bus

catch a cold / the flu
catch a criminal / thief
have / have got (an amount) left
leave (a person/thing) somewhere
leave (a thing) somewhere
leave (someone) alone
leave a message
leave home / the house / work / the office
leave school / a job / a husband / a wife
let me do something
let me see
let someone do something
let someone know
let's
not catch (a name / what someone said)

Unit 28

get a certificate
get a letter
get a new job
get along with
get dark
get divorced
get dressed
get here
get home
get it
get lost
get married
get on your nerves
get rid of
get the children
get to know
get up
getting better/worse
getting cold/hot
getting crowded
getting dark/light
getting hungry
getting late
getting ready
getting tired

Unit 29

come back home
Does this bus go to . . . ?
go (out) for a swim
go (out) on a date

go (out) to dinner
go (together) with
go bankrupt
go crazy/nuts
go in this room
go running / shopping / swimming
go to lunch
go to school
go to the game
going bald
going blind
How's it going?
It's going OK
What's going on here?

Unit 30

can't see a thing
feels (like)
hear
hearing
hold
listen (to)
look (at)
look everywhere
looks (like)
press (v.)
see
senses
sight
smell (v.)
smells (like)
sounds (like)
taste (v.)
tastes (like)
the feel of
the look of
the smell of
the sound of
the taste of
touch (v.)
watch

Unit 31

a (little) bit
a bit of luck
a little bit (of butter/time)
bottle (of cough syrup)
bowl (of sugar)
box (of chocolates)
bunch (of flowers/grapes)
can (of cola)
carton (of orange juice)

cup (of coffee)
gang (of kids / teenagers / youngsters / youths)
glass (of water)
group (of people)
herd (of cows)
jar (of jam)
pair (of gloves / pants / shoes / skis)
partitive
piece (of advice / cake / information / wood)
sheet (of paper)
slice (of bread)
tube (of toothpaste)
vase (of flowers)

Unit 32

a bit of
a pair of
a piece of
advice
countable noun
equipment
furniture
hair
headphones
homework
information
jeans
knowledge
luggage
news
pajamas
pants
plural noun
progress
scissors
shorts
sunglasses
uncountable noun
weather
work

Unit 33

admit
avoid
can't stand
decide
deny
(don't) mind
enjoy
expect

feel like
finish
forget
give
hate *(v.)*
imagine
let
like
love *(v.)*
make (someone do something)
manage
mean (to do something)
need
offer
prefer to
prefer (+ *ing*)
promise
refuse
remember
seem
try
want

Unit 34

advise
apologize
ask
blame
complain
confirm
convince
discuss
explain
insist
mention
persuade
propose
say
send
suggest
tell
want
warn

Unit 35

a little
absolutely
astonishing/astonished
bad
big
boiling
boring/bored

cold
confusing/confused
delighted
disappointing/disappointed
embarrassing/embarrassed
enormous
exciting/excited
exhausting/exhausted
extremely
fascinating
freezing
frightening/frightened
good
great
happy
hard
hot
hungry
interesting/interested
not (adjective) at all
not so/very
small
sort of
starving
surprising/surprised
terrifying/terrified
tiny
tired
very

Unit 36

across
along
around
at (a point/place)
at a party
at home/school/work
at the bus stop
behind / in back of
between
down
in (Africa/Taipei)
in front of
in my pocket
in the box
in the kitchen
into
near
next to
on (a surface)
on the desk
on the floor
opposite
out of

over
over/above
past
through
toward
under/below
up

Unit 37

a (little) bit
a little
adverb
almost (always/never)
always
extremely
fairly
frequently
generally
hardly (ever)
just about
kind of
nearly
never
occasionally
often
pretty
quite
rarely
rather
really
regularly
seldom
slightly
sometimes
somewhat
sort of
usually
very

Unit 38

after (that)
afterwards
(and) besides
and for another (thing)
anyway
as soon as
before
eventually
finally
first
first of all
for one thing
in the end

farm animal
fish
fly
giraffe
goat
goldfish
gorilla
hamster
horse
in the wild
lamb
leopard
lion
monkey
mosquito
parakeet
pet
pig
shark
sheep
snail
snake
spider
tiger
whale
zebra

Unit 45

Argentina
Australia
Brazil
Canada
Chile
China
Colombia
East Asia
Egypt
Europe
France
Great Britain
Indonesia
Iraq
Israel
Italy
Japan
Latin America
Mexico
nationality
region
Russia
Saudi Arabia
South Korea
Spain
Thailand

the Caribbean
the Mediterranean
the Middle East
the Philippines
the United States
Turkey
Vietnam

Unit 46

ankle
arm
back
bend (your knees)
bite (your nails)
blow (your nose)
breathe
buttocks
cheek
chest
chin
comb (your hair)
cry
elbow
eyebrow
fingers
fold (your arms)
foot
forehead
hand
heel
hip
keep (your back straight)
knee
laugh
lips
neck
nod (your head)
shake (hands / your head)
shoulder
smile (v.)
thigh
thumb
toes
waist
wrist
yawn (v.)

Unit 47

attractive
beard
beautiful
black
blond

broad shoulders
build
complexion
curly
dark brown
fat
good-looking
gray
handsome
height
How much does (someone)
    weigh?
How tall is . . . ?
light brown
medium
muscular
mustache
overweight
pale skin
pounds
pretty
red
scar
short
skinny
slim
straight
tall
thin
ugly
wavy
weigh
weight
What does (someone) look
    like?

Unit 48

anxious
bright
character
cheerful
cold
common sense
dependable
dishonest
disorganized
dumb
easygoing
flexible
friendly
generous
gloomy
grumpy
happy

hardworking
honest
humorous
inflexible
insensitive
intelligent
kind
late
lazy
mean
nervous
nice
optimistic
organized
pessimistic
pleasant
punctual
relaxed
reliable
sensible
sensitive
smart
smiling
stingy
strong
stupid
takes (the) initiative
tense
undependable
unfriendly
unhappy
unkind
unpleasant
unreliable
warm
weak

Unit 49

afraid (of)
anger
angry
clap
embarrassing/embarrassed
embarrassment
fear
frightened (of)
glance
happiness
happy
hate
hateful
jealous (of)
jealousy
knock

love
loving
march
point
press
pride
proud (of)
push
sad
sadness
shout
stare
stroll
wave (goodbye)
whisper

Unit 50

aunt
best friend
brother-in-law
classmate
close friend
colleague
cousin
co-worker
ex-boyfriend/girlfriend/
    husband/wife
family tree
family/last name
father-in-law
first/given name
grandchild(ren)
granddaughter
grandfather
grandmother
grandparent
grandson
inherited
maternal
middle initial/name
mother-in-law
nephew
niece
old friend
only child
paternal
personal name
related by marriage
relative
roommate
sister-in-law
stepfather
stepmother
surname

twin
uncle
widow
widower

Unit 51

adolescence
adult
baby
born
boyfriend
broke up
child
childhood
early teens
elderly
fall in love
fight
get divorced
get married
get pregnant
girlfriend
grow up
in your twenties/thirties
late thirties
middle age
middle-aged
mid-twenties
old age
retirement
senior citizen / senior
separated
split up
teenager
toddler

Unit 52

breakfast
brush (my teeth)
coffee break
come over
dinner
do the dishes / laundry /
    shopping / vacuuming
fall asleep
feed
get home
get off work
get to sleep/work
get up
go to bed
have friends over
ironing

ruin
run out (of)
spill
spoil
stain
There's something wrong
    with . . .
trip over

Unit 57

afford (can't afford . . .)
bill
borrow
charge
cheap
coin
cost
cost of living
Could I borrow . . . ?
Could you lend me . . . ?
currency
dime
dollar (bill)
fortune
free
How much is (something)
    worth?
How much is . . . ?
inexpensive
lend
nickel
pay for
penny
pretty expensive
quarter
reasonable
rich
save (up)
spend (an amount) on
standard of living
waste
wealthy
well-off

Unit 58

a cold
ache (n., v.)
allergies
asthma
backache
blow (your nose)
cancer
cavity

cough (n., v.)
coughing
diarrhea
drugstore
earache
fever
hay fever
headache
health
heart
heart attack
hurt
illness
injection
injure
lungs
nauseous
over-the-counter
    medication
pain (in my chest)
painful/painless
pharmacy
pollen
prescription
runny nose
shot
sneezing
sore throat
stomach
stomachache
suffer from
temperature
the flu
throw up
toothache
virus
vomit

Unit 59

accident
ambulance
bandage/Band-Aid®
black eye
black-and-blue
bleeding
blood
break (my arm)
broken ribs
bruise
bullet wound
burn (my hand)
call 911
cast
collide

concussion
cut (my finger)
emergency room (ER)
hospital
ice pack
injury
knife wound
knock (someone) out
observation
painful
rush
shoot
sling
stab
stitches
swollen
twist (my ankle)
unconscious
weapon
wound

Unit 60

belt
blouse
boot
button
coat
collar
cuff
earring
extra large (XL)
fit
get dressed
glove
hang up (something)
hat
jacket
jeans
necklace
not (big/long) enough
overcoat
pants
pantyhose
pocket
pocketbook
pullover sweater
purse
put on (something)
scarf
shirt
shoe
skirt
sleeve
stockings

suit
take off (something)
tie
too (short/small)
top
try on (something)
V-neck

Unit 61

appliance
butcher shop
Can/May I help you?
cashier
checkout counter
clothes
department store
do the shopping
drugstore
electronics
fitting room
fruit
furniture
go shopping
grocery shopping
grocery store
household goods
I'm already being helped,
    thanks
I'm looking for
jewelry
medicine
newsstand
I'm just looking, thanks
office-supply store
pay by (check / credit card)
pharmacy
poultry
salesperson
shopping center
shopping list
(shopping) mall
store
store window
supermarket
toys
vegetables
window shopping

Unit 62

apple
banana
beef
broccoli

cabbage
calf
carrot
cauliflower
cherry
chicken
chop (up)
cow
crab
cucumber
eggplant
garlic
grape
green bean
lamb
lemon
lettuce
lobster
mango
melon
mushroom
oil
onion
orange
oyster
peach
pear
pea
peel
pepper
pig
pineapple
plum
pork
potato
raspberry
salad
salad dressing
salmon
shellfish
shrimp
slice
strawberry
tomato
veal
vegetarian
vinegar
watermelon
zucchini

Unit 63

appetizer
bake
bitter

bland
boil
broil
check
course
dessert
entrée
fattening
fatty
fresh
fry
grill
hot
in advance
lean
low-calorie
low-fat
main course
medium
medium-rare
microwave (v.)
microwave (oven)
neutral
put on weight
rare
raw
reservation
roast
salty
server
sour
spicy
sweet
taste
tasteless
tasty
tender
tip
tough
well-done

Unit 64

aggressive
bus system
business district
commute
congested
cost of living
crime rate
crowded
cultural activities
dangerous
diverse
downtown

factory
in a hurry
job opportunities
metro area
neighborhood
night life
noisy
park
parking garage/lot
plenty to do
polluted
public library
public transportation
railroad (train) system
resident
rude
rush hour
shopping center
(shopping) mall
suburb
subway
traffic
transportation
urban area
wide range (of shops)

Unit 65

appreciate nature
barn
crops
farm
farmhouse
farmland
fields
grow up
harvest
hills
in touch with (the seasons)
lake
large distances
milk
nature
orchard
pace of life
peace and quiet
plant
river
rural area
silo
surrounding area
till
tractor
valley
wildlife

woods

Unit 66

accident
brake (v.)
break down
buckle (your seat belt)
construction
crosswalk
damage
directions
expressway
fast lane
fasten (your seat belt)
freeway
full-service
gas station
go straight
highway
injure
intersection
keep going
miles per hour (mph)
on your left/right
overpass
passing
pedestrian
road sign
rush hour
seat belt
self-service
sidewalk
skid
slam on (the brakes)
slippery
speed limit
take the first left/right
traffic jam
traffic light/signal
turn right/left

Unit 67

airfare
airport
bicycle/bike
boarding
bus
bus station
bus stop
cab [taxi]
car
catch (a bus)
cyclist

delay
drive (in)
driver
due to
engineer
fare
final call
fly
full
gas station
get in / out of
get on/off
go on
motorcycle
on time
pilot
plane
ride (in)
run
running
SUV (sport utility vehicle)
take (a taxi)
taxi [cab]
taxi stand
track
train
train station
truck
vehicle

Unit 68

attend
bank
banker
day/night shift
deal with
earn
engineer
flextime
get off
holidays
hourly wage
I'm a(n) (banker / engineer /
    teacher)
in charge of
income
income tax
job
make
manage
marketing
meet with
minimum wage
nine-to-five job

business news
celebrity
comics
cut
daily
deliver
edition
editor
editorial
entertainment
feature
freelancer
headline
international news
journalist
key
link
national news
newspaper
online edition
photographer
prove
publish
quit
reporter
review
sports news
tabloid
talks
weather forecast
weekly

Unit 78

cable TV
cartoon
change channels
channel surf
commercial
current affairs
documentary
game show
highlights
live
network
news magazine
plug (it) in
quiz show
reality show
remote (control)
repeat
rerun
satellite TV
series
soap opera

switch channels
talk show
television (TV)
turn it down/up
turn it on/off
What time is the movie on?
What's on TV tonight?

Unit 79

answering machine
be back
call
Can/Could/May I speak to/
  with . . . ?
cellular/cell phone
conversation
directory assistance (411)
get in touch
hold
land line
line is busy
pay phone
phone tag
return a call
ring
take a message
telephone book/number
text message
voicemail
wrong number

Unit 80

bounce back
browser
CD-ROM
click on
copy
CPU (central processing
  unit)
cut
delete
document
download
e-mail
erase
rile
flash drive
hard copy
hard disk/drive
hardware
icon
in-box
Internet
junk

keyboard
laptop
monitor
mouse
Net
online
open
operating system
paste
print (out)
printer
reply
save
screen
search engine
software
spam
store
turn it off
USB port
Web site (website)
wireless/Wi-Fi access
wireless connection
World Wide Web (the
  Web)

Unit 81

charter school
college
compulsory
core subjects
course requirements
dropout
elective
elementary school
English
graduate
high school
higher education
history
K–12
kindergarten (K)
math
middle school
nursery school
parochial school
PE (physical education)
pre-school
primary school
private school
public school
schedule
school district
science
secondary school

specialized high school
vocational high school

Unit 82

admit
agriculture
anthropology
application
architecture
art history
associate's degree
Bachelor of Arts (B.A.)
Bachelor of Science (B.S.)
business
college
community college
degree
doctorate (Ph.D.)
education
engineering
get admission
graduate assistant
graduate school
higher education
hotel administration
in college
institution
instructor
junior college
lecturer
major
master's degree
philosophy
political science
private institution
professor
psychology
research
scholarship
sociology
teaching assistant
thesis
tuition
undergraduate
university

Unit 83

arrest
break the law
cell
charge with a crime
commit a crime
convict (v.)
court

criminal
defendant
defense attorney/lawyer
evidence
felony
fine
go to court
guilty
illegal
innocent
investigate
jail
judge
jury
law
minor offense
murder
not guilty
offender
police
prison
prisoner
prosecutor
prove
punishment
question
render a verdict
sentence
suspect
ticket
trial

Unit 84

against the law
break into
breaking and entering
burglar/burglary
burglar alarm
burglarize/burgle
capital punishment
checkpoint
crime prevention
fight crime
gun
handbag
harsh
illegal
install
intruder
lawmakers
lock
manslaughter
murder/murderer
pocketbook
prevent

prison term
property
protect
punishment
purse
rob
robbery/robber
safe
shoplift
shoplifting/shoplifter
steal
theft/thief
tough
valuables
wallet

Unit 85

coalition
communism/communist
congressperson
conservatism/conservative
democracy
dictatorship/dictator
elect
in opposition
in power
in the center
left of center
legislative branch
liberal
liberalism/liberal
majority
middle of the road
monarch/monarchy
on the left/right
parliamentary government
political party
politics
president
presidential government
prime minister
representative
right of center
rule
senator
socialism/socialist
take office
vote for

Unit 86

application form
birth certificate
bureaucracy
bureaucrat

certificate
check
country of origin
customs form
date of arrival/departure
date of birth
document
driver's license
fill in/out forms
fishing license
gender
identification (ID)
income tax form
marital status
marriage certificate
obtain
passport
registration form
sex
signature
visa

Unit 87

aid
air force
alive
allies
army
blow up
bomb
break out
capture
ceasefire
civilians
conflict
defend
demands
explode
fire
hijack
hostage
hostilities
invade
killed
military forces
negotiate
peace
peace talks
peace treaty
plant a bomb
refuse
release
retreat
run out

shoot
suicide bomber
supplies
terrorism
territory
troops
war
wounded

Unit 88

acid rain
atmosphere
carbon dioxide (CO_2)
carpool
chlorofluorocarbons (CFCs)
conservation
conserve
contribute
damage
emission
environment
exhaust fumes
factory
fuel-efficient
gas
gas-guzzling
global warming
greenhouse effect
harm
human resources
industrial waste
long-term
natural resources
ozone (O_3) layer
plastics
pollution
public transportation
recycle
resource
smoke
soil
throw away
trap

Unit 89

accelerate
altitude
announce
baggage claim
boarding pass
cabin crew
captain
carry-on

check
check-in counter
claim slip
cruising
customs
destination
e-ticket
flight
flight attendant
gate number
get off
go through security
ground transportation
land
luggage
metal detector
overhead compartment
paper ticket
photo ID
portable electronic devices
remind
rent a car
runway
screen
seat number
store
stow
take off
taxi
terminal building
ticket agent
upright

Unit 90

bed and breakfast (B&B)
bellman
book a room
call a taxi
check in/out
double occupancy
double room
front desk
full
fully booked
hotel
housekeeping
included
inn
king-size bed
motel
non-smoking room/floor
pay the bill
porter
put it on the bill

registration desk
reservation
reserve a room
single room
suite
tip
tourist season
wake-up call
youth hostel

Unit 91

buy souvenirs
cathedral
cosmopolitan
famous building
tourist
get lost
go out (most evenings)
go shopping
guidebook
have a good/great time
historical monument
lively
map
market
nightlife
packed
palace
place
sightseeing
spend a lot of / lots of
     money
statue
take photographs/pictures
temple
tour of a town
touristy
worth + -ing

Unit 92

beach
beach resort
beach umbrella
cabin
campsite
cliff
close to nature
country/countryside
get away
hiking
palm tree
peace and quiet
picnic
put (your) feet up

rock
sand
sea
skin
sunbathing
sunblock / sunscreen /
     suntan lotion
sunburn
surfing
tent
vacation home
various
waves

Unit 93

a long time ago
at (+ a specific time)
at midnight
at night
by
century
day
decade
during
for (+ a period of time)
for ages
for the time being
hour
in (+ a period)
in the morning/afternoon/
     evening
last
lately
millennium
minute
month
on (+ a day)
on weekdays/weekends
recently
second
since (+ a period of time)
take
the other day
throughout
until/till
week
year

Unit 94

addition
arithmetic
below zero
billion
cardinal number

decimal
degrees
divided by
division
equals
even number
fourth
fraction
half
hundred
majority
math problem
mathematics
million
minority
minus
multiplication
nothing
odd number
oh (e.g., 0724)
ordinal number
percent
percentage
plus
quarter
subtraction
third
thousand
thousand
three quarters
times
zero

Unit 95

a long way
deep
deep/shallow end
depth
fairly long way
fat
great
height
high
high-rise building
How far is it?
How long/wide/tall/deep/
     big is . . . ?
just around the corner
length
long
narrow
over a mile
shallow
short
short walk

Answer key

Unit 1

1.1   1. It's better to establish a regular study schedule.
      2. *Answers will vary.*
      3. *Answers will vary.*
      4. Possible answers: Write your answers in pencil and then erase them so you can do the exercises again. Test yourself with vocabulary games. Review each word in bold on the left-hand page. Keep lists of new words and definitions.
      5. It's better to review vocabulary frequently for short periods of time.

1.2   *Answers will vary.*

1.3   1. T
      2. T
      3. F A **routine** means doing certain things in a similar way each time.
      4. T
      5. F If something is **effective**, it works well.
      6. F "**At least** 50 people" means "a minimum of 50 people."
      7. T
      8. T
      9. F **Reviewing** means studying something again (not for the first time).
      10. T

1.4   *Answers will vary.*

Unit 2

2.1   *Answers will vary. One possible arrangement:*

Clothing	Air travel	Adjectives with *-ful* or *-less*
shirt	ticket	homeless
glove	plane	painful
jacket	trip	careful
jeans	airport	helpful
put on	get on	careless

2.2   1. c) playing tennis
      2. b) beautiful weather
      3. c) schedule
      4. b) took
      5. c) pinkie
      6. a) fell
      7. c) shoes
      8. b) arrow curving up sharply

2.3   *Answers will vary.*

2.4   *Possible answers:*
      take a picture, a bath, a bus, a shower, a nap
      make a mistake, breakfast, noise, a cake, the bed
      do my job, the dishes, your best, the laundry, your homework

Unit 3

3.1   *Possible answers:*
      1. very bad, terrible
      2. the same as *choose*; o = /uː/

3. a verb
4. an adjective
5. uncountable
6. total, utter
7. two
8. *ch* = /k/, as in *character*
9. between, from
10. You have to choose between A and B. *or* You can choose from ten different colors.

3.2 *Possible answers:*
1. choice
2. advise
3. piece
4. chaotic
5. clean
6. Homework is schoolwork that you do at home; housework is work that is necessary in a home (e.g., washing, ironing, cleaning).
7. win a game
8. gain / put on weight
9. order
10. Take a seat. / Have a seat.

3.3 *Possible answers:*
1. grungy – informal
2. bye-bye – informal/spoken
3. childish – disapproving
4. thereby – formal
5. incision – technical
6. put someone down – informal

3.4 *Possible answers:*
1. the <u>tip</u> of my <u>tongue</u>
2. in other <u>words</u>
3. better <u>late</u> than never
4. on second <u>thought</u>
5. <u>break</u> a <u>promise</u>
6. no hard <u>feelings</u>
7. the <u>sooner</u> the <u>better</u>
8. a <u>matter</u> of <u>opinion</u>
9. every <u>now</u> and <u>then</u>
10. <u>beside</u> the <u>point</u>

Unit 4

4.1 *Possible answers:*

Last year I went to∧for my vacation.
I spent the first week∧Seville staying with a couple of friends, and then I took a train to Barcelona where∧spent another ten days. It is∧beautiful city and I had a marvelous time. I stayed in a very∧hotel right in the center of town, but I didn't mind spending a lot∧money because it has a relaxed∧and is also very convenient. My brother recommended it; he goes∧Spain a lot and he∧stays anywhere else.

1. Spain (noun)
2. in (preposition)
3. I (pronoun)
4. a (article)
5. nice (adjective)
6. of (preposition)
7. atmosphere (noun)
8. to (preposition)
9. never (adverb)

4.2 *Possible answers:*

A: What <u>time</u> is it? *uncountable noun*
B: It's 8:00. We'd better <u>hurry up</u> to make the 8:30 show. *phrasal verb*
A: OK, just let me go change into some <u>jeans</u> real quick. *plural noun*
B: No. We don't have time. I don't want <u>to be</u> late. *infinitive*
A: <u>Take it easy</u> about the time. We'll be all right. *idiom*

4.3
1. transitive
2. transitive
3. intransitive
4. transitive
5. intransitive
6. intransitive

4.4	b<u>r</u>ackets	2	<u>r</u>oot	1	<u>h</u>yphen	2	pa<u>r</u>entheses	4

4.4
b<u>r</u>ackets	2	<u>r</u>oot	1	<u>h</u>yphen	2	pa<u>r</u>entheses	4
unde<u>r</u>stand	3	<u>p</u>eriod	3	<u>c</u>omma	2	pronunc<u>i</u>ation	5
be<u>f</u>ore	2	<u>o</u>pposite	3	prepo<u>s</u>ition	4	semi<u>c</u>olon	4

4.5

Word	Part of speech	Adverb with "-ly" suffix	Prefix for "opposite"	Synonym
happy	adjective	happily	un- (unhappy)	cheerful
correct	adjective	correctly	in- (incorrect)	right
lucky	adjective	luckily	un- (unlucky)	fortunate
sure	adjective	surely	un- (unsure)	certain
probable	adjective	probably	im- (improbable)	likely

Unit 5

5.1 *Answers will vary.*

5.2
1. I didn't bring my book, can I *borrow* yours?
2. Remember to use a *pencil* to write your answers in this book.
3. I like to *repeat* vocabulary after my teacher pronounces it.
4. We need to *plug in* the OHP before we can use it.
5. I like to *highlight* words in my vocabulary *notebook*.
6. Hiro likes to help the teacher *erase* the board.
7. The teacher couldn't get the *LCD projector* to work.

5.3
1. look up – a word
2. sharpen – a pencil
3. turn in – homework
4. share with – a classmate
5. erase – the board
6. do – an exercise
7. make – mistakes

5.4 *Answers will vary.*

5.5
A: What does *borrow* mean?
B: It means to use something that belongs to someone else and then return it.

A: How do you pronounce it?
B: /ˈbɑr·oʊ/ Like *tomorrow*.

A: How do you spell *borrow*?
B: B-O-R-R-O-W.

A: What's the difference between *borrow* and *lend*?
B: If you borrow something, you take it. If you lend something, you give it.

Unit 6

6.1
1. unhappy
2. impatient
3. impolite
4. illegal
5. incorrect
6. irregular
7. invisible
8. impossible
9. illogical
10. unfriendly
11. unemployed
12. dishonest
13. disappear
14. unpack
15. unlock
16. dislike

6.2
1. he's unemployed
2. illegal
3. overcharged
4. invisible
5. illogical
6. impatient
7. impolite

6.3
1. misunderstand
2. unpacked
3. disappeared
4. disagree
5. redo
6. overslept
7. informal
8. misspell

6.4 *Possible answers:*

re-	un-	in-	im-	ir-
reopen	undressed	incorrect	impossible	irrelevant
rewrite	unclear	inefficient	imperfect	irrational
resend	unfamiliar	indecisive	immoral	irreplaceable

Unit 7

7.1
1. educate/education
2. improve/improvement
3. discuss/discussion
4. inform/information
5. spell/spelling
6. hesitate/hesitation
7. arrange/arrangement
8. stupid/stupidity
9. dark/darkness
10. weak/weakness
11. similar/similarity
12. punctual/punctuality
13. happy/happiness
14. popular/popularity

7.2
1. posting
2. selection
3. management
4. weaknesses
5. activity
6. administration
7. improvements
8. education

7.3 *Possible answers:*
1. studies economics
2. acts in movies, etc.
3. directs movies
4. manages a bank
5. makes (software)/programs for computers
6. writes songs
7. translates from one language to another
8. plays the guitar
9. drives a car, truck, or bus
10. creates art
11. reports the news

Unit 8

8.1
1. industrial
2. attractive
3. creative
4. foggy
5. homeless
6. dirty
7. careful, careless
8. dangerous
9. political
10. enjoyable
11. painful, painless
12. knowledgeable
13. (in)comprehensible
14. thoughtful, thoughtless
15. musical
16. (un)comfortable
17. famous
18. (un)reliable
19. washable
20. (un)breakable

8.2
1. careful
2. famous
3. knowledgeable *or* helpful
4. dangerous
5. painful
6. reliable
7. practical
8. undrinkable
9. inflexible
10. homeless

8.3 painless; careless; useless; hopeless; thoughtless

8.4 *Possible answers:*
1. cloudy, sunny, foggy
2. dangerous, careless, thoughtless, awful
3. beautiful, enjoyable, dangerous
4. famous, creative, knowledgeable
5. reliable, comfortable, practical
6. *Answers will vary.*
7. thoughtful, incomprehensible, enjoyable
8. dirty, famous, industrial, attractive

Unit 9

9.1 *Possible answers:*
1. It rained a lot yesterday.
2. We waited a long time.
3. Can you answer my question?
4. This orange tastes strange.
5. I usually laugh at jokes even if they are not funny.
6. I replied to his letter yesterday.
7. When the door gets stuck, you have to push it.

9.2 *Possible answers:*
1. I'll give her a call tonight.
2. The coach gave us a smile after we scored our second goal.
3. We were very tired, so we took a rest after lunch.
4. I took a turn to the right and entered a large room.
5. I had a dream about our class last night.
6. My teacher puts my homework in a file with my name on it.
7. We had a chat online last night.

9.3 *Possible answers:*
1. I often <u>walk</u> to the grocery store. It's not a great distance from my home. Besides, the <u>walk</u> gives me some exercise so I can keep my weight down without going on a <u>diet</u>.
2. I <u>look</u> for "use-by" dates on <u>packages</u>. I know that milk with today's date on it is probably not safe to <u>drink</u>. I don't buy fruit and vegetables that <u>smell</u> bad. If I'm buying things like cabbages or lettuce, I check the outside leaves.
3. Sometimes I make a <u>guess</u> how much something will <u>cost</u>. The only sure way to know, however, is to <u>look</u> at the price <u>tag</u>.

Unit 10

10.1 *Possible answers:*
schools: math teacher, admissions office, textbook
things we wear: wedding ring, tennis shoes, dress shoes, running shoes, sunglasses
places: dining room, post office, admissions office, front office, bedroom, coffee shop
machines: traffic light, DVD player, washing machine, laptop, cell phone, alarm clock
people: brother-in-law, father-in-law, mother-in-law, babysitter, math teacher

10.2
1. stop sign *or* traffic light
2. cell phone
3. alarm clock
4. coffee break
5. babysitter
6. haircut
7. income tax
8. paper clip

10.3 *Possible answers:*
1. *wedding ring:* earring, wedding invitation
2. *credit card:* credit bureau, business card
3. *toothbrush:* toothpaste, hairbrush.
4. *traffic light:* traffic jam, street light
5. *sunglasses:* sunshine, reading glasses
6. *front office:* front porch, corner office

Unit 11

11.1 *Possible answers:*
1. good-looking
2. well-written (-done, -known)
3. easygoing
4. short-sleeved (-handed)
5. part-time
6. first-hand (-time)

7. ten-dollar
8. badly done (written)

9. right-hand (-handed)
10. nicely done (written)

11.2 *Possible answers:*
1. poorly planned, poorly understood
2. part-time, half-time
3. badly injured, badly behaved
4. twenty-minute, twenty-dollar, twenty-year-old
5. right-handed, left-handed
6. ten-inch, half-inch.

11.3 *Possible answers:*

1. five-star	5. badly behaved	9. minute
2. second-hand	6. part-time	10. hundred-dollar
3. first-class	7. well known	11. short-sleeved
4. 32-inch	8. well paid, well off	12. brand new

11.4 *Answers will vary.*

Unit 12

12.1 *Possible answers:*
start: a family, a car, a fight
deep: trouble, breath, sleep
hard: time, work, look

12.2 *Possible answers:*

1. tell the truth	3. a heavy accent	5. an easy time	7. miss the bus
2. a deep sleep	4. highly unlikely	6. a heavy rain	8. run a computer program

12.3 *Possible answers:*

1. time; straight	3. start	5. start	7. commits	9. heavy
2. tell; face	4. runs	6. tells	8. utterly	10. seriously

12.4 *Answers will vary.*

Unit 13

13.1 *Possible answers:*
1. **feel like** = want/desire
2. **for good** = forever
3. **change my mind** = change my decision/plan
4. **tied up** = busy
5. **make do** = manage / get by

13.2
1. go ahead	3. What's up?	5. make up your mind
2. make it	4. get a move on	6. keep an eye on

13.3
1. starters, matters	3. offhand	5. do; run
2. turns	4. small	

13.4 *Suggested answers:*
have something/nothing/little in common = to have or not have similar interests. (If you have nothing/little in common, it means you don't have similar interests.)
crazy about something = to like something very much
get on someone's **nerves** = to make someone angry or irritable by your behavior

Unit 14

14.1 *The correct prepositions and possible answers:*
1. about   B: Her exams, I think.

2. for	B: Her friend.
3. on	B: More than $500.
4. to	B: An interview show, I think.
5. for	B: The fact that I forgot your name.
6. to	B: Yes, it does.
7. at	B: A man who threw some paper on the lawn.
8. with	B: I think it's out of gas.
9. on	B: Whether I can work from home.
10. for	B: My car keys.

14.2
1. b	3. f	5. h	7. a	9. g
2. j	4. i	6. c	8. d	10. e

14.3 *Possible answers:*
1. about it to the waiter
2. at solving math problems
3. for a job as a tour guide
4. to a teammate, who scored a basket
5. about rock concerts
6. in coins from other countries
7. of spiders
8. from people in smaller cities
9. of answering e-mail
10. with taking a nap

14.4
fond of responsible for
concentrate on rely on

Unit 15

15.1
1. on	5. by	9. on	13. by	17. at
2. by	6. by	10. by	14. by	18. at
3. on	7. for	11. in	15. on	19. by
4. on	8. in	12. on	16. in	20. at

15.2 *Possible answers:*
1. on time
2. in time
3. by phone
4. on TV
5. by mistake
6. in the end
7. at the end
8. at the moment
9. by chance / by accident

15.3 *Possible answers:*
1. No, the woman in the white blouse.
2. No. She did it by accident.
3. No. They went by train.
4. No. They're here on business.
5. No. I heard about it on TV.
6. No. He went by himself.
7. No. Its employees are all on strike.
8. No, it's at night.
9. No, you can reach me by e-mail.

Unit 16

16.1 *Possible answers:*
1. so/very/terribly, etc.
2. I'm; stuck; mind
3. keep; don't worry
4. kind
5. apologize; matter
6. sorry; lost track; worry

16.2 *Possible answers:*
1. I'm terribly sorry. I should be more careful.
2. I'm sorry I'm late, but I missed the bus.

3. Oh, thank you. That's very kind of you.
4. Don't worry. It doesn't matter.
5. Thank you for inviting me. / Thank you for a lovely dinner/evening.
6. Please accept our apologies for the delay in sending the information we promised you. Unfortunately we have experienced a much higher volume of business this month than usual, and this has resulted in . . .

16.3 *Possible answers:*
1. I'm so sorry. Are you OK? I'll get a cloth.
2. I'm sorry about the mess. I'll clean it up soon.

Unit 17
17.1
1. Do you want
2. I wish I could
3. How about going
4. don't we go
5. I guess
6. I'd rather see
7. what about
8. I'd love to

17.2 *Possible answers:*
1. A: Could; B: problem
2. A: wondering; B: love to
3. A: should; A: don't; B: good idea
4. A: should; B: How about; A: could; B: rather; A: see

17.3 *Possible answers:*
1. Sure, go ahead. / I'm sorry, but I don't have one.
2. No problem.
3. I'm sorry, but I don't have one. / Yes, sure.
4. Yes, I'd love to. / I'd love to but . . .
5. I'd love to, but I have to work late. / Yeah, great.
6. Sounds good. / I'll see.
7. I think I'd rather work in the language lab. / Sure. That's a great idea.
8. Yes, if you like. / I guess.

Unit 18
18.1 *Possible answers:*
1. What do you think of . . .
2. How do you feel about . . .
3. What are your feelings about . . .
4. What's your (honest) opinion of . . .

18.2
1. A: of; B: personally
2. opinion
3. extent
4. concerned
5. totally
6. mean

18.3 *Possible answers:*
1. Personally, I don't think you can learn a language in three months.
2. You may be right, but then again it costs a lot.
3. I don't agree with you at all about that.
4. That's true, but don't you think the story was interesting?
5. I don't think the homework was easy.
6. Yes, you could be right, but I'm not sure about that.
7. I agree that Sara is lying.
8. Don thinks the weather is too hot, but I can't go along with that.

18.4 *Possible answers:*
1. Yes, I think you're right.
2. Yes, possibly, but don't you think that older drivers have more experience?
3. I agree. I think if you are born in a country you have the right to be one of its citizens.

Unit 19

19.1 *Possible answers:*
1. so do I
2. I like it very much
3. I'd prefer to stay here
4. looking forward to seeing you
5. over / instead of / to tea
6. interested
7. me neither / neither do I
8. helping

19.2 *Possible answers:*

1. stand	3. in	5. forward	7. likes
2. thing/stuff	4. like	6. interest	8. hearing

19.3 *Possible answers:*
1. I can't stand these new shoes.
2. They'd rather go home.
3. His books don't interest me.
4. I don't like art and things like that.
5. I'm very interested in art history.
6. I don't mind this new building.

19.4 1. So do I. / Me too.
2. So do I. / Me too.
3. Neither do I. / Me neither.
4. Neither can I. / Me neither.
5. So am I. / Me too.
6. Neither am I. / Me neither.

Unit 20

20.1 *Possible answers:*
1. Good to see you.
2. Hi. How are you?
3. You too.
4. Good night.
5. Nice meeting you too.
6. Excuse me. Can I ask a question?
7. Not much.
8. See you later.

20.2 *Possible answers:*
1. Nice to meet you. / Nice to meet you too.
2. Excuse me, please.
3. Have a nice weekend.
4. Good morning.

20.3 *Possible answers:*
1. Excuse me. I'll be right back.
2. Sorry. Pardon me.
3. Excuse me. What was that?
4. Excuse me. Pardon me. (repeatedly, to one person after another)
5. Good night. See you in the morning.
6. Goodbye. It was nice to meet you.
7. Hi. How are you?
8. Excuse me. Excuse me. Could I just get a little more coffee here, please?

Unit 21

21.1 *Involves pronunciation practice only.*

21.2 1. so   2. so   3. not   4. it   5. so   6. not

21.3 1. c   2. f   3. e   4. b   5. d   6. a

21.4 *Possible answers:*
1. too bad
2. If you like / whatever
3. that's great
4. doubt it
5. Whatever you like
6. that's bad / that's terrible

21.5 *Possible answers:*
1. That's great. / That sounds like fun.
2. Oh, what a nuisance/pain.
3. If you like. / I don't mind.
4. I don't care. / Wherever.
5. That's fantastic! / That's great news. / That's wonderful.
6. That's too bad. / What a pain.
7. Really? That's awful. / That's bad news.
8. Oh, too bad. / That's a shame.

Unit 22

22.1 *Possible answers:*
1. picked
2. found
3. called
4. getting
5. gone
6. look
7. go
8. used
9. lying; stood
10. Sit
11. put
12. see

22.2 *Possible answers:*
1. his soccer team's loss
2. by 6:30
3. her legs hurt
4. his shoes and socks
5. what we have now
6. to be late
7. hand in your papers
8. on that wet floor

22.3 1. definition 2
2. definition 3
3. definition 5
4. definition 4
5. definition 1

Unit 23

23.1 *Possible answers:*
1. excuses/stories
2. very late last night
3. the light
4. The city
5. your address
6. The car
7. Until we can go shopping
8. if you are cold

23.2 1. OK
2. pick them up
3. stood up fast
4. OK
5. OK
6. stayed up late
7. OK
8. broke down yesterday

23.3 1. increasing – going up, manage – get by
2. failed – broke down; discover – figure out; established – set up
3. invent – make up; recorded – wrote down; rejected – turned down

23.4 *Answers will vary.*

Unit 24

24.1　　1.　I've got an old computer.
　　　　2.　I haven't got a job at the moment.
　　　　3.　Does he have any change for the machine?
　　　　4.　She doesn't have much money.
　　　　5.　We haven't got wireless Internet at school.
　　　　6.　A: Have you got an English dictionary?
　　　　　　B: Yes, I have.

24.2　　1.　Have you got a car?
　　　　2.　*no change*
　　　　3.　We've got a small garden.
　　　　4.　I think I've got a cold.
　　　　5.　Have you got a cell phone?
　　　　6.　Someone told me she's got a new boyfriend.
　　　　7.　no change
　　　　8.　no change

24.3　　*Possible answers:*
　　　　1.　problem　　　　　　　　4.　party
　　　　2.　a shower　　　　　　　　5.　have / have got
　　　　3.　Have you got / Do you have　6.　time

24.4　　*Possible answers:*
　　　　1.　Fred had a heart attack.
　　　　2.　Mary is having / will have a baby.
　　　　3.　Fred had a problem with the video projector.
　　　　4.　Mary had a look at my bad shoulder
　　　　5.　Fred had a really great time in Japan.
　　　　6.　I'll have the bill.

Unit 25

25.1　　1.　took　　3.　make　　5.　take　　7.　made　　9.　took
　　　　2.　take　　4.　made　　6.　take　　8.　take　　10.　doing

25.2　　*Possible answers:*
　　　　1.　Dan <u>did nothing</u> all day.
　　　　2.　I <u>took my time</u> in completing my homework.
　　　　3.　A good manager can <u>make a lot of money</u>.
　　　　4.　I'm going to <u>make</u> lunch for some friends tomorrow.
　　　　5.　I <u>did a favor for</u> my neighbor: I watered his garden.
　　　　6.　I'll <u>do the house-cleaning</u> on the weekend.
　　　　7.　In the end, he <u>made the decision to live in</u> Chicago.
　　　　8.　<u>It usually takes me 20 minutes to get to school</u> from my house.
　　　　9.　He is definitely <u>making progress</u>.
　　　　10.　I usually <u>do my shopping</u> on Saturdays.

25.3　　*Possible answers:*
　　　　1.　Maria did her homework after dinner.
　　　　2.　Bill took a break/nap/rest after he cut the grass.
　　　　3.　The neighbors made a lot of noise at their party.

25.4　　*Answers will vary.*

Unit 26

26.1　　*Possible answers:*
　　　　1.　break a record / the law / a promise
　　　　2.　give someone a hand / someone a call
　　　　3.　keep a record / a promise / quiet

26.2 *Possible answers:*
1. see   3. give   5. I'll see / See you.   7. keeps
2. keep   4. see   6. see   8. break

26.3 *Possible answers:*
1. keep his promise   3. keep in touch; give you a call
2. broke the law   4. give me a hand; give it some thought

26.4 *Possible answers:*
1. warm   3. quiet   5. forgetting
2. leaving; safe 4. breaking   6. saying

Unit 27

27.1 1. catch   3. let   5. left   7. catch
          2. leave   4. caught   6. leave   8. let; Let's

27.2 1. alone   3. know   5. left   7. catch
          2. catch   4. see   6. message 8. cold

27.3 1. e and h   2. a and f   3. c and g   4. b and d

27.4 *Answers will vary.*

Unit 28

28.1 1. find/obtain   5. annoys me   9. receive
          2. bring   6. receive   10. becoming healthier
          3. arrive   7. becoming
          4. became   8. divorced; marrying

28.2 1. It's getting cold in here.   5. I'm getting tired.
          2. I'm getting hungry.   6. It's getting dark.
          3. I'm getting hot.   7. It's getting crowded.
          4. It's getting late.

28.3 1. getting ready to go out
          2. get dressed very quickly
          3. get to know people in this country
          4. get along (very) well with my boss
          5. get rid of most of these chairs
          6. get it, do you

Unit 29

29.1 1. going   3. go   5. go *or* come
          2. coming   4. go   6. come

29.2 *Possible answers:*
          1. shopping   4. dancing; for dinner *or* to eat
          2. for breakfast   5. (out) on a date
          3. swimming (*or* for a swim)   6. riding / for a ride

29.3 *Possible answers:*
          1. blind   3. crazy   5. nuts
          2. bankrupt   4. bald   6. together

29.4 *Possible answers:*
          1. How are you?   3. travels to
          2. lead to   4. What is happening?

Unit 30

30.1
1.	ripe	5.	fresh	9.	doorbell
2.	new	6.	photo	10.	silk
3.	horrible	7.	donkey		
4.	water	8.	laundry detergent		

30.2 *Possible answers:*
1. sounds terrible/bad
2. looks sad/unhappy
3. looks/feels soft
4. tastes horrible/awful

30.3
1.	listening to; heard	5.	listening
2.	heard	6.	press
3.	hear	7.	hold
4.	watch	8.	watch/look; see

30.4 *Answers will vary.*

Unit 31

31.1
1.	carton	3.	bowl	5.	bottle	7.	can
2.	cup	4.	box	6.	glass	8.	jar

31.2 *Possible answers:*
The most surprising and unlikely are: a glass of soup, a tube of milk, a vase of coffee, a cup of toothpaste.

31.3 *Possible answers:*
1.	bunch	3.	slices/pieces	5.	sheet/piece	7.	pair
2.	gang/group	4.	piece	6.	group	8.	bit

31.4
1.	piece	2.	bit/piece	3.	slices/pieces; bunch	4.	bit	5.	herd

Unit 32

32.1 *Possible answers:*
1. I need some information.
2. We had great weather.
3. I'm looking for a new pair of jeans. *or* I'm looking for some new jeans.
4. Your hair is getting very long.
5. I can't find my sunglasses.
6. We had a lot of homework yesterday.
7. Is she making (any) progress with her English?
8. These pajamas are too big for me.

32.2 *countable:* cup; building; grape; television; people
uncountable: butter; spaghetti; paperwork; work; vocabulary
Sentences will vary.

32.3
1. a pair of shorts / some shorts
2. a pair of scissors / some scissors
3. a pair of sunglasses / some sunglasses
4. some advice
5. some furniture
6. some headphones / a pair of headphones
7. homework/work

32.4 *uncountable nouns:* traffic; construction; news
plural nouns: outskirts; authorities
The summaries will vary.

Unit 33

33.1
1. to work
2. to help
3. going
4. to drive / driving
5. to make
6. to work / working
7. going
8. to study / studying

33.2 *Possible answers:*
1. to be happy
2. going to the dentist
3. going shopping
4. to live a long life
5. cleaning the house
6. get up at a certain time in the morning
7. get up when they like

33.3 *Suggested answers:*
1. He let her go on vacation with two friends.
2. He offered to lend her the money for a hotel.
3. He refused to pay for the flight and her entertainment.
4. She promised to bring him back a present and repay the loan in six months.
5. They decided to go to Hawaii for two weeks.
6. She forgot to buy a present for her father.

Unit 34

34.1
1. She said (that) the movie was terrible.
2. He told me (that) it was not possible.
3. Can you explain what to do?
4. He suggested (that) we go home.
5. I want him to leave.
6. I need to confirm the flight.
7. I apologized for my mistake.
8. She advised me to buy a dictionary.

34.2 *Possible answers:*
1. discussed
2. complain
3. apologize
4. warn
5. persuaded
6. insisted
7. confirms
8. blamed

34.3 *Possible answers:*
1. that we go out to eat
2. a plan
3. (that) it was great
4. me a copy
5. on going with her
6. them to go
7. him to go home
8. the manager for the loss
9. where I live
10. how it works

34.4 *Possible answers:*

ask	+ indirect object + question word	I asked her who was coming to the party.
	+ object + infinitive	He asked another student to help him.
	+ preposition	Lee asked the waiter for a glass of water.
order	+ object	Our table ordered a pizza.
	+ indirect object + object	When Ed arrived, I ordered him a lemonade.
	+ object + infinitive	The judge ordered him to be quiet.
	+ that clause	The boss ordered that the meeting should start early.

Unit 35

35.1 *Possible answers:*
1. fascinating
2. small
3. terrifying
4. hard at all / very hard
5. cold; freezing

35.2 *Possible answers:*
1. exhausted; absolutely exhausting
2. very/extremely disappointing; very/extremely disappointed
3. embarrassed; embarrassing
4. confusing; confused
5. (absolutely) astonished; (absolutely) astonishing
6. (very/extremely) bored; (very/extremely) boring

35.3 *Possible answers:*

Dear Sandy,

Arrived Sunday evening. We were <u>starving</u> and had dinner right away. We are <u>delighted</u> with our hotel. We have <u>an enormous</u> room and the food is <u>great</u>. It's been <u>boiling</u> every day so far, so we've spent most of the time on the beach. But the water is actually <u>freezing</u> – that's because it's the Pacific coast, I suppose. Tomorrow we're going to walk to a <u>tiny</u> town about three miles from here – I'm sure I'll be <u>exhausted</u> by the time we get back, but it sounds like a <u>fascinating</u> place and I'm looking forward to it. It's so small that I was <u>astonished</u> to find it on a map! I'll write again in a couple of days and tell you about it.   Benita

Unit 36

36.1
1. in
2. at
3. at
4. in
5. on
6. at
7. on
8. in

36.2 *Possible answers:*
1. No, behind the statue.
2. No, it's down the hill.
3. No, I came in under the fence.
4. No, out of the car.
5. No, above the clouds.
6. No, in the apartment below me.
7. No, on the desk.
8. No, in front of it.

36.3 *Possible answers:*
1. around
2. in
3. past
4. across/over
5. into/to
6. across
7. along (*or* down)
8. at/in
9. across

Unit 37

37.1 *Possible answers:*
1. My brother often visits us on Sundays.
2. She hardly ever calls me.
3. I hardly saw him during his visit.
4. I occasionally get up early.
5. I have never ridden a motorcycle.

37.2 *Possible answers:*
1. almost never
2. hardly
3. nearly
4. somewhat
5. really

37.3 *Possible answers:*
1. John said the apartment was a bit small.
2. They said it was slightly boring.
3. The clothes were rather expensive.
4. I felt extremely happy at the wedding.
5. He's been getting very good marks on his exams.

37.4 *Possible answers:*
1. I sometimes buy clothes I don't wear.
2. I polish my shoes occasionally.

3. I hardly ever remember my dreams.
4. I often give money to people on the street if they ask me.
5. I rarely speak to strangers on buses and trains.
6. Sometimes I'm rude to people who are rude to me.

37.5 *Answers will vary.*

Unit 38

38.1
1. get
2. while
3. leaving
4. eventually/finally
5. After that
6. as soon as / when

38.2 *Possible answers:*
1. we went for a swim
2. I've finished here
3. you leave
4. I was getting out of the car
5. my boyfriend studied
6. the bus arrived
7. I was coming around the corner

38.3 *Possible answers:*
1. And for another, I've got lots of work to do.
2. After that, we stopped in Kyoto for a couple of days.
3. besides/anyway, no one really wants to go

38.4 *Possible answer:*

Ms. M. Watson
Owner, Park Royal Restaurant

Dear Ms. Watson:
Last weekend, some friends and I had dinner at the Park Royal. I am writing to express my dissatisfaction with the food and service in your restaurant. For one thing, our dinners were undercooked. I ordered chicken, and the middle of the meat was still pink. For another, the service was terrible. We could not get our server's attention when we needed something. And then, when we finally got her attention, our server was rude to us when we complained. Finally, we just paid our bill and left. It was not a nice experience.
Sincerely,

Unit 39

39.1
1. Although
2. in spite of
3. in spite of / despite
4. even though
5. whereas
6. In addition,
7. However,
8. too / as well

39.2 *Possible answers:*
He went to school today even though he didn't feel very well.
He always did his best at school, whereas most of his classmates were very lazy.
He has the right qualifications. What's more, he's the most experienced.
He didn't pass the exam in spite of the help I gave him.
He decided to take the job. However, the pay isn't very good.

39.3 *Possible answers:*
1. Despite
2. whereas
3. Furthermore
4. even though
5. however
6. as well

39.4 *Possible answers:*
1. she spoke very quickly
2. the others couldn't
3. the bad weather
4. it's much cheaper
5. I think I passed
6. I wasn't bored at all

Unit 40

40.1 *Possible answers:*
1. similar
2. different from
3. a lot in common
4. in common
5. live at home
6. goes to college

40.2 *Possible answers:*
1. She's very similar to the others.
2. Hong is very different from her sister.
3. The apartments are a very good value compared with/to the houses.
4. Everyone passed the exam except (for) Carla.
5. They have nothing in common.

40.3 *Possible answers:*
1. otherwise
2. in case
3. unless
4. as long as
5. otherwise

40.4 *Possible answers:*
1. are a member.
2. have to do it over the weekend.
3. pay me back by next week.
4. my cousin comes to stay for a few days.
5. I have to.

Unit 41

41.1 *Possible answers:*
1. I didn't call because it was very late.
2. I turned up the radio in the living room so I could hear it in the kitchen.
3. Since the restaurant was full, we went to the coffee shop next door.
4. There has been a drop in profits because the company has poor management.
5. Because it is a very large city, you have to use public transportation a lot.
6. I learned to drive so that my mother wouldn't have to take me to school every day.

41.2 *Possible answers:*
1. He couldn't play soccer because of his injured shoulder.
2. Her success in her job was due to her excellent training.
3. Because of the awful weather, we couldn't eat outside.
4. She couldn't go to work due to a broken ankle.
5. The flowers died because of the dry weather.
6. I was half an hour late because of the heavy traffic.
7. The referee stopped the game due to the rain.

41.3 *Possible answers:*
1. Since
2. result in
3. so that
4. lead to / cause
5. Therefore / As a result

41.4 *Possible answers:*
1. I will need it in my job very soon.
2. I can/could download English songs.
3. I am very busy during the week.
4. help me remember them.
5. I find it difficult to remember everything I study.
6. he gets a lot of opportunities to practice his English.

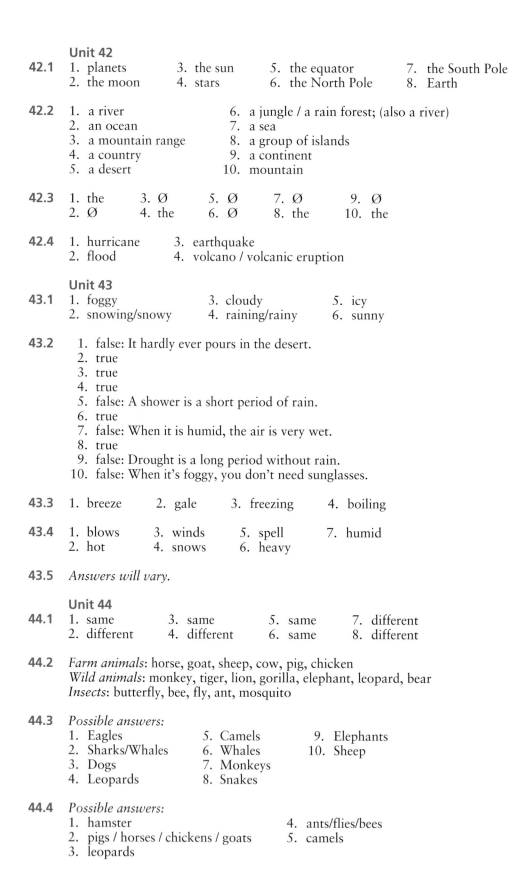

Unit 42

42.1
1. planets   3. the sun   5. the equator   7. the South Pole
2. the moon   4. stars   6. the North Pole   8. Earth

42.2
1. a river
2. an ocean
3. a mountain range
4. a country
5. a desert
6. a jungle / a rain forest; (also a river)
7. a sea
8. a group of islands
9. a continent
10. mountain

42.3
1. the   3. Ø   5. Ø   7. Ø   9. Ø
2. Ø   4. the   6. Ø   8. the   10. the

42.4
1. hurricane   3. earthquake
2. flood   4. volcano / volcanic eruption

Unit 43

43.1
1. foggy   3. cloudy   5. icy
2. snowing/snowy   4. raining/rainy   6. sunny

43.2
1. false: It hardly ever pours in the desert.
2. true
3. true
4. true
5. false: A shower is a short period of rain.
6. true
7. false: When it is humid, the air is very wet.
8. true
9. false: Drought is a long period without rain.
10. false: When it's foggy, you don't need sunglasses.

43.3
1. breeze   2. gale   3. freezing   4. boiling

43.4
1. blows   3. winds   5. spell   7. humid
2. hot   4. snows   6. heavy

43.5 *Answers will vary.*

Unit 44

44.1
1. same   3. same   5. same   7. different
2. different   4. different   6. same   8. different

44.2 *Farm animals*: horse, goat, sheep, cow, pig, chicken
Wild animals: monkey, tiger, lion, gorilla, elephant, leopard, bear
Insects: butterfly, bee, fly, ant, mosquito

44.3 *Possible answers:*
1. Eagles   5. Camels   9. Elephants
2. Sharks/Whales   6. Whales   10. Sheep
3. Dogs   7. Monkeys
4. Leopards   8. Snakes

44.4 *Possible answers:*
1. hamster
2. pigs / horses / chickens / goats
3. leopards
4. ants/flies/bees
5. camels

44.5 golden eagle = 168 mph
lion = 50 mph
shark = 40 mph
rabbit = 35 mph
elephant = 25 mph
pig = 11 mph
spider = 1.17 mph
snail = 0.03 mph

Unit 45

45.1 *Possible answers:*
1. Australia, Canada, Great Britain, the United States
2. Portuguese
3. Israelis
4. Arabic
5. Thai
6. Spanish
7. (South) Korean(s)
8. China
9. Colombia, Chile, Mexico
10. the Turkish/Turks

45.2 Ja<u>pan</u>, Japa<u>nese</u>, Bra<u>zil</u>ian, E<u>gyp</u>tian, <u>A</u>rabic
Chi<u>nese</u>, Aus<u>tral</u>ia, Indo<u>ne</u>sia, Indo<u>ne</u>sian, Vietna<u>mese</u>

*Words ending -***ian***: The main stress is on the syllable before -***ian***.*
*Words ending -***ese***: The main stress is on the final syllable, i.e., on the -***ese***.*

45.3 *For most items, answers will vary.*
Items with limited answer possibilities:
3. Canadians / Canadian people
5. (the) Mexicans / Mexican people
6. The Japanese / East Asians
8. Brazilians / Brazilian people

45.4
1. Thailand	5. Australia	9. Spain
2. Argentina	6. the United States	10. Japan
3. Turkey	7. Russia	
4. South Korea	8. the Caribbean	

45.5 *Answers will vary.*

Unit 46

46.1
1. forehead	7. thigh	13. back	19. finger
2. cheek	8. knee	14. elbow	20. heel
3. chin	9. foot	15. waist	
4. arm	10. toes	16. buttocks	
5. chest	11. neck	17. wrist	
6. hip	12. shoulder	18. hand	

46.2
1. blow your nose	5. bend your knees
2. nod your head	6. shake hands
3. comb your hair	7. bite your nails
4. fold your arms	

46.3 *Possible answers:*
1. they're happy or think something is funny
2. running or exercising

3. someone says something funny
4. they're nervous
5. they want to say "no"
6. they mean "yes"
7. they're tired or bored

46.4 *Words across:* elbow, neck, ankle, chest, cheek
Words down: chin, toe, lip, back, knee, eye, nail, arm, heel

Unit 47

47.1 *Possible answers:*

1. hair	4. medium	7. beard/mustache	10. complexions
2. skin	5. shoulders	8. scar	
3. curly	6. muscular	9. blue/brown	

47.2 *Possible answers:*

1. beautiful   3. overweight   5. handsome
2. not very good-looking   4. thin

47.3 *Possible answers:*
1. What does she/he look like?
2. How tall is she/he?
3. How much does she/he weigh?

47.4 *Answers will vary.*

Unit 48

48.1 *Possible order:*

Positive	Negative
smart	stupid
cheerful	cranky
nice	unpleasant
generous	stingy
relaxed	tense
hard-working	lazy

48.2 unkind; unreliable; disorganized; inflexible; undependable; insensitive; unpleasant; dishonest

48.3 *Possible answers:*
1. She has no common sense.
2. He is unreliable/undependable.
3. He doesn't take initiative.
4. She is very punctual.
5. He's very lazy.
6. She seems easygoing.
7. He is very flexible.
8. She is a sensitive person.

48.4

1. kindness	4. optimism	7. reliability	10. laziness
2. generosity	5. organization	8. stupidity	11. weakness
3. sensitivity	6. strength	9. flexibility	12. friendliness

48.5 *Answers will vary.*

Unit 49

49.1

a. anger	c. happiness	e. jealousy
b. sadness	d. pride	f. embarrassment

49.2   1. c   2. f   3. e   4. a   5. b   6. d

49.3   *Possible answers:*
1. I would feel embarrassed and upset.
2. I was once a passenger in a speeding car; I was/felt frightened.
3. Sometimes I get upset or angry when others talk to me while I'm trying to concentrate.
4. I might be embarrassed, or I might not worry about it.
5. I'm very proud of getting good grades in all my classes.
6. Yes. Once, I was embarrassed when my teacher asked me to stand up in front of the class.

49.4   1. people strolling
2. people clapping
3. someone pressing a button
4. people whispering
5. people waving

49.5   1. glanced
2. whispered
3. strolled
4. marched
5. stared

Unit 50

50.1   1. brother-in-law
2. nephew
3. cousins
4. niece
5. grandfather
6. uncle
7. aunt
8. widow
9. grandson
10. by marriage

50.2   *Answers will vary.*

50.3   *Answers will vary.*

50.4   *Answers will vary.*

Unit 51

51.1   1. a toddler
2. retired
3. mid-twenties
4. in her late forties / middle-aged
5. their early thirties
6. a senior citizen / a senior
7. a baby
8. a teenager / an adolescent
9. an adult / 18 / 21
10. adolescence

51.2   1. false: He was born in Chicago.
2. true
3. true
4. false: They split up because they had lots of fights.
5. true
6. false: Marie got pregnant a year after they got married.
7. false: Marie is now expecting her second child.
8. false: Sam left Marie.

51.3   *Possible answers:*
1. e   3. a   5. d   7. h
2. c   4. f   6. g   8. b

51.4   *Answers will vary.*

Unit 52

52.1   *Possible answers:*
have breakfast, lunch, dinner; a snack, friends over
take a nap, a shower, a bath, a coffee break, out the garbage/trash
do the dishes, the shopping, the laundry, the ironing, the vacuuming

52.2   1. b   2. e   3. a   4. f   5. d   6. c

52.3 *Answers will vary.*

52.4 *Answers will vary.*

52.5 *Possible answers:*
1. The man is getting up.
2. The woman is brushing her teeth.
3. The woman is leaving for work.
4. The two people are taking a (coffee) break.
5. The two people are taking out the garbage/trash.

Unit 53
53.1 1. yes
2. no, a fence around the backyard
3. yes
4. shut
5. yes
6. yes
7. no, on the ground floor / first floor
8. no, a view of a park

53.2 *Possible answers:*

1. front door; doorbell	3. view	5. belongs; condition
2. climb; elevator	4. rent	6. mortgage

53.3 *Possible answers:*

Positive	*Negative*
It's bright and sunny.	It's very dark.
It has a good view.	It doesn't have an elevator.
It is in good condition.	It is noisy.
It has huge closets.	It has tiny rooms.

53.4 *Answers will vary.*

Unit 54
54.1 *Possible answers:*

1. bath; shower	3. cooking	5. have meals	7. work
2. sleep	4. sit and relax	6. guests stay/sleep	8. under the house

54.2 *Possible answers:*
1. in the refrigerator
2. in a frying pan on the stove / in the oven
3. in the freezer
4. in the dishwasher
5. in a cabinet
6. in a cabinet
7. on the counter
8. in a blender

54.3

1. in	3. on; in	5. in
2. out; back	4. through/at; on	6. out; on

54.4 *Answers will vary.*

54.5 *Answers will vary.*

Unit 55

55.1
1. I brushed my teeth.
2. I went to sleep.
3. I set the alarm clock.
4. I turned out the light.
5. I took a shower.
6. I put on my pajamas.
7. I got into bed.

Order will vary. Possible order:
5 → 1 → 6 → 3 → 7 → 4 → 2

55.2 *Possible answers:*
1. He dusted the furniture.
2. He vacuumed the carpet/rug.
3. He ironed his clothes.
4. He did the laundry.
5. He did/washed the dishes.
6. He made the bed.

55.3 *Answers will vary.*

55.4 *Answers will vary.*

Unit 56

56.1

Infinitive	*Past tense*	*Past participle*
to burn	burned	burned
to break	broke	broken
to forget	forgot	forgotten
to run	ran	run
to lose	lost	lost
to leave	left	left

56.2 1. d   2. f   3. e   4. a   5. b   6. c

56.3 *Possible answers:*
1. Julia broke her glasses.
2. She had/got a stain on her skirt. *or* She spilled something (on her skirt).
3. She burned something (that) she was cooking.

56.4 *Possible answers:*
1. I dropped it
2. There's something wrong with it. / It isn't working.
3. I lost it.
4. I left it at home.
5. It's out of order.

56.5 *Answers will vary.*

Unit 57

57.1
1. saved up
2. cost
3. paid; is worth
4. borrowed; spent
5. charged
6. wasted

57.2 *Possible answers:*
1. The restaurant was pretty expensive.
2. How much is your laptop worth?
3. I'm sorry, but I can't afford it. *or* I'm sorry, but I can't afford to go.
4. Could you please lend me $10?
5. How much did your dictionary cost?

57.3　1. no　　3. yes　　5. yes　　7. no
　　　　2. no　　4. no　　6. no　　8. no

57.4　*Answers will vary.*

Unit 58
58.1　*Possible answers:*
　　　　1. sneezing, a runny nose, a sore throat, a cough
　　　　2. sneezing, a sore throat, a cough, a runny nose, aching muscles, a temperature/fever
　　　　3. sneezing, a runny nose, itchy eyes
　　　　4. a stomachache, keep going to the bathroom
　　　　5. difficulty breathing / breathing problems

58.2　1. same /eɪ/　　　　　5. same /ɜr/
　　　　2. different /ɑ/, /ʌ/　　6. different /ɑɪ/, /ɪ/
　　　　3. different /ɪ/, /ɑɪ/　　7. same /f/
　　　　4. same /f/　　　　　　8. different /ɔ:/, /ʌ/

58.3　*Possible answers:*
The man had a terrible toothache, which was very painful, so he went to the dentist. She looked at (*or* examined) the tooth and said he had a cavity. It needed a filling. He had an injection (*or* The dentist gave him an injection), so the drilling was painless. Afterward, his tooth felt much better and he was happy.

58.4　1. hurts　　　　　5. lung
　　　　2. attack　　　　6. prescription
　　　　3. stomachache　7. asthma
　　　　4. pain　　　　　8. myself (*or* my leg, my arm, etc.)

58.5　*Answers will vary.*

Unit 59
59.1　| *Noun* | *Verb* | *Noun* | *Verb* |
|---|---|---|---|
| cut | cut | injury | injure |
| bandage | bandage | shot | shoot |
| blood | bleed | treatment | treat |
| bruise | bruise | wound | wound |

59.2　1. c　　2. e　　3. d　　4. b　　5. a

59.3　*Possible answer:*
Paul somehow fell out of the tree where he was picking apples and knocked himself out. His wife immediately called 911 for an ambulance. It arrived quickly and rushed him to the hospital. He was suffering from a concussion and had to have some stitches for a large cut on the side of his head. Fortunately he's going to be fine.

59.4　*Answers will vary.*

Unit 60
60.1　*Possible answers:*
I need a pair of shoes, boots, socks, jeans, pants, shorts, gloves, pantyhose / stockings, earrings.

60.2　*Suggested answers:*
　　　　2. g　　5. e　　8. h
　　　　3. a　　6. i　　9. f
　　　　4. c　　7. b

60.3 *The order of answers will vary.*
1. a button   4. a necklace
2. a belt   5. (a pair of) gloves
3. a pocket

60.4 *Possible answers:*
1. skirt; blouse *or* top   4. enough; size
2. suit; pants   5. too; enough
3. tie; shirt

60.5 *Possible answers:*
1. worn by women: dress, blouse, skirt, pantyhose/stockings
2. worn by men and women: hat, gloves, jeans, pants, jacket, scarf, coat, pullover sweater, overcoat. (Earrings and necklaces are worn by both men and women in some cultures.)
3. *Answers will vary.*

Unit 61

61.1
1. fruit   5. household goods
2. clothes/clothing   6. toys
3. furniture   7. stationery / office supplies
4. appliances   8. electronics

61.2 *Possible answers:*
butcher shop: chicken, steak
department store: an armchair, a shirt, an MP3 player, a notebook
grocery store: aspirin, bananas, a loaf of bread, carrots
pharmacy: aspirin
office-supply store: envelopes, a notebook
Some other things you could buy in each store:
butcher shop: ground beef, lamb
department store: a washing machine, perfume
grocery store: onions, canned soup
pharmacy: soap, medicine
office-supply store: pens, paper clips

61.3
1. salesperson or salesclerk   4. (shopping) mall
2. fitting room   5. window shopping
3. cashier / checkout counter   6. newsstand

61.4 1. looking for   2. size   3. pay by   4. looking

Unit 62

62.1 *Possible answers:*
Vegetable	*Fruit*
1. potato	pear
2. broccoli	banana
3. green bean	grape
4. carrot	cherry
5. lettuce	lemon

62.2 banana / watermelon /ə/   onion / mushroom /ʌ/
peach / zucchini /iː/   salmon / lamb /æ/
pepper / lemon /e/   oysters / oil /ɔɪ/

62.3 *Possible answers:*
1. Salmon is the only fish. The others are types of meat.
2. Chicken is the only animal meat. The others are types of shellfish.
3. Eggplant. The others are used in salad.

4. Peach is the only fruit. The others are vegetables.
5. Oyster is a shellfish. The others are types of meat.

62.4   *Possible answers:*

Always	*Sometimes*	*Never*
cherries	apples	pineapples
grapes	pears	bananas
strawberries	oranges	watermelons
peaches		mangoes
		lemons

62.5   *Answers will vary.*

Unit 63

63.1   *Answers will vary.*

63.2   *Possible answers:*
lemon – sour
chicken – bland or tender
honey – sweet
bacon – salty *or* fatty *or* tasty
ice cream – sweet *or* fattening
steak – tender *or* fatty *or* lean
chili peppers – hot and spicy
avocado – bland

63.3   1. homemade chicken liver pâté
2. entreé
3. grilled steak with a pepper sauce
4. baked salmon
5. grilled steak with a pepper sauce
6. baked salmon with spinach and breast of chicken in white sauce with mushrooms
7. grilled steak with a pepper sauce
8. chocolate mousse and ice cream
9. fruit salad
10. probably green salad, baked salmon with spinach, and fruit salad

63.4   *Answers will vary.*

Unit 64

64.1
1.	rush	d.	hour
2.	public	f.	transportation
3.	night	h.	life
4.	cost	g.	of living
5.	crime	c.	rate
6.	shopping	e.	mall
7.	job	b.	opportunity
8.	bus	a.	system

64.2   *Possible answers:*
1. I've met all the <u>residents</u> of the building.
2. I usually <u>commute</u> by bus.
3. She lives in a <u>suburb</u> called Elmdale.
4. The mall has <u>a wide range</u> of shops.
5. The houses in my <u>neighborhood</u> are small.
6. The residents of the city are <u>diverse</u>.

64.3 *Answers will vary.*

64.4 *Answers will vary.*

Unit 65

65.1
1. live in   f. a farmhouse
2. pick   b. apples / d. crops
3. flow through   a. a valley
4. milk   h. cows
5. harvest   d. crops / b. apples
6. plant   g. seeds / d. crops
7. till   c. the soil
8. travel   e. large distances

65.2
1. rural   3. cows   5. silos   7. plant seeds
2. grow   4. river   6. Woods   8. picking

65.3 *Possible answers:*
1. thing   3. planting   5. harvest   7. meet
2. appreciate   4. crops   6. quiet   8. nightlife

65.4 *Answers will vary.*

Unit 66

66.1 Go <u>straight</u> and <u>turn left</u> at the intersection. Then you keep <u>going</u> and <u>turn</u> right when you <u>get</u> to the <u>school</u>. Then <u>turn right</u> again at <u>Green</u> Street, and the bank is <u>on your/the</u> left, just after the <u>movie theater</u>.

66.2 *Possible answers:*
1. fasten/buckle; seat   5. crosswalk
2. injured; damaged   6. broke down
3. rush hour   7. traffic jam
4. braked; crashed/slammed   8. passed; lane

66.3
1. turn left   3. signal/light   5. airport
2. slippery   4. speed   6. pedestrian crossing

66.4 *Answers will vary.*

Unit 67

67.1
1. ride   3. run   5. take
2. get in   4. fly   6. missed

67.2 *Possible answers:*
1. miss the bus / the train   4. taxi/truck driver
2. bus/train station   5. get on the bus / the plane
3. get in the car / the SUV / taxi   6. airfare / taxi fare

67.3
1. truck   3. bus   5. motorcycle
2. SUV   4. bicycle/bike

67.4
1. bus stop   3. full   5. on time   7. by; took/caught
2. track   4. delay; to   6. passengers   8. departing; stops

67.5 *Answers will vary.*

Unit 68

68.1
1. earn   e. a salary
2. work   a. overtime

3. pay   f. income tax
4. attend   b. meetings
5. see   d. clients
6. run   c. a store

68.2 *Possible answers:*
1. I work in a bank.
2. What do you do for a living? / What do you do?
3. My salary is $35,000.
4. My (total) income is $50,000.
5. I work for an engineering company/firm.
6. I'm in charge of one of the smaller departments.

68.3 *Possible answers:*
1. What hours do you work?
2. Do you ever work overtime?
3. Do teachers earn very much?

68.4 *Answers will vary.*

Unit 69
69.1 *Possible answers:*
1. a doctor, an architect, a lawyer, an engineer, a professor
2. a surgeon, a dentist, a soldier, a sailor, a pilot, a police officer, a firefighter
3. a sailor
4. a mechanic
5. a doctor, a soldier, a sailor, a pilot, a police officer, a firefighter
6. a vet
7. a pilot, a firefighter
8. an accountant
9. a doctor, a nurse, a surgeon, a vet
10. a soldier, a sailor, someone in the air force

69.2 *Possible answers:*
1. designs buildings
2. teaches in a university
3. keeps and examines financial records of people and companies
4. treats / takes care of animals
5. advises people on legal problems
6. plans the construction of roads, bridges, machines, etc.
7. builds walls with bricks
8. buys and sells stocks
9. repairs cars
10. operates on people in a hospital

69.3 *Possible answers:*
1. Really? When did he join the police force?
2. Really? When did she join the army?
3. Really? When did he join the navy?
4. Really? When did he join the air force?
5. Really? When did she join the fire department?

69.4 *Possible answers:*
an architect to design your house
a lawyer to give you legal advice
a carpenter to make shelves and cabinets
a plumber to install pipes in the kitchen and bathroom

an electrician to do all the electrical work
an accountant to calculate how much everything will cost

69.5 *Answers will vary.*

Unit 70

70.1
1. fired / let go
2. an intern
3. unemployed
4. resigned/quit
5. promoted
6. prospects
7. retired
8. employees
9. a raise
10. abroad

70.2   1. b   2. e   3. d   4. a   5. c

70.3 *Possible answers:*
1. part-time
2. training/experience
3. challenge
4. her
5. over

70.4

Verb	General noun	Person noun(s)
retire	retirement	retiree
promote	promotion	–
employ	employment	employer [boss]; employee [worker]
resign	resignation	–
train	training	trainer [gives the training]; trainee [receives it]

70.5 *Answers will vary.*

Unit 71

71.1
1. phone calls
2. arranges
3. the office
4. A retailer
5. break room
6. set up
7. paperwork
8. Our floor

71.2
1. copy room
2. corner office
3. bookshelf
4. filing cabinet
5. break room
6. wastebasket
7. keyboard
8. corner office

71.3
1. co-worker
2. coffeemaker
3. receptionist
4. workstation
5. boss
6. invoice

71.4 *Answers will vary.*

Unit 72

72.1
1. a loan
2. interest
3. inflation
4. aims/objectives/goals
5. (it) breaks even
6. (in) recession

72.2 *Possible answers:*
1. gradual
2. sharp
3. thriving
4. expanding
5. goals
6. increased

72.3 *Possible answers:*
1. increased
2. fell
3. decrease
4. increase/rise
5. dramatically
6. rose/increased

72.4 *Possible answers:*
1. break even
2. political stability
3. make a profit
4. interest rate
5. raw material(s)
6. profit and loss

72.5 *Answers will vary.*

Unit 73

73.1　*Possible answers:*
1. cards, board games, musical instruments
2. stamps, coins, antiques
3. hiking, camping, rock climbing

73.2　*Possible answers:*
1. photography　　　　　5. making jewelry
2. collecting antiques　　6. playing chess
3　playing a musical instrument　7. carpentry
4. running/jogging　　　8. shells

73.3
1. go　　　　　　　　5. go
2. took up; gave it up　6. play
3. made　　　　　　　7. joined
4. collects　　　　　　8. do

73.4　*Answers will vary.*

Unit 74

74.1　throw it
head it
pass it
hit it
catch it
kick it

74.2　*Possible answers:*
1. baseball, table tennis, golf
2. football, soccer, basketball
3. football, baseball, basketball
4. football, soccer
5. soccer

74.3
1. false: They are the crowd / the spectators.
2. true
3. true
4. false: It has a referee.
5. false: The Blue team is behind/trailing.
6　false: It is played on a court.
7. true
8. true

74.4　*Possible answers:*
1. beat　　　3. loss　　　5. leading
2. score　　4. victory　6. tied

74.5　*Answers will vary.*

Unit 75

75.1　1. the orchestra　　2. C8　　3. the aisle　　4. on the stage

75.2
1. a musical　　　　6. critics/reviewers
2. the cast　　　　　7. reviews
3. the audience　　　8. subtitles
4. clap/applaud　　　9. to reserve
5. director　　　　　10. stars

75.3 *Possible answers:*
1 B. action; C. exciting, suspenseful
2 B. drama; C. funny, fast-paced
3 B. comedy; C. moving, powerful
4–6 *Answers will vary.*

Unit 76

76.1
1. pianist
2. violinist
3. guitarist
4. drummer
5. saxophonist
6. cellist

76.2
1. a landscape 2. a portrait 3. sculpture

76.3 *Possible answers:*
1. conductor
2. classical; composer
3. jazz
4. playwright; play
5. gallery/museum; exhibit/show
6. pop/rock; songwriter
7. opera
8. novel/book/work; fiction
9. artist/painter; portraits

76.4 *Answers will vary.*

Unit 77

77.1 *Answers will vary.*

77.2 *Possible answers:*
1. The mayor will leave his/her job.
2. The legislature has reduced/lowered taxes.
3. There is a new attempt/try to reduce teenage smoking.
4. The U.S. supports a European plan.
5. A study has made a connection between stress and heart disease.
6. The police have discovered a very important witness.

77.3 *Answers will vary.*

Unit 78

78.1 *Possible answers:*
1. Could you turn the TV on / turn on the TV?
2. Could you turn it up, please?
3. Could you change the channel?
4. Could you turn it down?
5. Could you turn it off?

78.2
1. drama series: *FBI Files, Crime City*
2. news magazine: *60 Minutes*
3. game show: *Guessing Game!*
4. sports program: *NASCAR Racing*
5. talk show: *The Tonight Show*
6. cartoon show: *Springfield*
7. reality show: *Reality House*
8. current affairs program: *Washington Week in Review, 60 Minutes*
9. soap opera: *Times in Our Lives*
10. comedy series: *Jerry's Show, Springfield*

78.3 *Answers will vary.*

Unit 79

79.1 *Possible answers:*
1. telephone number
2. cell phone
3. pay phone
4. telephone book
5. on the phone
6. phone tag

79.2 *Possible answers:*

A
1. This is
2. message
3. out / not here / away from his desk / busy

4. call you back
5. number

B
6. this is
7. be back
8. leave; message
9. call me / call me back

C
10. Is this / Can I speak to
11. This is
12. tried/called/dialed

13. busy
14. on

79.3 *Answers will vary.*

Unit 80

80.1 *Possible answers:*
1. word processing
2. software
3. hard drive / disk / copy / ware
4. flash drive
5. World Wide Web

6. e-mail address
7. operating system
8. CD-ROM
9. bounce back
10. laptop

80.2 1. paste   2. print   3. cut   4. copy   5. save

80.3 *Possible answers:*
1. laptop
2. online
3. Wi-Fi/wireless/Internet
4. checked
5. messages
6. deleted

7. read
8. replied
9. sent
10. back
11. address
12. turned

80.4 *Answers will vary.*

80.5 *Answers will vary.*

Unit 81

81.1 1. math   3. science   5. art
        2. history   4. English   6. music

81.2
1. kindergarten through twelfth grade
2. 3 or 4
3. 5 or 6
4. kindergarten
5. vocational; specialized
6. English, reading, writing, math, science, social studies
7. public
8. middle school or junior high school

81.3 *Answers will vary.*

81.4 1. to school
        2. graduated; to college

3. dropped out
4. compulsory/required

81.5 *Answers will vary.*

Unit 82

82.1
1. architecture
2. agriculture
3. hotel administration
4. psychology
5. business
6. art history
7. political science
8. engineering

82.2
1. tuition
2. bachelor's degree: B.A. or B.S.
3. undergraduates
4. professors, lecturers, instructors
5. application
6. graduate students
7. research
8. community college / junior college

82.3 *Possible answers:*
1. graduate student
2. a scholarship
3. an associate's degree
4. Which college/university did you go to?
5. She's majoring in physics. / Her major is physics.
6. a bachelor's degree

82.4 *Answers will vary.*

Unit 83

83.1
_1_ Last week $100,000 was stolen from a bank on Main Street.
_7_ they found both men guilty.
_4_ and charged them with the robbery.
_6_ After the jury listened to all the evidence,
_8_ They were sent to prison for seven years.
_5_ The trial took place six months later.
_3_ They finally arrested two men
_2_ The police questioned a number of people about the crime.

83.2
1. the police
2. the judge
3. prisoners
4. the jury
5. the prosecutor and defense attorney/lawyer
6. criminals

83.3
1. broken; committed
2. against/breaking
3. fine
4. prove
5. guilty
6. evidence
7. convicted; sentence
8. offense

83.4 *Answers will vary.*

Unit 84

84.1

Crimes	*People*	*Places*
murder	burglar	cell
manslaughter	thief	prison
robbery	judge	court
shoplifting	criminal	police station
	prisoner	
	attorney	
	jury	

84.2
1. burglary
2. murder
3. shoplifting
4. manslaughter
5. theft/robbery

84.3 *Answers will vary.*

84.4 *Answers will vary.*

Unit 85

85.1

Abstract noun	Person	Adjective
politics	politician	political
dictatorship	dictator	dictatorial
socialism	socialist	socialist
conservatism	conservative	conservative
liberalism	liberal	liberal

85.2
1. Congress
2. party
3. majority
4. elections
5. held
6. system
7. party
8. majority
9. Prime

85.3 *Answers will vary.*

85.4 *No discrete answers.*

Unit 86

86.1 *Possible answers:*
1. identification / landing / membership card
2. birth/marriage certificate
3. driver's/fishing license
4. application / registration / income tax form

86.2 *Possible answers:*
1. obtain
2. checked
3. fill in / fill out / sign
4. sign
5. runs out / expires; renew
6. lines
7. application

86.3 *Answers will vary.*

86.4 *Possible answers:*
1. When were you born?
2. Where do you come from?
3. Are you male or female?
4. Are you single or married?
5. When did you arrive?
6. When will you leave?

86.5 *Answers will vary.*

Unit 87

87.1
1. f
2. c
3. g
4. e
5. h
6. d
7. a
8. b

87.2 *Possible answers:*
1. (still) alive
2. hostilities
3. retreat
4. run out
5. exploded; break out; planted; attack
6. hijacked; hostages; release; demands

87.3

First mention	repeated as . . .
war	conflict
food and medicine	supplies
ordinary people	civilians
soldiers	troops
blew up	exploded
fire	shoot
aid	help
wounded	injured

87.4 *Answers will vary.*

Unit 88

88.1
1. the ozone layer
2. acid rain
3. industrial waste
4. public transportation
5. global warming
6. exhaust fumes
7. the greenhouse effect
8. natural or human resources

88.2

Noun	Verb
waste	waste
conservation	conserve
destruction	destroy
pollution	pollute
damage	damage

Noun	Adjective
damage	damaging
environment	environmental
harm	harmful
danger	dangerous
nature	natural

88.3 *Possible answers:*
1. plants; water/air
2. smoke from factories
3. the earth
4. the sun's heat
5. the average temperature of the planet
6. damages the ozone layer

88.4 We should:
recycle paper, etc.
use/take public transportation instead of cars.
save/conserve water and energy.

We shouldn't:
throw away paper, etc.
destroy the ozone layer.
waste water and energy.

88.5
1. false
2. false
3. true
4. true

Unit 89

89.1
1. check-in counter
2. baggage claim
3. ground transportation
4. boarding pass
5. metal detector
6. photo ID
7. take off
8. go through security

89.2
1. overhead compartment
2. customs
3. e-ticket
4. carry-ons / carry-on luggage
5. runway
6. flight attendants (or cabin crew)
7. terminal building
8. cruising altitude

89.3 *Possible answers:*
1. took off / departed
2. captain/pilot
3. fasten
4. flew

5. landed/arrived   7. flight
6. get off

89.4 *Answers will vary.*

Unit 90
90.1 *Possible order of answers:*
  <u> 1 </u> I reserved a single room at the hotel.
  <u> 7 </u> I watched TV until I fell asleep.
  <u>11 </u> I paid my bill at the front desk and checked out.
  <u> 3 </u> I checked in at the registration desk.
  <u> 4 </u> I went up to my room.
  <u> 8 </u> I had a wake-up call at seven o'clock.
  <u> 2 </u> I arrived at the hotel.
  <u> 9 </u> I got up and took a shower.
  <u>10 </u> I had breakfast.
  <u> 5 </u> A bellman took my luggage upstairs.
  <u> 6 </u> I gave the bellman a $2 tip.

90.2 *Possible answers:*
  1. I'd like to make a reservation for a double room, nonsmoking, for two nights. I'd like two beds, please. Arriving next Thursday and checking out Saturday.
  2. I'm checking out. Could I have my bill, please?
  3. Could I have a wake-up call tomorrow at 7 a.m., please?
  4. Could you put it on my bill, please?
  5. There's something wrong with the shower in my room.
  6. How do I get to the nearest bank from here?

90.3 *Answers will vary.*

Unit 91
91.1 *Possible answers:*
  1. great time   7. lost
  2. sightseeing   8. market
  3. packed   9. go out
  4. shopping   10. spent
  5. souvenirs   11. taken
  6. galleries/museums

91.2 *Answers will vary.*

91.3 *Possible answers:*
  1. Yes, we took lots of pictures.   4. Yes, the nightlife is fantastic.
  2. Yes, it's very cosmopolitan.   5. Yes, we had a great time.
  3. Yes, it was (absolutely) packed.

91.4 *Answers will vary.*

Unit 92
92.1 *Possible answers:*
suntan
sunburn
sunbathe
sunblock
sunscreen

92.2 1. c   2. d   3. e   4. f/a   5. b   6. a/f

92.3 *Possible answers:*
1. to spend time lying on the beach, sunbathing, and swimming
2. because they want a suntan
3. to protect themselves from the sun
4. very painful
5. surfing

92.4 *Possible answers:*
1. get away   3. quiet   5. walk/stroll
2. country/countryside   4. sit/sunbathe   6. picnic

92.5 *Possible answers:*
1. resort   4. hiking
2. different/various   5. peace
3. tent

Unit 93
93.1 1. at   3. at   5. on   7. On   9. On   11. in
2. in   4. in   6. on   8. at   10. at   12. on

93.2 1. by   3. since   5. in   7. for
2. until   4. for   6. during   8. throughout

93.3 *Readers are not expected to know exact answers.*
Possible answers:
1. 10   4. The answer depends on what year it is, e.g., 47 years in 2010.
2. two   5. 12 1/2 hours
3. 19th

93.4 *Possible answers:*
1. the other day   4. for ages (You could also say "in ages.")
2. for the time being   5. a long time ago
3. recently/lately

93.5 *Answers will vary.*

Unit 94
94.1 1. four hundred (and) sixty-two
2. two and a half
3. two thousand three hundred (and) forty-five
4. six point seven five
5. zero point two five *or* point two five
6. one million two hundred (and) fifty thousand
7. ten point oh four
8. forty-seven percent
9. September (the) tenth or the tenth of September
10. July (the) fourth *or* the fourth of July
11. five five five, eight oh seven seven *or* five five five, eight oh double seven
12. five (degrees) below zero *or* minus five (degrees) Fahrenheit
13. nineteen oh three
14. twenty thirty-six *or* two-thousand thirty-six

94.2 1. thousand
2. on the tenth of September / on September (the) tenth
3. two thousand nine / twenty oh nine.
4. the thirty-first of August / August (the) thirty-first
5. two and a half hours long

94.3 1. 59   2. 192   3. 60   4. 5   5. 8   6. 15

94.4 *Answers will vary.*

Unit 95
95.1 *Answers will vary.*

95.2 *Possible questions:*
What size shoes/dress does she take/wear?
How high are the mountains? / What's the height of the mountains?
How far is it from one side of the lake to the other?
How big is the lake? / What's the size of the lake?
How deep is it? / What's the depth of the lake?
How long is the swimming pool? / What's the length of the swimming pool?
How wide is the pool? / What's the width of the pool?
How deep is the pool at the deep end / at the shallow end? *or* What's the depth of the pool at the deep end / at the shallow end?

95.3 *Possible answers:*
1. No, it's pretty short.
2. No, he's fairly thin/slim.
3. No, it's very shallow
4. No, it's in a tall building. *or* No, it's in a high-rise building.
5. No, it's very narrow.
6. No, it's very thin.
7. No, she's pretty short.
8. No, it's a (great) big place.

Unit 96
96.1
1. a rectangular table
2. a star-shaped ring
3. a round window
4. a checked shirt
5. a plaid tie
6. an oval / oval-shaped mirror
7. diamond-shaped earrings
8. a floral sofa / a rectangular sofa
9. a pointed hat

96.2
1. a pencil / a pen
2. a football field (tennis court, etc.)
3. the moon
4. a carrot
5. the sea (a lake, etc.)
6. an egg
7. a coat hanger
8. a square
9. a triangle
10. a salmon (trout, etc.)

96.3 *Answers will vary.*

Unit 97
97.1
1. European Union
2. personal computer
3. United States of America
4. automated teller machine
5. United Nations
6. Organization of Petroleum Exporting Countries
7. personal identification number
8. high definition

97.2 Michael,
Peter had a math exam this afternoon, and then he had to take his bike to the repair shop, so he'll probably get home a little late. You can watch TV or read the paper while you're waiting for him. If there's a problem (e.g., if Dr. Brown calls about the flu vaccination), my office phone number is next to the photos in the dining room. I've got my cell with me too. Peter's dad and I should be home by about five o'clock. Margaret (Peter's mom)

97.3 1. etc.   2. e.g.   3. St.   4. i.e.   5. Mr.   6. Dr.

97.4 1. e.g.   3. rep   5. etc.   7. ad   9. bye
         2. ID   4. board   6. flu   8. St.; i.e.   10. plane; St.

Unit 98

98.1 *Possible answers:*
1. Beware of pickpockets
2. Watch your step
3. Do not disturb; Do not feed the animals; Do not leave luggage unattended
4. No parking; No vacancy; No smoking
5. Thank you for not smoking
6. Handle with care
7. Out of order
8. Keep off the grass

98.2 *Possible answers:*
1. outside a motel
2. on a container of food, milk, medicine, etc.
3. on a sidewalk
4. on a package/bottle/tube of medicine
5. on an ATM, public phone
6. outside a theater
7. on the outside of a package
8. in a park, outside a building

98.3 *Possible answers:*
1. Do not feed the animals.
2. Do not leave luggage unattended. / No smoking
3. Please do not disturb.
4. No parking
5. Thank you for not smoking
6. Watch your step

98.4 *Answers will vary.*

98.5 *Answers will vary.*

Unit 99

99.1 *Possible answers:*
1. perfume / after-shave lotion
2. a key
3. knife and fork
4. flour
5. stereo/radio
6. clothes/belongings
7. a toy/game
8. shampoo / conditioner

99.2 *Possible additions:*
A: How many people were at the conference?
B: <u>Around/About/Approximately</u> 400.
A: Did you enjoy it?
B: Yes, <u>sort of / kind of</u>.
A: You don't seem very sure.
B: Well, there were some good <u>things</u>, but it was <u>kind of</u> long.
A: And how did John's talk go?
B: Well, he was <u>kind of / sort of</u> nervous at the beginning, but then he got more confident, and I think it went really well.
A: Did he have a big audience?
B: <u>About/Around</u> seventy-five.
A: That's pretty good.
B: I think John was <u>kind of / sort of</u> disappointed – he wanted <u>around</u> a hundred.

99.3 *Possible answers:*
1. kind of
2. more or less
3. sort of / kind of
4. more or less / approximately
5. kind of / sort of
6. a vague memory (of it)

Unit 100

100.1

Formal	Informal
purchase	kids
thus	five bucks
apprehend	handy
resume	guy
commence	
patron	

buy – purchase   catch/stop – apprehend   dollar – buck
man – guy   easy to reach – handy   start again – resume
therefore – thus   customer – patron.   children – kids

100.2 *Possible answers:*
1. Is that your bike?
2. I bet the show will start pretty soon.
3. Wanna go out for dinner?
4. What's up?
5. The guy in the market sold me this ring for 20 bucks.
6. Where did you buy/get that book?
7. They'll never catch him.
8. On our vacation, we're going to hang out at the pool every day.
9. Where did the kids get that video game?

100.3 *Possible answers:*

Dear Mr. Kim:

We regret to inform you that we are unable to lend you the sum of 500 dollars that you require, but it may be possible to grant you a loan for part of the sum. If you are still interested, perhaps you would like to contact our assistant manager. She will be happy to discuss the matter further.

Sincerely,

100.4
1. a drag (*informal*) "boring / a bore"
2. restroom (*formal*) "bathroom"; on the premises (*formal*) "in this building"
3. shut up (*informal*) "be quiet"
2. ripped off (*informal*) "stole"
5. prohibited (*formal*) "not allowed"